COLLECTIONS
FOR YOUNG SCHOLARS
VOLUME 5, BOOK 2

The Civil War

The American West

Journeys and Quests

Art by Susan Keeter

COLLECTIONS FOR YOUNG SCHOLARS

VOLUME 5, BOOK 2

PROGRAM AUTHORS
Carl Bereiter
Ann Brown
Marlene Scardamalia
Valerie Anderson
Joe Campione

CONSULTING AUTHORS
Michael Pressley
Iva Carruthers
Captain Bill Pinkney

OPEN COURT PUBLISHING COMPANY
CHICAGO AND PERU, ILLINOIS

CHAIRMAN
M. Blouke Carus

PRESIDENT
André W. Carus

EDUCATION DIRECTOR
Carl Bereiter

VICE-PRESIDENT AND PUBLISHER
Barbara Conteh

EXECUTIVE EDITOR
Shirley Graudin

MANAGING EDITOR
Sheelagh McGurn

PROJECT EDITOR
Janette McKenna

ART DIRECTOR
John Grandits

VICE-PRESIDENT, PRODUCTION
AND MANUFACTURING
Chris Vancalbergh

PERMISSIONS COORDINATOR
Diane Sikora

COVER ARTIST
Susan Keeter

Printed in the United States of America

ISBN 0-8126-5248-7

10 9 8 7 6 5 4 3 2 1

ACKNOWLEDGMENTS

Grateful acknowledgment is given to the following publishers and copyright owners for permission granted to reprint selections from their publications. All possible care has been taken to trace ownership and secure permission for each selection included.

Bradbury Press, a division of Macmillan, Inc.: *Death of the Iron Horse* by Paul Goble, copyright © 1987 by Paul Goble.

Clarion Books, an imprint of Houghton Mifflin Co.: "Half Slave and Half Free" from *Lincoln: A Photobiography* by Russell Freedman, copyright © 1987 by Russell Freedman. An excerpt entitled "So I Became a Soldier" from *The Boys' War: Confederate and Union Soldiers Talk about the Civil War* by Jim Murphy, text copyright © 1990 by Jim Murphy.

Dillon Press, Inc., a division of Macmillan, Inc.: An excerpt entitled "Sacagawea's Journey" from *Sacagawea* by Betty Westrom Skold, copyright © 1977 by Dillon Press, Inc.

Farrar, Straus & Giroux, Inc.: "When Shlemiel Went to Warsaw" from *When Shlemiel Went to Warsaw and Other Stories* by Isaac Bashevis Singer, translated by Isaac Bashevis Singer and Elizabeth Shub, text copyright © 1968 by Isaac Bashevis Singer.

William Graves: "The Greatest Snowball Fight in History" by William Graves from the January 1981 issue of *Cricket* magazine, copyright © 1980 by William Graves.

Harcourt Brace Jovanovich, Inc.: "Wander-Thirst" by Gerald Gould from *Stars to Steer By* by Louis Untermeyer, copyright 1941 by Harcourt, Brace & World, Inc.

HarperCollins Publishers: "Harriet Tubman" from *Honey, I Love and Other Love Poems* by Eloise Greenfield, text copyright © 1978 by Eloise Greenfield. Excerpts entitled "The Hospital" and "Under Siege" from *Voices from the Civil War* by Milton Meltzer, copyright © 1989 by Milton Meltzer. "Old Yeller and the Bear" from *Old Yeller* by Fred Gipson, copyright © 1956 by Fred Gipson. "The West Begins" from *By the Shores of Silver Lake* by Laura Ingalls Wilder, text copyright 1939 by Laura Ingalls Wilder, copyright © renewed 1967 by Roger L. MacBride. An excerpt entitled "The Search" from *And Now Miguel* by

Joseph Krumgold. "Travel" by Edna St. Vincent Millay from *Collected Poems*, copyright 1922 by Edna St. Vincent Millay.

Holiday House, Inc.: Excerpts from *Buffalo Hunt* by Russell Freedman, copyright © 1988 by Russell Freedman.

Henry Holt and Co., Inc.: "Younde Goes to Town" from *The Cow-Tail Switch and Other West African Stories* by Harold Courlander and George Herzog, copyright © 1975 by Harold Courlander.

Houghton Mifflin Co.: An excerpt entitled "The Coming of the Long Knives" from *Sing Down the Moon* by Scott O'Dell, copyright © 1970 by Scott O'Dell. "Roads Go Ever Ever On" from *The Hobbit* by J.R.R. Tolkien, copyright © 1966 by J.R.R. Tolkien.

James Houston: "The Whole World Is Coming" from *Songs of the Dream People: Chants and Images from the Indians and Eskimos of North America*, edited and illustrated by James Houston, Atheneum, New York, copyright © 1972 by James Houston.

Alfred A. Knopf, Inc.: "Carrying the Running-Aways" from *The People Could Fly: American Black Folktales*, retold by Virginia Hamilton, illustrated by Leo and Diane Dillon, text copyright © 1985 by Virginia Hamilton, illustrations copyright © 1985 by Leo and Diane Dillon.

Lothrop, Lee & Shepard Books, a division of William Morrow & Co., Inc.: An excerpt entitled "The Siege of Vicksburg" from *The Tamarack Tree* by Patricia Clapp, copyright © 1986 by Patricia Clapp. *The Story of Jumping Mouse: A Native American Legend*, retold and illustrated by John Steptoe, copyright © 1984 by John Steptoe.

Macmillan Publishing Co., a division of Macmillan, Inc.: "The Adventures of Odysseus" from *The Children's Homer* by Padraic Colum, copyright renewed 1946 by Padraic Colum and Willy Pogany.

Morrow Junior Books, a division of William Morrow and Co., Inc.: An excerpt from *Charley Skedaddle* by Patricia Beatty, text copyright © 1987 by Patricia Beatty.

continued on page 368

5

THE CIVIL WAR

❧ 7 ❧

THE AMERICAN WEST

JOURNEYS AND QUESTS

❧ *10* ❧

THE CIVIL WAR

The Departure of the Seventh Regiment, April 19, 1861. 1869. Thomas Nast.

Oil on canvas. Photo: The Seventh Regiment Fund, Inc.

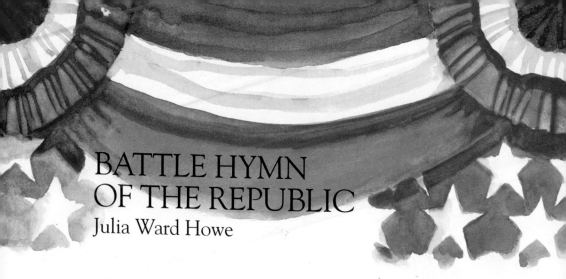

BATTLE HYMN OF THE REPUBLIC

Julia Ward Howe

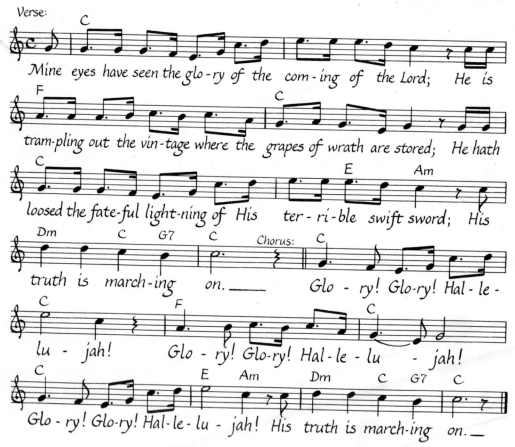

Verse:

Mine eyes have seen the glo-ry of the com-ing of the Lord; He is tram-pling out the vin-tage where the grapes of wrath are stored; He hath loosed the fate-ful light-ning of His ter-ri-ble swift sword; His truth is march-ing on.___

Chorus:

Glo-ry! Glo-ry! Hal-le-lu-jah! Glo-ry! Glo-ry! Hal-le-lu-jah! Glo-ry! Glo-ry! Hal-le-lu-jah! His truth is march-ing on.___

DIXIE
Daniel Decatur Emmett

musical notation by Christina T. Davidson

HALF SLAVE AND HALF FREE

from LINCOLN: A PHOTOBIOGRAPHY
by Russell Freedman

Wanted poster for a runaway slave.

"If slavery is not wrong, nothing is wrong. I cannot remember when I did not so think, and feel."
—ABRAHAM LINCOLN

When Abraham Lincoln took his seat in Congress in 1847, Washington was a sprawling town of 34,000 people, including several thousand slaves. From the windows of the Capitol, Lincoln could see crowded slave pens where manacled blacks waited to be shipped south.

Southern planters had built a cotton kingdom on the shoulders of enslaved blacks, and they meant to preserve their way of life. Many white Southerners claimed a "sacred" right to own Negroes as slaves. Slavery was a blessing for blacks and whites alike, they said, "a good—a positive good," according to Senator John C. Calhoun of South Carolina.

Slave uprisings and rebellions had resulted in tough measures to control blacks and silence white critics of slavery. Throughout the South, antislavery writings and societies were suppressed or banned.

Slavery had never prospered in the North and had been outlawed there. Some Northerners wanted to abolish slavery everywhere in the land, but abolitionists were still a small and embattled minority. Most people in the North were willing to leave slavery alone, as long as it was confined to the South.

While the North was free soil, it was hardly a paradise for blacks. Racial prejudice was a fact of everyday life. Most

Yankee states had enacted strict "black laws." In Illinois, Lincoln's home state, blacks paid taxes but could not vote, hold political office, serve on juries, testify in court, or attend schools. They had a hard time finding jobs. Often they sold themselves as "indentures" for a period of twenty years—a form of voluntary slavery—just to eat and have a place to live.

Even in northern Illinois, where antislavery feelings ran strong, whites feared that emancipation of the slaves would send thousands of jobless blacks swarming into the North. Abolitionists were considered dangerous fanatics in Illinois. Lincoln knew that to be branded an abolitionist in his home state would be political suicide.

Early in his career, Lincoln made few public statements about slavery. But he did take a stand. As a twenty-eight-year-old state legislator, he recorded his belief that slavery was "founded on both injustice and bad policy." Ten years later, as a congressman, he voted with his party to stop the spread of slavery, and he introduced his bill to outlaw slavery in the nation's capital. But he did not become an antislavery crusader. For the most part, he sat silently in the background as Congress rang with angry debates over slavery's future.

Lincoln always said that he hated slavery. He claimed he hated it as much as any abolitionist, but he feared that efforts to force abolition on the South would only lead to violence. He felt that Congress had no power to interfere with slavery in states where it already existed.

He wanted to see slavery done away with altogether, but that would take time, he believed. He hoped it could be legislated out of existence, with some sort of compensation given

Slave market in Atlanta. The slaves were held in pens until
they were auctioned off.

Library of Congress

to the slaveholders in exchange for their property. As long as Congress kept slavery from spreading, Lincoln felt certain that it would gradually die a "natural death."

When his congressional term ended in 1849, Lincoln decided to withdraw from public life. For the next five years he concentrated on his law practice and stayed out of politics. As he traveled the Illinois circuit, arguing cases in country courthouses, slavery was becoming an explosive issue that threatened to tear the nation apart.

Vast new territories were opening up in the West, bringing the North and South into conflict. Each section wanted to control the western territories. The South needed new lands for the large-scale cultivation of cotton and other crops with slave labor. The North demanded that the western territories be reserved for the free labor of independent farmers and workers. Meanwhile, as the territories reached statehood and gained votes in Congress, they would hold the balance of political power in Washington. The admission of each new state raised a crucial question: Would it enter the Union as a free state or a slave state?

So far, Congress had managed to hold the country together through a series of uneasy compromises, such as the Missouri Compromise of 1820. These agreements permitted slavery in some western territories and barred it in others. But attitudes were hardening. Growing numbers of Northerners had come to regard slavery as a moral evil, an issue that could no longer be avoided. Southerners, meanwhile, were more determined than ever to protect their way of life.

An African-American family in slavery times.

The issue came to a head in 1854, when Congress passed the bitterly debated Kansas-Nebraska Act. Under the Missouri Compromise, the region that included the territories of Kansas and Nebraska had been declared off-limits to slavery. Under the new Act, however, the future of slavery in those territories would be determined by the people who settled there. They would decide for themselves whether to enter the Union as free states or slave states.

The Kansas-Nebraska Act had been introduced by Lincoln's old political rival, Stephen Douglas, now a U.S. Senator from Illinois. Douglas's policy of "popular sovereignty" caused a storm of protest in the North. By opening new territories to slavery, his measure overturned the Missouri Compromise, which had held slavery in check. With the passage of Douglas's Act, Lincoln ended his long political silence. "I was losing interest in politics," he said, "when the repeal of the Missouri Compromise aroused me again."

He was "thunderstruck and stunned," aroused as he had "never been before." Douglas and his followers had opened the gates for slavery to expand and grow and establish itself permanently. Now it would never die the "natural death" Lincoln had expected. He felt compelled to speak out. For the first time in five years he neglected his law practice. He traveled across Illinois, campaigning for antislavery Whig candidates and speaking in reply to Senator Douglas, who had returned home to defend his policies.

Lincoln told his audiences that slavery was a "monstrous injustice." It was a "cancer" threatening to grow out of control "in a nation originally dedicated to the inalienable rights of man." And it was not only wrong, it threatened the rights of everyone. If slavery was permitted to spread, free white workers would be forced to compete for a living with enslaved blacks. In the end, slavery would undermine the very foundations of democracy. "As I would not be a slave, so I would not be a master," Lincoln declared. "This expresses my idea of democracy. Whatever differs from this, to the extent of the difference, is not democracy."

He had been studying the history of the nation, pondering the words and ideals of the Founding Fathers. He believed that the cornerstone of the American experiment in democracy was the Declaration of Independence, which states that "all men are created equal," and that all are entitled to "Life, Liberty, and the pursuit of Happiness." Lincoln took this declaration personally. It meant that every poor man's son deserved the opportunities for advancement he had enjoyed. He felt that the Declaration of Independence expressed the highest political truths in history, and that blacks and whites alike were entitled to the rights it spelled out.

Although Lincoln was determined to oppose the spread of slavery, he admitted that he didn't know what to do about those states where slavery was already established, where it was protected by a complex web of state and national laws. "I have no prejudice against the Southern people," he said. "They are just what we would be in their situation. If slavery did not now exist amongst them, they would not introduce it. If it did now exist amongst us, we should not instantly give it up. . . . I surely will not blame them for not doing what I should not know how to do myself. If all earthly power were given me, I should not know what to do, as to the existing institution."

By 1856, open warfare had broken out in Kansas. Antislavery Northerners and proslavery Southerners had both recruited settlers to move into the territory. "Bleeding Kansas" became a battleground of rigged elections, burnings, lynchings, and assassinations as the rival forces fought for control of the territory.

Violence reached even to the floor of Congress. After delivering an impassioned anti-Southern speech on "The Crime Against Kansas," Senator Charles Sumner of Massachusetts was beaten with a cane and almost killed by Congressman Preston Brooks of South Carolina.

Then the U.S. Supreme Court handed down a decision that shocked antislavery forces everywhere. In 1857, the court ruled in the *Dred Scott* case that Congress had no power

A newspaper drawing shows Representative Preston Brooks attacking Senator Charles Sumner on the Senate floor.

New York Public Library

to prohibit slavery in any of the nation's territories, because that would violate property rights guaranteed by the Constitution. Scott was a slave who sued for his freedom on grounds that his master had twice taken him onto free soil in the North. The court declared that as a black man, Scott was not and never had been a citizen. He was not entitled to the rights spelled out by the Declaration of Independence. Slaves were private property, the court said, and Congress could not pass laws depriving white citizens of "the right of property in a slave."

The *Dred Scott* decision was a stunning setback for the opponents of slavery. But it also helped mobilize antislavery opinion. Lincoln spent two weeks studying the decision so he could prepare an argument against it. Speaking in Springfield, he pointed to the "plain unmistakable language" of the Declaration of Independence. When its authors declared that all men have equal rights, "This they said, and this they meant," Lincoln argued. He urged respect for the courts, but he added: "We think the *Dred Scott* decision is erroneous. We know the court that made it has often overruled its own decisions, and we shall do what we can to have it overrule this."

By now, Lincoln had become a leading antislavery spokesman in Illinois. And he had switched his political allegiance. Since entering politics he had been a Whig, but the Whigs had not been able to unite in opposition to slavery, and now the party was splintered and dying. Thousands of Whigs had gone over to the Republicans, a new party founded in 1854 to oppose the spread of slavery. Lincoln remained loyal to the Whigs until 1856, when he made up his mind to leave his "mummy of a party" and join the Republicans himself.

He wanted to be in office again so he could influence public policy, and this time he was after Stephen Douglas's Senate seat. The two men had been rivals for twenty years now. Douglas had risen to national prominence. He had been a judge of the Illinois Supreme Court, a congressman and a senator, an outstanding leader of the Democratic party. Lincoln's political career had floundered after his solitary term in Congress. "With *me*, the race of ambition has been a failure— a flat failure," he remarked. "With *him* [Douglas] it has been one of splendid success. His name fills the nation and is not unknown, even, in foreign lands."

Lincoln had made an unsuccessful bid for the Senate as a Whig, in 1855. As a Republican he tried again, and in 1858 he won his new party's nomination. He launched his campaign on a sweltering June evening with a rousing speech before twelve hundred shirt-sleeved delegates at the state Republican Convention in Springfield.

Where was the nation headed? Lincoln asked them. More than four years had passed since the passage of the Kansas-Nebraska Act, yet agitation over slavery had not ceased. "In my opinion," he sang out, "it *will* not cease, until a *crisis* shall have been reached, and passed.

"A house divided against itself cannot stand.

"I believe this government cannot endure, permanently half *slave* and half *free*.

"I do not expect the Union to be *dissolved*—I do not expect the house to *fall*, but I *do* expect it will cease to be divided.

"It will become *all* one thing, or *all* the other."

Lincoln warned that the opponents of slavery must stop its westward expansion. They must put slavery back on the "course of ultimate extinction." Otherwise slavery would spread its grip across the entire nation, "till it shall become lawful in *all* the States, *old* as well as *new—North* as well as *South*."

There could be no fair fight between slavery and freedom, because one was morally wrong and the other morally right. Senator Douglas and the Democrats did not care about the advance of slavery, said Lincoln. The Republicans did care. The issue facing the country was the spread of slavery across the nation and into the future.

Some Republicans felt that the speech was too extreme, too much "ahead of its time." But most of the delegates in Lincoln's audience cheered him on. It was the strongest statement he had ever made about slavery. And it set the stage for his dramatic confrontation with Stephen Douglas.

The campaign between them during the summer of 1858 was to capture the attention of the entire nation. In July, Lincoln challenged Douglas to a series of public debates. Douglas accepted the challenge, agreeing to seven three-hour debates in small Illinois towns.

At least twelve thousand people were on hand for the first debate at Ottawa on August 21. More than fifteen thousand showed up at Freeport a week later, even though it rained. At every stop, people came from miles around in wagons and buggies, on horseback and on foot, to see and hear the candidates and decide who was the better man. Town squares were festooned with banners and flags. Peddlers hawked Lincoln and Douglas badges, bands played, cannons roared, and marshals on horseback tried to maintain order among huge crowds as the candidates arrived in town.

With his opponent, Douglas, seated to his right, Lincoln addresses
the crowd at Charleston, Illinois, on September 18, 1858. Lincoln
and Douglas held seven debates, each lasting three hours.
Painting by Robert Marshall Root.
Illinois State Historical Library

Douglas traveled in high style, riding from town to town in
a private railroad car, sipping brandy and smoking cigars, surrounded by friends and advisors and accompanied by his
beautiful wife. Lincoln traveled more modestly, as an ordinary
passenger on the regular trains. His wife Mary stayed home
with their sons Willie and Tad. She heard her husband speak
only once, at the final debate in Alton.

Newspaper reporters trailed the candidates, taking down
their speeches in shorthand and telegraphing stories to their
newspapers back east. What the debaters said in remote Illinois towns could be read the next day in Boston or Atlanta.

The striking contrast between Douglas and Lincoln—The Little Giant and Long Abe, as reporters called them—added color and excitement to the contests. Douglas was Lincoln's opposite in every way. Barely five feet four inches tall, he had a huge round head planted on massive shoulders, a booming voice, and an aggressive, self-confident manner. He appeared on the speakers' platform dressed "plantation style"—a navy coat and light trousers, a ruffled shirt, a wide-brimmed felt hat. Lincoln, tall and gangly, seemed plain in his rumpled suit, carrying his notes and speeches in an old carpetbag, sitting on the platform with his bony knees jutting into the air.

The give and take between them held audiences spellbound. Douglas defended his doctrine of popular sovereignty. The nation could endure half slave and half free, he argued. Each state had the right to decide for itself the question of slavery.

Lincoln replied that popular sovereignty was just a smoke screen to allow the spread of slavery. The country had endured for decades half slave and half free only because most people believed that slavery would die out. Besides, slavery wasn't just a matter of states' rights. It was a moral issue that affected the whole country. "This government was instituted to secure the blessings of freedom," said Lincoln. "Slavery is an unqualified evil to the Negro, to the white man, to the soil, and to the State."

Douglas argued that the constitutional guarantee of equality applied only to white citizens, not to blacks. The Supreme Court had ruled that blacks weren't citizens at all. "I am opposed to Negro equality," said Douglas. "I believe

Left: Five feet four—Senator Stephen A. Douglas, nicknamed The Little Giant. His booming voice and confident manner made up for his small stature.
Right: Six feet four—A. Lincoln, also known as Long Abe or The Tall Sucker. His eventual victory over Douglas earned him another nickname—The Giant Killer.

Illinois State Historical Library

this government was made by the white man for the white man to be administered by the white man."

Douglas pressed the issue of white supremacy. Was Lincoln in favor of Negro equality? Did he advocate a mixing of the races? In Illinois, where many voters opposed equal rights for blacks, these were touchy questions. Across the state, Douglas kept race-baiting Lincoln, warning white crowds that he was a "Black Republican" who wanted to liberate the slaves so they could stampede into Illinois to work, vote, and marry with white people.

Lincoln complained bitterly that Douglas was twisting and distorting the issue through a "fantastic arrangement of words, by which a man can prove a horse chestnut to be a chestnut horse." The issue was not the social or political equality of the races, he protested defensively. He had never advocated that Negroes should be voters or office holders, or that they should marry whites. The real issue was whether slavery would spread and become permanent in America, or whether it would be confined to the South and allowed to die out gradually.

Lincoln appealed to the voters to "discard all this quibbling about this man and the other man—this race and that race and the other race as being inferior." And he added: "There is no reason in the world why the Negro is not entitled to all the natural rights enumerated in the Declaration of Independence, the right to life, liberty, and the pursuit of happiness. I hold that he is as much entitled to these as the white man."

At the time, senators were elected by state legislatures, not by popular vote. When the returns came in, the Republicans had not won enough seats in the legislature to send Lincoln to the Senate. Douglas was reelected by a narrow margin. "The fight must go on," Lincoln told a friend. "The cause of civil liberty must not be surrendered at the end of one or even one hundred defeats." Even so, the defeat hurt. "I feel like the boy who stumped his toe," he said. "I am too big to cry and too badly hurt to laugh."

Lincoln lost the election, but the debates had catapulted him to national prominence. He continued to speak out on the issues in Illinois and throughout the North, and by 1860, he was being mentioned as a possible candidate for president. At first he doubted that he could win. "I must, in all candor, say I do not think myself fit for the presidency," he told an Illinois newspaper editor. But powerful Republican leaders felt that Lincoln had a good chance to carry the party banner to victory. As they began to work for his nomination, he did not interfere. "The taste *is* in my mouth a little," he admitted.

When Illinois Republicans held their state convention on May 9, 1860, Lincoln was chosen unanimously as their favorite-son candidate. The cheering delegates lifted his long frame overhead and passed him hand-by-hand down to the speaker's platform.

A week later, the national convention of the Republican party met in Chicago. Several prominent Republicans were competing for the presidency, and Lincoln was not the first choice of many delegates. But he was acceptable to all factions of the party, and after some backstage maneuvering, he was nominated on the third ballot. He had spent the day quietly down in Springfield, waiting for news from the convention, and passing the time playing handball.

Meanwhile, the Democratic party had split in two. Northern Democrats meeting in Baltimore nominated Stephen Douglas for president. Southern Democrats, unwilling to accept any Northerner, held their own convention in Richmond, Virginia, and nominated John C. Breckinridge of Kentucky. Another group, the Constitutional Union party, also entered the contest with John Bell of Tennessee as their candidate.

It wasn't customary in those days for a presidential candidate to campaign on his own behalf. Lincoln didn't even leave Springfield until after Election Day. But his supporters carried on a spirited campaign, playing up Lincoln's humble background. At Republican rallies and parades all over the North, he was hailed as Honest Abe, the homespun rail-splitter from Illinois, a man of the people who was born in a log cabin and was headed for the White House.

A crowd of well-wishers gathers in front of Lincoln's home at a campaign rally in 1860. Lincoln is standing to the right of the doorway in a white summer suit.

Chicago Historical Society

The presidential candidate, June 1860. Of this photograph Lincoln said, "That looks better and expresses me better than any I have seen; if it pleases the people, I am satisfied."

The Bettmann Archive

Shortly before the election, Lincoln received a letter from Grace Bedell, an eleven-year-old girl in Westfield, New York, suggesting that he grow a beard. " . . . you would look a great deal better for your face is so thin," she wrote. "All the ladies like whiskers and they would tease their husbands to vote for you." As he waited for the nation to vote, Lincoln took her advice.

On Election Day—November 6, 1860—Lincoln waited in the Springfield telegraph office until he was certain of victory. Then he went out into the streets of Springfield to be greeted by fireworks and torchlight parades. Mary joined him, radiant and beaming, at a Republican Ladies' supper that evening. A guest reported that the women paid "solicitous attention" to the president-elect, fetching him coffee, serving him sandwiches, and serenading him with "vigorous Republican choruses."

Lincoln received 1,866,000 votes and carried every Northern state. Douglas had 1,377,000 votes, and Breckinridge, the candidate of the Southern Democrats, 850,000 votes. The North had swept Lincoln into office. In the South, his name hadn't even appeared on the ballot.

Douglas had warned that a Republican victory would bring on "a war of sections, a war of the North against the South, of the free states against the slave states—a war of extermination." Southern leaders were saying that they would never accept this "Black Republican" as president. They were already threatening to withdraw from the Union and form an independent slave nation. An Atlanta newspaper declared: "Let the consequences be what they may . . . the South will never submit to such humiliation and degradation as the inauguration of Abraham Lincoln."

In December—three months before Lincoln took his oath of office—South Carolina led the way. The state announced that it had seceded from the Union. It was now a sovereign nation, dedicated to the preservation of slavery.

MEET RUSSELL FREEDMAN, AUTHOR

Freedman outlines his research process when preparing to write a book: "I start out at the library. I usually start with the most recent books on the subject and go through their bibliographies, working my way backward. I try to familiarize myself . . . with literature that goes back as far as I want to go. Whenever possible, I do field research. For Lincoln. . . . I tried to visit every place that Lincoln had lived, starting with his log-cabin birthplace in Kentucky. . . . I just think that the more you can see with your own eyes, the stronger your feeling for the subject and the more authentic the writing is going to be. . . . I want to tell a compelling story, not simply write books that are used for reports. That's boring."

Harriet Tubman Series, #10. c. 1939–40. Jacob Lawrence.

Casein tempera on gessoed hardboard. Hampton University Museum. © Jacob Lawrence/VAGA, NY

HARRIET TUBMAN
Eloise Greenfield

Harriet Tubman didn't take no stuff
Wasn't scared of nothing neither
Didn't come in this world to be no slave
And wasn't going to stay one either

"Farewell!" she sang to her friends one night
She was mighty sad to leave 'em
But she ran away that dark hot night
Ran looking for her freedom

She ran to the woods and she ran through the woods
With the slave catchers right behind her
And she kept on going till she got to the North
Where those mean men couldn't find her

Nineteen times she went back South
To get three hundred others
She ran for her freedom nineteen times
To save Black sisters and brothers

Harriet Tubman didn't take no stuff
Wasn't scared of nothing neither
Didn't come in this world to be no slave
And didn't stay one either

And didn't stay one either

CARRYING THE RUNNING-AWAYS

from THE PEOPLE COULD FLY
by Virginia Hamilton
illustrated by Leo and Diane Dillon

Never had any idea of carryin the runnin-away slaves over the river. Even though I was right there on the plantation, right by that big river, it never got in my mind to do somethin like that. But one night the woman whose house I had gone courtin to said she knew a pretty girl wanted to cross the river and would I take her. Well, I met the girl and she was awful pretty. And soon the woman was tellin me how to get across, how to go, and when to leave.

Well, I had to think about it. But each day, that girl or the woman would come around, ask me would I row the girl across the river to a place called Ripley. Well, I finally said I would. And one night I went over to the woman's house. My owner trusted me and let me come and go as I pleased, long as I didn't try to read or write anythin. For writin and readin was forbidden to slaves.

Now, I had heard about the other side of the river from the other slaves. But I thought it was just like the side where we lived on the plantation. I thought there were slaves and masters over there, too, and overseers and rawhide whips they used on us. That's why I was so scared. I thought I'd land the girl over there and some overseer didn't know us would beat us for bein out at night. They could do that, you know.

Well, I did it. Oh, it was a long rowin time in the cold, with me worryin. But pretty soon I see a light way up high. Then I remembered the woman told me to watch for a light. Told me to row to the light, which is what I did. And when I got to it, there were two men. They reached down and grabbed the girl. Then one of the men took me by the arm. Said, "You about hungry?" And if he hadn't been holdin me, I would of fell out of that rowboat.

Well, that was my first trip. I was scared for a long time after that. But pretty soon I got over it, as other folks asked me to take them across the river. Two and three at a time, I'd take them. I got used to makin three or four trips every month.

Now it was funny. I never saw my passengers after that first girl. Because I took them on the nights when the moon was not showin, was cloudy. And I always met them in the open or in a house with no light. So I never saw them, couldn't recognize them, and couldn't describe them. But I would say to them, "What you say?" And they would say the password. Sounded like "Menare." Seemed the word came from the Bible somewhere, but I don't know. And they would have to say that word before I took them across.

Well, there in Ripley was a man named Mr. Rankins, the rest was John, I think. He had a "station" there for escaping slaves. Ohio was a free state, I found out, so once they got across, Mr. Rankins would see to them. We went at night so we could continue back for more and to be sure no slave catchers would follow us there.

Mr. Rankins had a big light about thirty feet high up and it burned all night. It meant freedom for slaves if they could get to that bright flame.

I worked hard and almost got caught. I'd been rowin fugitives for almost four years. It was in 1863 and it was a night I carried twelve runnin-aways across the river to Mr. Rankins'. I stepped out of the boat back in Kentucky and they were after me. Don't know how they found out. But the slave catchers, didn't know them, were on my trail. I ran away from the plantation and all who I knew there. I lived in the fields and in the woods. Even in caves. Sometimes I slept up in the tree branches. Or in a hay pile. I couldn't get across the river now, it was watched so closely.

Finally, I did get across. Late one night me and my wife went. I had gone back to the plantation to get her. Mr. Rankins had him a bell by this time, along with the light. We were rowin and rowin. We could see the light and hear that bell, but it seemed we weren't gettin any closer. It took forever, it seemed. That was because we were so scared and it was so dark and we knew we could get caught and never get gone.

Well, we did get there. We pulled up there and went on to freedom. It was only a few months before all the slaves was freed.

We didn't stay on at Ripley. We went on to Detroit because I wasn't takin any chances. I have children and grandchildren now. Well, you know, the bigger ones don't care so much to hear about those times. But the little ones, well, they never get tired of hearin how their grandpa brought emancipation to loads of slaves he could touch and feel in the dark but never ever see.

"The Drinking Gourd" sounded like a simple folk song but was really a map to freedom. Hidden in its lyrics were directions along the Underground Railroad. The "drinking gourd" refers to the constellation called the Big Dipper, which points to the North Star. "When the sun comes back and the first quail calls" meant spring, when travel was safest. The "old man" was Peg Leg Joe, who left tracks of "left foot, peg foot," along the riverbank and who carved signs in dead trees. The river that "ends between two hills" was the Tombigbee River, and the "great big river" was the Ohio River, where Peg Leg Joe waited to carry the escaped slaves across to the free states on the other side.

THE DRINKING GOURD

musical notation by Christina T. Davidson

Chorus:
Fol-low ____ the drink-ing gourd! ____ Fol-low ____ the drink-ing gourd. ___ For the old man is a-wait-ing for to car-ry you to free-dom If you fol-low the drink-ing gourd. **Verse:** When the sun comes back, and the first quail calls, ____ Fol-low ____ the

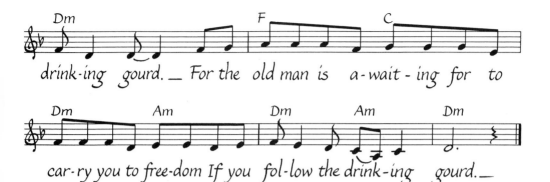

drink-ing gourd. __ For the old man is a-wait-ing for to
car-ry you to free-dom If you fol-low the drink-ing gourd. __

Chorus: Follow the drinking gourd! etc.

The riverbank makes a very good road,
The dead trees will show you the way.
Left foot, peg foot, traveling on,
    Follow the drinking gourd.

Chorus: Follow the drinking gourd! etc.

The river ends between two hills,
Follow the drinking gourd.
There's another river on the other side,
Follow the drinking gourd.

Chorus: Follow the drinking gourd! etc.

When the great big river meets the little river
Follow the drinking gourd.
For the old man is a-waiting for to carry you to freedom,
    If you follow the drinking gourd.

SO I BECAME A SOLDIER

from THE BOYS' WAR by Jim Murphy

"Then the batteries opened on all sides [of Sumter] as if an army
of devils were swooping around it."

On April 12, 1861, thousands of Confederate troops were assembled in the still darkness of early morning, looking out toward the mouth of Charleston Harbor. The object of their attention was a squat brick structure sitting on an island one mile away: Fort Sumter. Inside, Robert Anderson, a major in the Union army, along with sixty-eight soldiers, braced for the attack.

Slowly, darkness lifted and Sumter's shape became more and more distinct. Confederate gunners adjusted the firing angle of their weapons, torches poised near the fuses. At exactly 4:30 A.M., General P. G. T. Beauregard gave the command, and the bombardment—and with it the Civil War—began.

An officer inside Fort Sumter described the war's opening shot:

"The eyes of the watchers easily detected and followed the shell as it mounted among the stars, and then descended with ever-increasing velocity, until it landed inside the fort and burst. It was a capital shot. Then the batteries opened on all sides [of Sumter] as if an army of devils were swooping around it."

Thirty-four hours and over four thousand shot and shells later, Sumter's forty-foot-high walls were battered and crumbling. Fires consumed portions of the interior and were moving closer to the powder magazine. No one inside the fort had been seriously injured in the bombardment, but the outcome of the fight was inevitable. The battle for Fort Sumter ended with the surrender of Union forces on April 14.

Before leaving the fort, Union troops were allowed a brief flag-lowering ceremony accompanied by a cannon salute of fifty guns. (Oddly enough, a freak accident during this ceremony caused an explosion that killed two men—the first victims of the Civil War.) Then, with banners flying and the drums beating the rhythm to "Yankee Doodle," Anderson's small force marched aboard the steamship *Baltic* and headed for New York. Beauregard's soldiers entered the burning fort triumphantly and raised the Confederate Stars and Bars. Even before the smoke had a chance to clear, the nation—including its boys—was ready to go off to war.

When word of Fort Sumter's fall reached him in Washington, President Abraham Lincoln acted quickly, issuing a call for seventy-five thousand volunteers to put down the insurrection. News of the president's call to arms spread with surprising speed—by telegraph, newspaper headlines, and word of mouth. Thomas Galway was fifteen years old and living in Cleveland, Ohio, when he heard.

"As I was coming from Mass this morning," Galway wrote in his journal, "I saw bulletins posted everywhere announcing the bombardment of Fort Sumter. Large crowds were gathered in front of each bulletin board, people peering over one another's heads to catch a bit of the news. All seemed of one mind. Everyone talked of war."

Over in Indiana, fourteen-year-old Theodore Upson was working in the cornfield with his father when a neighbor came by. "William Cory came across the field (he had been to town after the Mail). He was excited and said, 'the Rebs have fired upon and taken Fort Sumpter.' Father got white and couldn't say a word.

"William said, 'The President will soon fix them. He has called for 75,000 men and is going to blocade their ports, and just as soon as those fellows find out that the North means business they will get down off their high horse.' "

Much the same was happening in the South. Newspapers hailed the victory at Sumter and predicted that the North would not risk any sort of military action. Public meetings were held to whip up support for the Confederate government.

T. G. Barker, then just thirteen, was attending a small private school in South Carolina. "We were in class," Barker remembered, "all bent over our books, when Headmaster Hammond entered. He did not knock to announce himself, which was unusual, and he did not speak to our teacher either. This was also unusual. He went instead to the middle of the room and said in a serious voice: 'We have had word this morning. Fort Sumter has surrendered and is now a part of the Confederate States of America.' Then he smiled. A second passed and not a sound. Then, as if shot from a cannon, the class stood as one and cheered Hooray! Hooray!"

The political and social causes of the war were numerous and complex, and still produce arguments among historians. Certainly, the profound cultural differences between the North and South were a factor, as were their opposing views on the issue of states' rights. And there is little doubt that an important element of the split was the institution of slavery. Many in the North saw slavery as evil and wanted it abolished completely. Others would accept slavery if it could be confined to the South or if the South agreed to phase it out over a number of years.

For its part, the South viewed slavery as vital to its economic survival. Agriculture, especially the growing of cotton, was its most important business. Slavery provided the cheap labor needed to bring in crops at a profit. Without slavery, Southerners argued, their entire way of life would crumble and be destroyed.

Intensifying matters was the fact that Southern interests were trying to introduce slavery in the newly settled western regions. Many in the North felt that slavery had to be stopped before it had a chance to spread and take hold in the West. As far as Southerners were concerned, the federal government was nothing more than an interfering bully trying to force its views on them.

The slavery question was not a new one at all. It had been discussed and debated, argued and fumed over for nearly fifty years. Tempers were frayed to the point of exploding, and fights had even taken place on the floor of the Senate. When war actually broke out, it was like a pressure-release valve. At last, the country seemed to sigh with relief, something concrete was finally going to settle the dispute.

The result on both sides was an enthusiastic rush to enlist. Men crowded the recruitment centers in the nearest cities or signed on with locally organized units. Emotions ran so high that everywhere enlistment quotas were being met and surpassed easily. Caught up in all of this were boys.

Generally, boys from the North did not join the army because they felt a burning desire to stamp out slavery. One boy's comment about slavery is fairly typical: "I do not know anything about it, whether it is a good thing or a bad thing," he wrote in a letter, "and when talk gets around to it I say very little." Many joined because they wanted to take the defiant South and "set them straight." But most signed up for a simpler reason—to escape the boring routine of farm life and take part in an exciting adventure.

The same spirit of adventure and glory motivated Southern boys as well. A Mississippi recruit said he had joined "to fight the Yankies—all fun and frolic." But underneath the festive attitude was another, deeply felt reason for serving—to defend their homes from a large invading army. One Southern boy made his feelings clear, "I reather die then be com a Slave to the North."

Each side had recruitment rules that expressly banned boys from joining and fighting. At the start of the war, for instance, the Union held that a recruit had to be at least eighteen years old. In spite of this, a tall fourteen- or fifteen-year-old could easily blend into a crowd of men and slip through in the hurry to form a unit. Those questioned about their age might be

A regiment of young Confederate soldiers drills under the walls of Castle Pinkney, South Carolina, 1861.

Library of Congress

A Union drummer boy
in full uniform.

Sixteen-year-old Edwin Francis
Jennison was killed at Malvern Hill,
Virginia, in July 1862.

able to bluff their way past a wary recruiting sergeant. Anyway, how would a recruiter check on an applicant's facts? The
standard forms of identification we have today, such as driver's license, social security number, and credit cards, did not
exist back then. There were no computers or telephones
either, so verifying someone's birthday was nearly impossible.

By far the easiest way for a boy to slip into the army was as
a musician, especially as a drummer or bugler. These were
considered nonfighting positions, so recruiters often allowed a
boy to sign on without worrying about his age. The Union
army alone had need of over forty thousand musicians, while
an estimated twenty thousand served for the South.

Many boys found it surprisingly simple to enlist for duty that would take them into the thick of the fighting. Thomas Galway did. The day after the surrender of Fort Sumter, Galway visited a nearby armory run by a group called the Cleveland Grays. "But they did not seem to me to be the sort of stuff that soldiers are made of, so I went away." That evening, "I went to the armory of the Hibernian Guards. They seemed to like me, and I liked them. So together with Jim Butler and Jim O'Reilly, I enlisted with them. My name was the first on the company's roll to enlist. I didn't tell them that I was only fifteen. So I became a soldier."

On occasion, a boy would enter with the blessings of one or both parents. Ned Hutter went to join the Confederate army near his hometown in Mississippi. When the recruitment officer asked his age, Ned told him the truth: " 'I am sixteen next June,' I said. . . . The officer ordered me out of line and my father, who was behind me, stepped to the table. 'He can work as steady as any man,' my father explained. 'And he can shoot as straight as any who has been signed today. I am the boy's father.' It must have been the way he said the words . . . [because] the officer handed me the pen and ordered, 'sign here.' "

Such support was rare, however, and most boys had to get in by less honest means. A fifteen-year-old Wisconsin boy, Elisha Stockwell, Jr., was one of them. "We heard there was going to be a war meeting at our little log school house," Stockwell recalled. "I went to the meeting and when they called for volunteers, Harrison Maxon (21), Edgar Houghton (16), and myself, put our names down. . . . My father was there and objected to my going, so they scratched my name

L. William Ambrose and Jamie C. Calaise were drummer boys for the Union army.

out, which humiliated me somewhat. My sister gave me a severe calling down . . . for exposing my ignorance before the public, and called me a little snotty boy, which raised my anger. I told her, 'Never mind, I'll go and show you that I am not the little boy you think I am.' "

Elisha's hurt and anger calmed after his sister and mother apologized for what had been said. He even promised not to enlist again if he could attend school that winter. They agreed, and Elisha put aside his zeal to fight the Confederacy.

Unfortunately, Elisha's father had other plans for Elisha's winter. He'd signed up himself and his son to burn charcoal, a tedious, dirty, and backbreaking job. When Elisha learned this, he devised a new plan to enlist. First he told his parents he was going to a dance in town. Then he persuaded a friend's father, a captain in the Union army, to accompany him to a nearby recruitment center.

"The Captain got me in by my lying a little, as I told the recruiting officer I didn't know just how old I was but thought I was eighteen. He didn't measure my height, but called me five feet, five inches high. I wasn't that tall two years later when I re-enlisted, but they let it go, so the records show that as my height."

Elisha went home to gather up some clothes and found his sister in the kitchen preparing dinner. He did not mention anything about fighting for the Union, and after a brief conversation, "I told her I had to go down town. She said, 'Hurry back, for dinner will soon be ready.' But I didn't get back [home] for two years."

Major General Johnny Clem began his army career as a drummer.

CHARLEY SKEDADDLE

from the book by Patricia Beatty
illustrated by Tom LaPadula

*Twelve-year-old Charley Quinn has run away
from his sister in New York City, lied about his age, and joined
the 140th New York Volunteers as a drummer boy. Charley is
proud of his abilities as a fighter and longs to get even with the
Confederates for the death of his brother Johnny, who died at
Gettysburg while serving in the 140th. On May 5, 1864,
Charley experiences his first battle.*

Charley awoke trembling at sunrise to find a hand on his shoulder, shaking him. Over the crackle of musket fire in the distance, a man's voice said into his ear, "Boy, get up and go to the colonel."

Charley got up, fastened on his drum, and hurried to where he'd seen his colonel lie down on a blanket like any other soldier. Something important was happening for sure. Fallon was there with his bugle when he arrived.

Colonel Ayres, a medium-sized, handsome, bearded man, turned from his officers to the two boys. "The Confederates know we're here. That's skirmish fire you're hearing. They must have been just a few miles from us during the night. We're waiting to hear what orders General Griffin will give us."

Charley dared ask, "Will we be fighting here in the Wilderness, sir?"

"It appears so. Go out with your instruments and get the men up and ready. It doesn't matter how much noise you make now."

"Yes, sir," said Charley softly.

Together he and the bugler left the officers. Fallon blew reveille, and Charley beat out the signal Silas had shown him to assemble the men.

Things happened quickly after that. A rider came at a gallop down the Orange Turnpike to the 140th and the other units of the 1st Division. Griffin had ordered them to advance at seven-thirty with their entire force—to attack along the road.

By that hour, the whole division, thousands of men, was in full battle array. A moment after Charley heard the buglers of the various units sound the "advance," the 140th and all the others started forward down the turnpike and through the forest lining its sides, as they'd been ordered.

Then came what men feared most about this part of Virginia—getting lost. As soldiers moved forward, picking their way through the forest where twisting vines and thickets tore at their bodies and small trees grew so close to each other that it was impossible to squeeze through, their progress was slowed. Each part of the trackless Wilderness, though not far out of sight of the road, looked like every other part. Grimly, men walked onward, ever alert for the unseen enemy; but as they moved, they did lose sight of one another and their regiments.

Charley Quinn got lost with them, but by shouting and then by drumming his special signal, he finally was able to reassemble his scattered regiment in one spot. Pulling out Johnny's pocket watch, Charley saw that it was now late morning. They'd been lost for hours. He cursed the Wilderness.

When all of the lost regiments of the 1st Division eventually re-formed in the shelter of trees on the north side of the Orange Turnpike, two lines of attack were drawn up there. The 140th New York was on the left of the first long blue line, and behind them stood their old Gettysburg comrades, the 146th New York, nicknamed Garrard's Tigers.

At ten minutes to noon, Colonel Ayres gave Fallon and Charley the order to sound and beat the "charge." Charley drummed the long roll, a difficult signal that he had just mastered, and Fallon blew "forward." The hoarse cheer that roared up from the men thrilled Charley to the soles of his shoes. He cheered with them as they ran south out of their forest cover in a line of bright bayonets in the midday sunshine and into the trees across the turnpike. Sprinting beside the color-bearer, his heart beating as fast as his drum, Charley Quinn went forward with his regiment. As he ran and drummed, he whooped like an Indian or yelled "Hi-hee" along with the others around him.

Yankee cannon that had been brought down the Orange Turnpike from Culpeper sent shells screeching over their heads to smash into tree trunks, shattering them and sending limbs crashing down among the running men. Hundreds of sparrows fled shrieking from the mutilated trees. A red doe broke in

alarm from her thicket and darted across the march of the 140th into a tall brake in one graceful, bounding motion.

Now unseen Rebel skirmishers, sharpshooters sent out ahead of their regiments, commenced to fire on the advancing bluecoats. The crackle of rifles was suddenly all around Charley as he beat his drum with fingers slick with sweat. He saw men throw up their arms and fall on either side of him as he ran to keep pace with the color-bearer. He stared down at the fallen soldiers in horror, but his drumbeat drove him on as it did the others. Not realizing what he did, he moved along like the others, head downward, leaning forward as against a strong wind.

At Sanders Field, a clearing with a gully in it, the advancing boy caught sight of his first Johnny Rebs, men not in gray as he had expected but in butternut brown. They were running away, looking over their shoulders as they fled down the gully and up over the slope onto the other side. The 140th came after them without a pause. Charley heard Colonel Ayres shouting, "Steady. Steady, men, steady," and Charley came along steadily, his blood drumming in his ears and his thoughts disconnected and fleeting—of his sister Noreen and her sewing machine, of Broadway's traffic which he dodged so nimbly, of the boy from the Dead Rabbit gang he had fought.

The 140th soon learned why the Rebels had given up the fight and fled so easily before them. It had been a trap! Hundreds of Confederates lay at the top of the gully behind felled trees made into breastworks. Down in the gully, Charley Quinn's regiment drew a hideous cross fire from Rebel-filled stands of timber in front of them and to the right.

Driven in on itself, the 140th crowded to the left back toward the Orange Turnpike road. Charley went with them, keeping close to his colonel. As he stood next to the officer, drumming the long roll steadily, a Rebel minié ball—a small, round, hollow musket shell—whistled past his left elbow and smashed into the head of his drum. No sound could come from it now. Charley stood motionless, staring at it, his drumsticks lifted.

Then, all at once, a hoarse shout, "Hurrah, boys. Hurrah!" attracted his attention. To his right he saw Jem Miller, shouting for all he was worth, his legs pumping toward the Confederates' logs. The boy looked on in horror as Jem dropped his musket, spread wide his arms, and crumpled onto the ground at the bottom of the gully. Jem? Jem dead? Dead in the early-afternoon light of such a warm spring day? It could not be. In Charley's brain something howled, "No!"

Charley ran to his fallen friend. A quick glance showed him the red hole in his forehead, the mark of a sharpshooter. In a flash, Charley had Jem's musket to his shoulder. The man had been a careful soldier. He'd have a fresh charge in it if he was running to meet the enemy. Taking aim, little Charley Quinn chose his man, a lanky, brown-bearded Confederate standing atop the logs looking for a target for his own musket. Charley fired. The Rebel dropped his gun and clutched at his shoulder. Blood began to well between his fingers, and he fell backward over the breastworks.

Now the truth flooded Charley's consciousness. Gone were thoughts of heroism and revenge. He had shot a man! He was only twelve years old, and he'd shot and killed a human

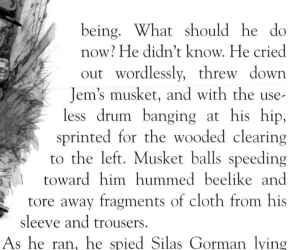

being. What should he do
now? He didn't know. He cried
out wordlessly, threw down
Jem's musket, and with the useless drum banging at his hip,
sprinted for the wooded clearing
to the left. Musket balls speeding
toward him hummed beelike and
tore away fragments of cloth from his
sleeve and trousers.

As he ran, he spied Silas Gorman lying
sprawled not thirty feet away. He could see him
clearly through drifting curls of smoke. Silas had torn away
the seams of one leg of his trousers and was staring down at a
bloody wound on his shin. He saw Charley and beckoned to
him, his mouth open in a call for help that could not be heard
over the shouting, screaming, crackling, and booming that
filled the gully. Silas wanted him! Silas needed him!

But Charley Quinn did not break his stride to go to his
friend. He ran on among the dead and wounded, racing faster,
stumbling forward.

Something strange had happened to his vision. Everything
he saw was crystal-clear—fluffy white smoke drifting over the
clearing from all the firing going on, falling leaves clipped by
musket balls, the open red mouths of the yelling, charging

men of the 140th—and the startled eyes of Con Sullivan as
he saw Charley fleeing.

As the boy ran by him, he heard Con's voice bellowing,
"Charley, skedaddle! Go on. Run away. Run, ye coward Bowery bummer!"

An officer picked up Sullivan's cry. "Run, run, ye whelp.
Run home to your mama!" he shouted, and lifted his pistol to
shoot at Charley but did not pull the trigger.

Running toward the end of the bluecoat troops, Charley
spotted Dan Whaley, the Dead Rabbit who had recognized
him that first day in Culpeper. He didn't shout at him but
watched as Charley streaked past. Other men who knew him
as the regimental drummer boy saw and marked him with
their eyes. An officer at the rear swatted at him with the flat
of his sword to drive him back and missed.

Charley Quinn kept on running to the left even when he'd
passed by all of the men of the 140th New York. He ran like
a fear-crazed animal up over the rim of the gully until a clump
of roots lying in his path brought him down to a crashing halt
flat on his face.

There he lay for a little while panting for breath. The
sound of firing and yelling behind him came clearly to his
ears. He got up, detached the useless drum from its sash, and
dropped both it and the sash onto the earth. The drumsticks
were behind him where he'd dropped them at the clearing.

61

He lurched over to the little creek coming out of a swamp, the creek he'd passed, drumming proudly, just a few minutes before. He bent down to cup water to soothe his burning face. Then he got up, waded across the water, and followed the swamp quite a distance to a particularly dense thicket of undergrowth.

Crawling inside it, Charley sat, with his head on his drawn-up knees, listening to the battle, trying to pray, sobbing in the shame and misery of his desertion. In his mind, he saw Johnny's and Jem's and Silas's accusing faces. He could hear Con's well-remembered voice taunting him. As the boy sat there, a terrorized rabbit came leaping into the thicket to snuggle wild-eyed up against his arm. Charley looked at its quivering sides and trembling whiskers. The battle had made a runaway, a skedaddler, out of it, too, but it was only a rabbit, not a soldier. A rabbit could be expected to run—but not Charley Quinn. That skedaddler had killed a man and then had turned and run—and everybody knew it.

Deep sobs racked Charley's body. He threw himself full-length onto the earth, pounding it, startling the rabbit that had sought refuge by him, making it pin back its ears and lope away. He'd failed this poor frightened creature, too. Charley sat up again, folded his arms on his knees, and lay his head on the blue cloth he was not fit to wear.

The night was quiet, but not the dawn of the sixth of May. The crackling of musket fire came to Charley's ears on all sides. More fighting. Not knowing what else to do, he stayed where he was until a new fear propelled him into action. Fire! Fires from the sparks of thousands of cannon shells had sprung up among the dry leaves of the Wilderness and roared over acres of timberland. Now the gray smoke billowing from them, mixing with gunpowder fumes, drove Charley Quinn out of his protective thicket.

Coughing, frightened by the smoke, he bent to wet his pocket handkerchief in swamp water and tie it around his nose and mouth. As he stooped at the edge of the stinking dark water, he heard a sharp clicking sound he recognized. The cocking of a pistol. Straightening and whirling around, Charley looked up into the face of a lantern-jawed, sallow, yellow-haired man in a brown-yellow short jacket, blue Union army trousers, and a gray forage cap. A Rebel, for sure! In his hand was a huge, long-barreled cavalry pistol. It was aimed at Charley's head. The boy froze.

First the man shot a wad of tobacco juice at Charley's feet, then he asked softly, "What've we got here? I'd say it was a redhead Yankee boy. Kinda small, ain'tcha? If you were a

turtle now, I'd throw you back in the swamp to grow up some. Who'd you be?"

Charley faltered. "I was a drummer boy. My name's Charley." After that he fell silent.

"Charley what?"

"Make it Skedaddle," Charley told him bitterly.

The Confederate laughed. "That's some queer old name you got. Come along with me, boy. My officer'll want to talk to you. Give me your knapsack and jest move out ahead of me."

"Who are you?" Charley asked.

"Who I am don't matter."

Was he a prisoner? Charley sank his teeth into his lower lip to keep from crying. What would happen to him now? What did the Johnny Rebs do with Yankee drummer boy prisoners?

Charley tied the wet cloth over his face and, hands in the air, began to walk ahead of his Rebel captor. It was hard going through the tangle of vines and hickory bushes that tore at his uniform. Twice he fell and was prodded to his feet by the toe of his captor's boot and the words, "Git on up, Yankee boy. I ain't got all day to fetch you back to where we got to go."

Deep among the thickets and trees, Charley could not see fifteen feet ahead of him, but on either side he saw clearly the dead bodies of men dressed in blue and butternut-brown and gray uniforms lying stiff and staring. Sometimes tongues of flame shot up so near that their clothing was singed. The brush hissed and popped in the heat as bright red sparks flew over their heads. Surely this was like the hell the sisters in school and the priest in church had warned him about.

After much turning and twisting, they arrived at a clearing filled with men dressed in the butternut-brown color of the Confederate Army. A half dozen bluecoat soldiers sat on the ground with their hands folded on top of their heads.

Charley's captor told him,"Git on over there and sit down with them other bluebellies."

The boy did as he was told. Looking from face to face, he was relieved to see no one he knew. He took the handful of skillet-parched corn a Reb gave him and tried to chew it. He couldn't and had to spit it out. Rebel soldiers watching him laughed. One said, "It's what we got to eat. Ain't it good enough for you, Yankee brat?"

A Rebel officer in a very tattered, soiled gray coat came over to the prisoners to warn, "Don't you Union men do any talking to one another. I'll personally shoot the man who does. Someone'll be coming to get you soon."

His words proved true. Very shortly three Confederate soldiers with muskets and shining bayonets came to roust the Yankees up and send them walking ahead of them.

An hour's marching of nearly three miles brought Charley and the others through the Wilderness to a large open space where they once again were told to sit. There was a farmhouse, a barn, and some other outbuildings here, as well as hundreds of shabbily dressed Confederate soldiers. Most were gaunt and grimy. Not a few were shoeless. Some wore gray forage caps; others wore brown slouch hats over a mixture of gray and butternut-brown jackets and coats. Some had on Union-blue trousers stripped from the enemy dead.

White smoke from the muskets firing among the trees mingled with the darker smoke from the Wilderness fires. Coming across the open space in acrid-smelling wreaths, it made men cough and sneeze. Charley put the handkerchief up over his nose and mouth again.

The boy was just settling himself onto the ground when he was forced to leap to his feet to keep from being run over by a host of men racing toward him. Rebels! Rebels retreating as fast as they could.

Then a great animal-like roar rose up from a thousand throats, and Charley saw other tattered Rebels racing forward through the ranks of their retreating comrades. A charge! As they ran, they screeched the famous Rebel yell, "Ee ee-ee-ee-ee!"

Behind them came a tall, gray-bearded officer in a gray uniform under a black cloak, riding a dapple-gray horse with a black mane and tail. As the officer reached the charging men, a few of them, hearing the hoofbeats, slackened their speed. At once, a wild shouting rose up from these men: "Go back, General Lee. Go back!"

Lee? Robert E. Lee? Charley Quinn gaped in amazement, as did the other prisoners. Generals were seldom seen anywhere, and certainly not in infantry charges.

Charley watched, fascinated, as a sergeant of the charging Texas Brigade sprang forward to grab hold of the bridle of Lee's horse, stopping the famous Traveller from going into battle with his master.

Now many Texans halted their attack to turn and shout, "We won't go unless you go back!"

A Confederate officer rode up to Lee's side and began to argue with him. When Lee slowly shook his head, the sergeant let go of the rein to release it to his commander-in-chief. An enormous cheer crashed into the smoky air as Robert E. Lee turned his horse around and began to ride toward some horsemen in a knoll to his right.

"Lee! Lee!" echoed soldiers' deep voices. While their comrades cheered, those men of the Texas Brigade who had forced Lee back to safety resumed their charge against the Yankees among the trees.

As for Charley Quinn, he sat down again at a bayonet's prod until a corporal came over, pointed to him, and then jerked him to his feet. Hustled along, he was taken to a tent where a sad-faced, balding Confederate officer sat at a little folding table. It was hot inside, and the front and rear tent flaps were open for ventilation.

Once the corporal had gone, the officer asked, "Who are you, lad?"

"Charley. Charley Skedaddle."

"I know that word. And I doubt that is your real last name."

Charley swallowed and said, "It's Quinn, sir."

"You are not a soldier, are you?"

"No, sir. I never signed any papers to enlist. I was only a drummer."

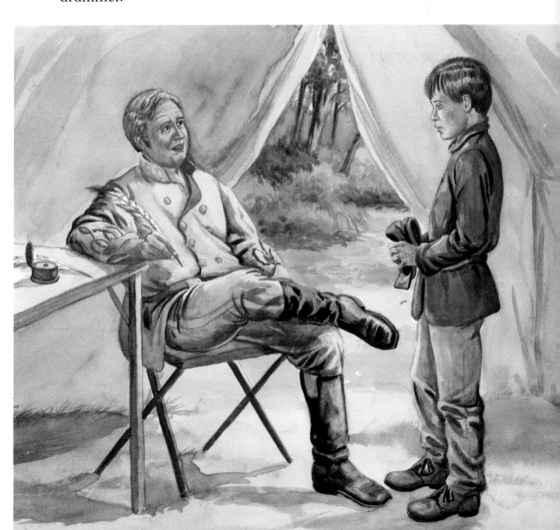

At this, the officer put down the pen he had in his hand. "A drummer boy. I thought as much. What is your age?"

"Twelve, sir."

"What is your regiment?"

Charley didn't answer. All soldiers had been warned that if they were ever captured, they were to tell only their name and rank. He had done that already, and now he said, "I can't tell you that, sir."

The officer smiled slightly. "Have you ever gone to school?"

"Oh, yes, sir. I can read and write just dandy."

"I'm glad to hear it. I was a schoolmaster at one time." He sighed. "How did you get separated from your regiment? I think you can tell me *that*, you know."

Blushing, Charley lowered his gaze. He stuttered, "I—I got scared when I saw my drum hit by a minié ball and saw my friend Jem get killed, so I ran away." No, he wouldn't dare say he'd picked up a musket and killed a Reb. That'd bring him more trouble, for sure.

"So you ran away? I thought you had. Well, you are only a child, after all. Have you ever heard of Andersonville Prison?"

"No, sir, I haven't."

The Confederate officer sighed again. "It's a prison camp for Yankee soldiers down in Georgia. It would be a very bad place to send a boy your age. You should be in a classroom. If any of the men from your regiment in Andersonville found out you were a deserter, it would be even worse for you. Well, then, I think I shall have to do something else with you. You will note that I have not written down one word about you. I'll have no record of you."

"What will you do with me, sir?"

"Have you any money with you?"

"A little bit."

"Good. Yankee money is worth quite a bit more here than our money. Do you see the open tent flap behind me?"

"Yes, sir, I do."

"Then be so good, Charley Skedaddle, as to skedaddle through it right now. As I see it, you are of no use to us. And I don't want it on my conscience that I sent a twelve-year-old boy to Andersonville."

"You're letting me go?"

"Yes, I am. There is a thicket of some size behind this tent. Get into it and stay there until this battle is over and we move on."

"But where'll I go after that, sir?"

"That is up to you." The officer frowned. "If you go north, you'll run into your own troops. If you go south, you'll be captured again and may fare differently with some other man. If you go east, you could run into battle after battle. That's where the fighting is going to be next, unless I miss my guess. What's left to you, then?"

"The west!" said Charley, unable to believe his good fortune.

"Then west it has to be. That's mountain country here in Virginia. You will find it very different from New York City, but I see it as your only refuge right now."

Charley gasped out, "How did you know I was from New York City?"

"Your manner of speaking and how you pronounce words. I've been there. I've made a study of accents. That's why I was given this particular chore with prisoners who will not talk. Get rid of your uniform if you know what is good for you. Now, my boy, do as I tell you. Skedaddle before I change my mind. I don't fancy deserters—no matter how young they may be."

"Thank you, thank you, sir." After lifting his hat, Charley Quinn shot like a bolt past the man's table and out the rear flap of the tent. He sprinted for the nearby hickory thicket and dived inside, all the while thanking the guardian angel the sisters said he always had with him for his deliverance. Once inside the thicket, he took off his blue uniform blouse, discarded his cap, and began to pick at the stripe sewn along the sides of his trousers as part of his splendid drummer boy's uniform.

Lying on his belly in the thicket on that long, hot day, Charley had a lot of time to think and wonder, and the heat of shame crept up to his cheeks as he thought of Silas and Jem. They had not run! They'd fought it out. Had Silas died, too? What had happened to the 140th? Where were they now? Still fighting here in the Wilderness? Were most of them dead, as his friends were?

Would Noreen get a letter from someone in the 140th telling her that he had run away, or would whoever wrote her be kind enough to say he was "missing in action," perhaps even mention that he had picked up a musket and used it?

Used a musket? Yes. Each time he closed his eyes, Charley could again see the man he'd shot and killed.

He'd committed a mortal sin. He wasn't a real soldier who had orders to do that to an enemy. Where could he confess his sin? Where could he find a priest? He should have gone back to the rear of his regiment and halted there, ready to be captured; or else he should have tried to get a new drum from the supply wagon. If he'd done that, he wouldn't be caught in this nightmare now.

But he hadn't. He'd killed a man, and then he'd run and kept on running. Now look at him—he was no longer in any uniform at all. And he was alone and nameless in a thicket somewhere in the dreaded Wilderness.

The fight went on and on till sunset, and while it did, Charley lay in his thicket, afraid to move lest he be discovered. Insects crawled over him, and once a brown-bodied little snake twisted by, not three feet from his motionless hand. Oh, how did he ever find himself in this vile place? Why did he ever leave the Bowery? How he missed New York! How he wished he were back in the Bowery among his friends. He'd give anything to be with Noreen. He'd even be glad to see Noreen's fiancé, Mr. Demarest. They would find him different now—they would. He would even give up his membership in the Bowery Boys if Noreen wanted.

Dozens of thoughts and recriminations, all of them sad or frightening, went through Charley's head as he lay there, until finally, worn out by anguish, fear, and hunger, he fell asleep, his face pressed to the red soil. And while he slept, the Battle of the Wilderness slowed and then petered out in the darkness.

THE GREATEST SNOWBALL FIGHT IN HISTORY

William Graves

illustrated by Arieh Zeldich

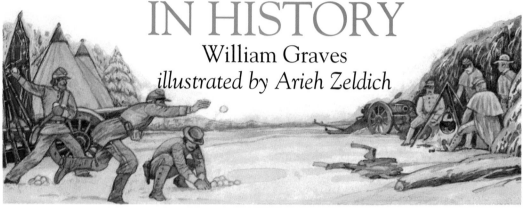

On the morning of 29 January 1863, a thick, wet blanket of snow covered the Union and Confederate armies camped on either side of the Rappahannock River in Virginia. The Yankees, used to cold, snowy winters, just groaned and clutched their heavy blankets more tightly about them. But many of the Confederate soldiers had never seen snow before; they were delighted with the cold white stuff and wasted no time leaving their huts and tents to throw a few snowballs.

It started out as just a small fight between a few men in the First and Fourth Regiments of the Texas Brigade. Then, like a giant snowball rolling down a mountain, the fight gained momentum until all the men in the two regiments were pelting each other with icy snowballs. After a while they joined forces to attack the still-sleeping Fifth Regiment and, with a murderous barrage of iceballs, charged their fellow Texans.

The Bloody Fifth, never one to avoid a fight, counterattacked vigorously.

It wasn't long before someone yelled, "Let's get the Porkers!" and with a shout of laughter the fight expanded still further. Even the officers entered into it now; some of them directing the enlisted men in preparing a huge supply of snowball ammunition, others sending out scouts and forming the wings as the three regiments prepared to descend on the unsuspecting "Porkers" of the Third Arkansas Regiment (also part of the Texas Brigade).

General John Bell Hood, commander of the entire brigade, watched the Texans attack the boys from Arkansas, but he stayed neutral as his men fought it out with thousands of sailing snowballs. Then, smiling, Hood turned to his staff and whispered instructions.

A great cheer arose from the men as the brigade battle flag unfurled in the crisp winter air. Bugles, fifes, and drums sounded as Hood's staff hurried to carry out orders. The enlisted men followed their general's instructions and formed into battle array, stuffing their haversacks with snow and ice and packing plenty of snowballs to carry in their arms.

Then, led by General Hood himself, the laughing, stumbling Texas Brigade pushed through two feet of snow for a surprise attack on General G.T. Anderson's Georgia Brigade which was calmly eating breakfast.

Fifteen hundred men strong, the Texas Brigade stormed the "Goober Grabbers," as the Georgia Brigade was known—laughing, yelling, pelting them with snowballs. General Anderson, always quick to see his duty and do it, rallied his men and ordered the Georgians to counterattack the cold,

wet avalanche of snowballs flying from the Texans and Arkansans.

The battle was spirited as the men heaved snowballs for all they were worth. Generals Hood and Anderson, bravely positioned in the heaviest fire and drenched with snow and icy melting water, directed their brigades masterfully; regimental colonels moved their men to best press the attack or shore up the defense.

At last a lull fell over the battlefield. The generals conferred, grinned, shook hands—and a truce was declared. The two brigades joined to form a division and moved forward against the ready and waiting division under General Lafayette McLaw's command.

The drums sounded like thunder, the bugles like shrill battle cries as the two divisions clashed together in the snowy woods. There were nine thousand men, shouting and laughing, soaked by countless wounds from the harmless white cannonballs. Generals and colonels tackled friends to rub their faces in the snow; enlisted men raced across enemy lines to liberate their captured leaders.

And across the Rappahannock River the Union Army stood to arms, fearing from the noise that an attack was imminent.

At last the battle drew to a close, and the Confederates retreated happily to their campsites. The biggest snowball fight in history had ended. Years later, when asked what was the hottest battle he had ever been in, many a grizzled veteran, remembering the snowy hills behind Fredericksburg, would say without hesitation, "The great snowball fight of '63."

TENTING ON THE OLD CAMP GROUND

Walter Kittredge

We're tent-ing to-night on the old Camp ground, Give us a song to cheer__ Our wear-y hearts, a song of home. And friends we love so dear. __ Man-y are the hearts that are wear-y to-night, __ Wish-ing for the war to cease,__ Man-y are the hearts look-ing for the right To see the dawn of peace.__ Tent-ing to-night, Tent-ing to-night,__ Tent-ing on the old Camp ground. __

musical notation by Christina T. Davidson

We've been tenting tonight on the old Camp ground,
    Thinking of days gone by,
Of the lov'd ones at home that gave us the hand,
    And the tear that said "Good bye!"

Chorus: Many are the hearts, etc.

We are tired of war on the old Camp ground,
    Many are dead and gone,
Of the brave and true who've left their homes,
    Others been wounded long.

Chorus: Many are the hearts, etc.

We've been fighting today on the old Camp ground,
    Many are lying near;
Some are dead, and some are dying,
    Many are in tears.

Chorus: (after last verse)
Many are the hearts that are weary tonight,
    Wishing for the war to cease,
Many are the hearts looking for the right
    To see the dawn of peace.
Dying tonight, Dying tonight,
    Dying on the old Camp ground.

THE HOSPITAL
Louisa May Alcott

*Many women on both sides volunteered as nurses
in army hospitals. One of those who volunteered was Louisa
May Alcott (later to write* Little Women *and other popular
novels for children). She reported for duty to a Washington
hospital late in 1862. She writes about her experiences.*

There they were! "Our brave boys," as the papers justly call them, for cowards could hardly have been so riddled with shot and shell, so torn and shattered, nor have borne suffering for which we have no name, with an uncomplaining fortitude, which made one glad to cherish each as a brother. In they came, some on stretchers, some in men's arms, some feebly staggering along propped on rude crutches, and one lay stark and still with covered face, as a comrade gave his name to be recorded before they carried him away to the dead house. All was hurry and confusion; the hall was full of these wrecks of humanity, for the most exhausted could not reach a bed till duly ticketed and registered; the walls were lined with rows of such as could sit, the floor covered with the more disabled, the steps and doorways filled with helpers and lookers-on; the sound of many feet and voices

A ward in the Armory Square Hospital in Washington, D.C.

U.S. Military History Institute, Carlisle Barracks, Pennsylvania

made that usually quiet hour as noisy as noon; and, in the midst of it all, the matron's motherly face brought more comfort to many a poor soul than the cordial draughts she administered, or the cheery words that welcomed all, making of the hospital a home. . . .

The house had been a hotel before hospitals were needed, and many of the doors still bore their old names; some not so inappropriate as might be imagined, for my ward was in truth a ball-room, if gunshot wounds could christen it. Forty beds were prepared, many already tenanted by tired men who fell down anywhere, and drowsed till the smell of food roused them. Round the great stove was gathered the dreariest group I ever saw—ragged, gaunt and pale, mud to the knees, with bloody bandages untouched since put on days before; many bundled up in blankets, coats being lost or useless; and all wearing that disheartened look which proclaimed defeat more plainly than any telegram of the Burnside blunder. I pitied them so much, I dared not speak to them, though, remembering all they had been through since the rout at Fredericksburg, I yearned to serve the dreariest of them all. Presently, Miss Blank tore me from my refuge behind piles of one-sleeved shirts, odd socks, bandages and lint; put basin, sponge, towels, and a block of brown soap into my hands, with these appalling directions:

"Come, my dear, begin to wash as fast as you can. Tell them to take off socks, coats and shirts, scrub them well, put on clean shirts, and the attendants will finish them off, and lay them in bed."

If she had requested me to shave them all, or dance a hornpipe on the stove funnel, I should have been less staggered; but to scrub some dozen lords of creation at a moment's notice, was really—really—. However, there was no time for nonsense, and, having resolved when I came to do everything I was bid, I drowned my scruples in my washbowl, clutched my soap manfully, and, assuming a businesslike air, made a dab at the first dirty specimen I saw. . . . I scrubbed away like any tidy parent on a Saturday night. Some of them took the performance like sleepy children, leaning their tired heads against me as I worked, others looked grimly scandalized, and several of the roughest colored like bashful girls. One wore a soiled little bag about his neck, and as I moved it, to bathe his wounded breast, I said, "Your talisman didn't save you, did it?"

"Well, I reckon it did, marm, for that shot would a gone a couple a inches deeper but for my old mammy's camphor bag," answered the cheerful philosopher.

Another, with a gunshot wound through the cheek, asked for a looking glass, and when I brought one, regarded his swollen face with a dolorous expression, as he muttered—

"I vow to gosh, that's too bad! I warn't a bad-looking chap before, and now I'm done for; won't there be a thunderin' scar! And what on earth will Josephine Skinner say?"

A nurse at a Union hospital in Tennessee.

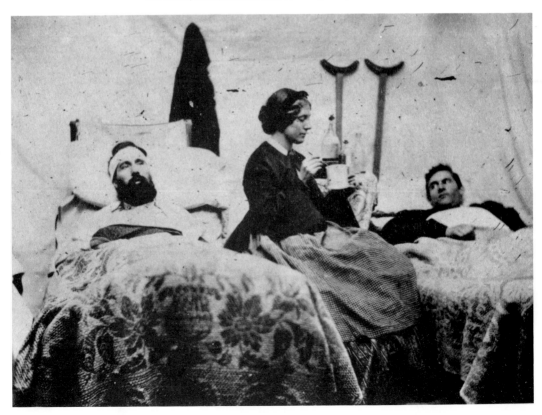

THE TELEGRAM

from LITTLE WOMEN
by Louisa May Alcott
illustrated by Larry Frederick

Meg, Jo, Beth, and Amy were the four daughters of Mr. and Mrs. March whom Mr. March lovingly called his "little women." When their father had to go away to war, the girls did their best to help their mother and their housekeeper, Hannah. Laurie, a wealthy, motherless neighbor boy, almost a member of the family, could never do enough for Mrs. March and the girls, whom he adored.

A sharp ring interrupted Mrs. March, and a minute after, Hannah came in with a letter.

"It's one of them horrid telegraph things, mum," she said, handing it as if she was afraid it would explode and do some damage.

At the word "telegraph," Mrs. March snatched it, read the two lines it contained, and dropped back into her chair as white as if the little paper had sent a bullet to her heart. Laurie dashed downstairs for water, while Meg and Hannah supported her, and Jo read aloud, in a frightened voice,—

"Mrs. March:
Your husband is very ill. Come at once.
S. Hale, Blank Hospital, Washington."

How still the room was as they listened breathlessly, how strangely the day darkened outside, and how suddenly the whole world seemed to change, as the girls gathered about their mother, feeling as if all the happiness and support of their lives was about to be taken from them. Mrs. March was herself again directly; read the message over, and stretched out her arms to her daughters, saying, in a tone they never forgot, "I shall go at once, but it may be too late. O children, children, help me to bear it!"

For several minutes there was nothing but the sound of sobbing in the room, mingled with broken words of comfort, tender assurances of help, and hopeful whispers that died away in tears. Poor Hannah was the first to recover, and with unconscious wisdom she set all the rest a good example; for, with her, work was the panacea for most afflictions.

"The Lord keep the dear man! I won't waste no time a cryin', but git your things ready right away, mum," she said heartily, as she wiped her face on her apron, gave her mistress a warm shake of the hand with her own hard one, and went away, to work like three women in one.

"She's right; there's no time for tears now. Be calm, girls, and let me think."

They tried to be calm, poor things, as their mother sat up, looking pale, but steady, and put away her grief to think and plan for them.

"Where's Laurie?" she asked presently, when she had collected her thoughts, and decided on the first duties to be done.

"Here, ma'am. Oh, let me do something!" cried the boy, hurrying from the next room, whither he had withdrawn, feeling that their first sorrow was too sacred for even his friendly eyes to see.

"Send a telegram saying I will come at once. The next train goes early in the morning. I'll take that."

"What else? The horses are ready; I can go anywhere, do anything," he said, looking ready to fly to the ends of the earth.

"Leave a note at Aunt March's. Jo, give me that pen and paper."

Tearing off the blank side of one of her newly copied pages, Jo drew the table before her mother, well knowing that money for the long, sad journey must be borrowed, and feeling as if she could do anything to add a little to the sum for her father.

"Now go, dear; but don't kill yourself driving at a desperate pace; there is no need of that."

Mrs. March's warning was evidently thrown away; for five minutes later Laurie tore by the window on his own fleet horse, riding as if for his life.

"Jo, run to the rooms, and tell Mrs. King that I can't come. On the way get these things. I'll put them down; they'll be needed, and I must go prepared for nursing. Hospital stores are not always good. Beth, go and ask Mr. Laurence for a couple of bottles of old wine: I'm not too proud to beg for father;

he shall have the best of everything. Amy, tell Hannah to get down the black trunk; and, Meg, come and help me find my things, for I'm half bewildered."

Writing, thinking, and directing, all at once, might well bewilder the poor lady, and Meg begged her to sit quietly in her room for a little while and let them work. Everyone scattered like leaves before a gust of wind; and the quiet, happy household was broken up as suddenly as if the paper had been an evil spell.

The short afternoon wore away; all the other errands were done, and Meg and her mother busy at some necessary needlework, while Beth and Amy got tea, and Hannah finished her ironing with what she called a "slap and a bang," but still Jo did not come. They began to get anxious; and Laurie went off to find her, for no one ever knew what freak Jo might take into her head. He missed her, however, and she came walking in with a very queer expression of countenance, for there was a mixture of fun and fear, satisfaction and regret in it, which puzzled the family as much as did the roll of bills she laid before her mother, saying, with a little choke in her voice, "That's my contribution towards making father comfortable and bringing him home!"

"My dear, where did you get it? Twenty-five dollars! Jo, I hope you haven't done anything rash?"

"No, it's mine honestly; I didn't beg, borrow, or steal it. I earned it; and I don't think you'll blame me, for I only sold what was my own."

As she spoke, Jo took off her bonnet, and a general outcry arose, for all her abundant hair was cut short.

"Your hair! Your beautiful hair!" "O Jo, how could you? Your one beauty." "My dear girl, there was no need of this." "She doesn't look like my Jo any more, but I love her dearly for it!"

As everyone exclaimed, and Beth hugged the cropped head tenderly, Jo assumed an indifferent air, which did not deceive anyone a particle, and said, rumpling up the brown bush, and trying to look as if she liked it: "It doesn't affect the fate of the nation, so don't wail, Beth. It will be good for my vanity; I was getting too proud of my wig. It will do my brains good to have that mop taken off; my head feels deliciously light and cool, and the barber said I could soon have a curly crop, which will be boyish, becoming, and easy to keep in order. I'm satisfied; so please take the money, and let's have supper."

"Tell me all about it, Jo. *I* am not quite satisfied, but I can't blame you, for I know how willingly you sacrificed your vanity, as you call it, to your love. But, my dear, it was not necessary, and I'm afraid you will regret it, one of these days," said Mrs. March.

"No, I won't!" returned Jo stoutly, feeling much relieved that her prank was not entirely condemned.

"What made you do it?" asked Amy, who would as soon have thought of cutting off her head as her pretty hair.

"Well, I was wild to do something for father," replied Jo, as they gathered about the table.

"I hate to borrow as much as mother does, and I knew Aunt March would croak; she always does, if you ask for a ninepence. Meg gave all her quarterly salary toward the rent, and I only got some clothes with mine, so I felt wicked, and was bound to have some money, if I sold the nose off my face to get it."

"You needn't feel wicked, my child; you had no winter things, and got the simplest with your own hard earnings," said Mrs. March, with a look that warmed Jo's heart.

"I hadn't the least idea of selling my hair at first, but as I went along I kept thinking what I could do, and feeling as if I'd like to dive into some of the rich stores and help myself. In a barber's window I saw tails of hair with the prices marked; and one black tail, not so thick as mine, was forty dollars. It came over me all of a sudden that I had one thing to make money out of, and without stopping to think, I walked in, asked if they bought hair, and what they would give for mine."

"I don't see how you dared to do it," said Beth, in a tone of awe.

"Oh, he was a little man who looked as if he merely lived to oil his hair. He rather stared, at first, as if he wasn't used to having girls bounce into his shop and ask him to buy their hair. He said he didn't care about mine, it wasn't the fashionable color, and he never paid much for it in the first place; the work put into it made it dear, and so on. It was getting late, and I was afraid, if it wasn't done right away, that I shouldn't have it done at all, and you know when I start to do a thing, I hate to give it up; so I begged him to take it, and told him why I was in such a hurry. It was silly, I dare say, but it changed his mind, for I got rather excited, and told the story in my topsy-turvy way, and his wife heard, and said so kindly: 'Take it, Thomas, and oblige the young lady; I'd do as much for our Jimmy if I had a spire of hair worth selling.' "

"Who was Jimmy?" asked Amy, who liked having things explained as they went along.

"Her son, she said, who was in the army. How friendly such things make strangers feel, don't they? She talked away all the time the man clipped, and diverted my mind nicely."

"Didn't you feel dreadfully when the first cut came?" asked Meg, with a shiver.

"I took a last look at my hair while the man got his things, and that was the end of it. I never snivel over trifles like that; I will confess, though, I felt queer when I saw the dear old hair laid out on the table, and felt only the short, rough ends on my head. It almost seemed as if I'd an arm or a leg cut off. The woman saw me look at it, and picked out a long lock for me to keep. I'll give it to you, Marmee, just to remember past glories by; for a crop is so comfortable I don't think I shall ever have a mane again."

Mrs. March folded the wavy chestnut lock, and laid it away with a short gray one in her desk. She only said "Thank you, deary," but something in her face made the girls change the subject, and talk as cheerfully as they could about the prospect of a fine day tomorrow, and the happy times they would have when father came home to be nursed.

No one wanted to go to bed, when, at ten o'clock, Mrs. March put by the last finished job, and said, "Come, girls." Beth went to the piano and played her father's favorite hymn; all began bravely, but broke down one by one, till Beth was left alone, singing with all her heart, for to her music was always a sweet consoler.

"Go to bed and don't talk, for we must be up early, and shall need all the sleep we can get. Good-night, my darlings," said Mrs. March, as the hymn ended, for no one cared to try another.

They kissed her quietly, and went to bed as silently as if the dear invalid lay in the next room. Beth and Amy soon fell asleep in spite of the great trouble, but Meg lay awake, thinking the most serious thoughts she had ever known in her short life. Jo lay motionless, and her sister fancied that she was asleep, till a stifled sob made her exclaim, as she touched a wet cheek,—

"Jo, dear, what is it? Are you crying about father?"

"No, not now."

"What then?"

"My—my hair!" burst out poor Jo.

MEET LOUISA MAY ALCOTT, AUTHOR

Louisa May Alcott was born in 1832 in Pennsylvania and lived most of her life with her parents and three sisters in Concord, Massachusetts. She supported herself and her parents by writing romantic adventure stories for adults. In 1867, a publisher asked her to write a story for girls. She wrote in her journal, "Mr. N. wants a girl's story, and I begin Little Women. *Marmee, Anna, and May all approve my plan. So I plod away, though I don't enjoy this sort of thing. Never liked girls or knew many, except my sisters; but our queer plays and experiences may prove interesting, though I doubt it." Years later, she wrote next to this entry: "Good joke."*

A Rainy Day in Camp. 1871.
Winslow Homer.

Oil on canvas. Gift of Mrs. William F.
Milton, 1923, The Metropolitan Museum
of Art. 23.77.1. Photo: © 1983 The
Metropolitan Museum of Art

*Filling Cartridges at the
U.S. Arsenal at Watertown,
Massachusetts.* 1861.
Winslow Homer.

Wood engraving. From *Harper's
Weekly*, July 20, 1861. Harris Brisbane
Dick Fund, 1929, The Metropolitan
Museum of Art. 29.88.1

FINE ART
THE CIVIL WAR

Ruins of Charleston, South Carolina.
c. 1865. Alexander Gardner.

Photograph. The Erwin Smith Collection,
Library of Congress. Photo: PHOTRI

Robert Gould Shaw Memorial on Boston
Commons. 1897. Augustus Saint-Gaudens.

Bronze bas-relief. Photo: Richard Avery/Stock, Boston

*A Ride for Liberty—
the Fugitive Slaves.*
1862. Eastman
Johnson.

Oil on board. Gift of Miss
Gwendolyn O.L. Conkling,
The Brooklyn Museum

THE SIEGE OF VICKSBURG

from THE TAMARACK TREE
by Patricia Clapp
illustrated by Lydia Halverson

*Seventeen-year-old Rosemary Leigh was born
in England, but has lived since her mother's death with her older
brother Derek in Vicksburg, Mississippi. Living with Rosemary
and Derek are their cook Amanda and Amanda's daughter
Betsy. Amanda's husband, Hector, is a free black man who was
once active in the Underground Railroad.*

It was midafternoon yesterday when Mary Byrd Blair and I stumbled up the hill on our way home from the hospital. We were untidy and stained from the work we had been doing, and so weary we could scarcely put one foot before the other. The firing was slight and I commented on it.

"I wonder why they have stopped so suddenly. I don't like it."

"I expect it's time for tea," Mary Byrd said airily. "Isn't it true that in England everything stops for tea?"

"If only we were in England now!" Then I giggled. "I wonder if the soldiers crook their little fingers when they hold their cups. And do you suppose they're having cucumber sandwiches with their tea?"

"Stop talking about food! If a chicken squawked by right now I'd eat it! Feathers and all!"

I laughed. "Once I would have considered that a disgusting thought."

"Well, maybe I'd pull some of the feathers off," she admitted. "I never knew before what it was to be truly hungry, did you, Rosemary?"

"Never. There may be *something* to eat at our house." Casually I added, "I don't know whether Derek is home or not," and glanced sideways at Mary Byrd. I saw her blush and smiled to myself.

"Well, I'll stop," she said, "but I can't stay long. Mamma goes into a real swivet when the shelling starts and she doesn't know where I am."

We walked across the broad lawn, untended now and full of weeds, and my dog Woof came slowly to meet us. How thin he was! I leaned and stroked him, and together we went into

the house. Amanda and Betsy were in the kitchen, Betsy on her mother's lap. Amanda looked up, her face worried.

"What is it?" I asked. "Is Betsy not feeling well?"

"She's so cold, Miss Rosemary. Seems like she can't stop shivering."

"Do you know what's the matter with her?"

"No. I sure wish I did."

I knelt beside the rocking chair and took Betsy's hand in mine. "Where does it hurt, Betsy? What is the trouble, baby, can you tell us?"

Betsy raised dark teary eyes. "I'm so hungry," she murmured, "and I'm so ascared of all the shootin', and my head aches." Burrowing that black curly head in Amanda's shoulder she sobbed quietly.

"I was just about to go get us the milk," her mother said, "and maybe I could get an egg or two. Those neighbors still have a few chickens nobody found yet." She smiled wryly. "They're keeping them in their back parlor so nobody knows. With a dab of milk and an egg I could fix something for the child here. But I can't take her, and I don't like to leave her alone."

"We'll watch her," Mary Byrd said. "You go along, Amanda. We'll take good care of Betsy." She gazed at Amanda in quiet wonder. "I didn't know there was a chicken or a cow left within a hundred miles," she added. "Amanda, you're amazing!"

"Seems I just know some real handy folks," she said rising, and gesturing for me to sit down, she placed Betsy in my lap. "I'll be back soon's I can," she said, gathering up her old cloth bag and going out the kitchen door.

I sat rocking, Betsy huddled in my arms. Mary Byrd sat on the floor beside us, and started to sing very softly. It was some sort of lullaby, and her sweet voice made it a tender, soothing melody. Betsy's eyes began to droop, and after a moment or two I felt her relax in sleep.

"I never heard you sing before," I said quietly. "You have a lovely voice."

"There hasn't been much to sing about lately, sugar. When is it ever going to be over, Rosemary?"

"There was talk about the fourth of July, remember? And that's the day after tomorrow. At least it's quiet now."

Just as I spoke those ill-timed words the guns started again, louder and closer than I had ever heard them. It seemed as if the earth shook with their thunder. Betsy jerked upright in

my arms and screamed, and I could not stop her. I cupped my hands over her ears, but it was no help.

"Let's take her down to the basement," I shouted at Mary Byrd. "It may shut out some of the noise."

Mary Byrd nodded, and together we managed to get a hysterical Betsy down the kitchen steps, Woof slinking along beside us. We laid the child on one of the mattresses and I sat beside her and tried to comfort her, but she was beyond hearing me. As the shelling continued, almost paralyzing in its intensity, shriek after shriek came from her, her eyes shifted like those of a frightened horse, her hands clutched at me. Mary Byrd moved close to us, and I don't think either of us knew whether we were huddling together for mutual solace or for protection.

And then a shell crashed through the cellar wall, rolled a few feet toward us, and lay there, round and ugly, hissing. If Betsy had not fainted I am sure I would have. Suddenly I was scanning the walls of the basement frantically, looking for the entrance to the secret tunnel I knew was there.

"The wine racks," I shouted at Mary Byrd. "Behind the wine racks."

She looked at me as if I had gone mad, but when I stood up, leaving Betsy unconscious on the mattress, she rose with me, her eyes on mine. I ran to the wall lined with racks and racks of dusty bottles, pushing against them, pulling at them, muttering to myself, unheard in that continuing racket, glancing over my shoulder at the sinister shell that lay across the basement from us, and I prayed. Oh, how I prayed! And then I felt one tier of shelves give a little under my hand, and as I struggled with it, it slowly came away from the wall, moving on hinges as a door does. Behind it another door opened slowly outward. Woof kept getting under my feet, Mary Byrd was at my shoulder, her blue eyes huge as she stared into the damp, musty-smelling darkness behind that door. When I ran back to the mattress on which Betsy lay, she was beside me,

helping drag child and mattress through the door, into that stygian blackness, helping me shut the door behind us, closing us in. Just as I sank down on the edge of the mattress there came an ear-splitting crash from the other side of the door, followed by the roar of falling wood and plaster, and the sharp sound of shattered glass. I threw myself across Betsy and my head knocked hard against another head, Mary Byrd's, as she did precisely the same thing.

For what seemed an eternity we lay that way, Woof shaking as he huddled close into me, until the noise stopped. I sat up, and when I spoke my voice seemed very loud in the sudden quiet.

"Betsy. Are you all right?"

Her voice was small but clear. "I think so, Miss Romy. But I'm a mite squashed. Why you two ladies pounce on me like that?"

Mary Byrd started to laugh, and after a second I laughed with her. "Squashed!" she said, and went off into another gale. We couldn't stop, until finally, with gasps for breath, she managed to speak. "Where in the name of heaven are we?"

"In a tunnel under the house," I told her.

"Oh." A pause. "Rosemary, *why* is there a tunnel under the house?"

"It's an escape tunnel for slaves."

"Oh." Another pause. "I see. I've heard of them."

There was not a glimmer of light anywhere. The blackness was as thick and heavy as a rug. I could feel Woof trembling against me, but I could not see him. I felt for Betsy's hand and held it tightly in mine, but I could not see her. I groped for Mary Byrd's hand, found it and clasped it. The darkness was absolute.

"I don't think I like this very much," Mary Byrd said. "I wonder what the basement is like. Perhaps we should open the door and look."

"I'll try."

"I'll help."

I stood up and stepped inch by inch toward where I thought the door must be, Mary Byrd clutching my skirt. I felt for the rough wooden surface of the door, and in a step or two, found it.

"It's here," I said, and pushed against the door. It didn't move. "It seems to be stuck."

"Let's push together. One, two, three—*push!*" It was useless. "Maybe if we put our backs against it," Mary Byrd suggested.

Together we leaned our backs against the stubborn door, pushing with all our strength. It did not give an inch. I felt a sudden movement from Mary Byrd and heard her gasp a quick "Oh!"

"What is it?"

"My foot slipped and I twisted my ankle. It's nothing."

"Are you all right?"

"Of course. Let's sit down for a moment and decide what to do next."

But when she tried to take the few steps to the mattress I could hear her inhale sharply, and I knew the ankle must be painful.

"Put your arm across my shoulders and hop," I told her. "I'll hold you up."

With my arm about her waist she hopped, and I helped her settle on a corner of the mattress.

"Is it very bad?" I asked.

"As you would say, Rosemary, don't worry. What do you think we should do now?"

"Be very brave," I answered aloud, and said silently to myself, Be *very* brave, Rosemary! I could feel the cold damp sweat breaking out on my forehead, my face, my arms. It was the old terrifying feeling that I thought familiarity with the cave had banished, but here it was again, worse than I had ever felt it. I clenched my teeth tightly together and tried to slow my breathing. I *had* to keep calm. If Betsy and Mary Byrd even suspected my terror it could affect them, too. My heart was beating so hard I was sure the others could hear it in the silence. In the dark stillness. When Betsy spoke I jumped.

"I've been in here before. Dada showed me this place."

"Your daddy showed you, Betsy?" Mary Byrd asked. "How did he know about it?"

The child's voice held pride. "Dada helped to dig it."

"Your *father*? Hector helped dig this tunnel?"

"Yes, Miss Mary Byrd. It's a great long tunnel, too."

"Does Derek know about it, Rosemary?"

"Yes," I managed, though my voice seemed to squeak.

"I see," Mary Byrd said after a pause. "He never told me."

"I wish there was a light in here," I said. It was almost a whisper.

Betsy moved and was sitting beside me, her hand on my shoulder. I wondered if she could feel me shaking.

"There might be," she said.

"There might be what?"

"A light. A candle maybe. I 'member. When I was here with Dada he showed me little . . . shelf things. In the walls. There was a box with candles and matches."

I looked around straining my eyes, but the darkness was impenetrable. "Where, Betsy? Where were the shelves? Can you remember?" As I spoke I found myself getting to my feet. Anything was better than sitting there shivering.

"They're just sort of stuck on the walls. I don't know where."

"Maybe I can find them."

Mary Byrd's hand grasped my skirt. "Rosemary, sit down! You'll get lost!"

I swallowed hard and tried to sound calm. "If this is a tunnel I can't get very far lost. If I don't find any shelves I'll . . . I'll just turn around and come back. Hold Woof's collar. I don't want to trip over him."

Mary Byrd's voice came in a mutter. "I wish somebody would hold *your* collar!"

My knees felt like water, but I forced myself to take a few steps in that solid blackness, stretching out my arms, my fingers brushing along the clay walls. From behind me Betsy spoke.

"The shelves are 'bout at the top of my head," she offered.

"Thank you," I said politely.

This is what it's like to be blind, I thought. Blind and buried alive. Step by trembling step I moved, fingers trailing along the walls. How far had I come? Not far—I could turn now and in a few steps be back with Betsy and Mary Byrd and Woof. In the dark. No, it was better to go on if there was any chance of light. What an atavistic fear it is, the fear of darkness! I wanted to claw through the walls to light and air. The fingers of my right hand stubbed against rough wood. "Ow!"

"What is it?" Mary Byrd's voice seemed a long way off.

"I think I found a—yes! A shelf! Wait . . . there's something . . . a box, I think. . . ." My hand, shaking uncontrollably, felt a square outline. I tried to lift it, but it seemed fastened to a wooden shelf projecting from the wall. "I can't see how it opens . . . wait, yes . . . I can." My blind fingers raised a lid, scrabbled in the box, felt the blessed smooth waxen shape of candles! Matches? Oh, please God, let there be matches! A smaller box, I could feel roughness on the outside. Gently, oh, so gently—I pushed at one end of it. If they should spill I'd never find them! The little drawer of the matchbox opened, inside . . . yes . . . oh, thank you God! Inside were matches.

"I found them. Candles—and matches! If I can just light one . . . "

"I knew they were there," came Betsy's smug voice.

"You are wonderful!" I said and meant each syllable. With icy cold fingers I took a match from the little box and struck it against the roughness. It sparked and went out. Another. This one broke in my shaking hand. A third. A tiny flame that wavered in my heavy breathing. I closed my mouth tight, held the match carefully until the flame strengthened, took the candle from the box—and lit it! It was like life after death! I had never, in all my life, been so proud of myself. I turned back to where the others must be.

"Look!"

"Just like Mamma tells from the Bible," Betsy remarked. "Let there be light."

"And there was light," Mary Byrd finished, her voice solemn.

Holding the lighted candle, shielding it with my other hand, I moved back. Six shining eyes watched as I approached. I felt exhausted and exhilarated—and almost in control of my fear.

"I 'membered, I 'membered," Betsy crowed, bright-eyed with excitement.

"Where does the tunnel go, Betsy? Can you remember that?"

"I don't know, Miss Romy. Dada and me, we never went all the way. He just showed it to me once, and said he helped dig it. He said it was very long."

I pushed my brain to recall what Hector had said. I could hear his deep voice: "About a mile . . ." Could I possibly walk a mile in this clammy place? "I could go along to the end and bring someone back to help us," I said.

"And you'd probably step out right spang in the middle of Yankeedom!" Mary Byrd said flatly. "Don't you move! We're going to sit right here on this mattress until someone gets us out." She stopped suddenly, and when she went on her voice was very small. "Someone *will* get us out, won't they?"

"Of course," I said, trying to sound confident.

How long would it take Amanda to get back? When would Derry come home? It might not be for hours. Would anyone think to look for us here? And if they found us, could they get the door open? There must be piles of rubbish against it. . . . I tipped the candle until a little wax dripped onto the floor, and then set the candle in it. My hand felt too weak to hold it any longer. In the small circle of flickering light we all looked at each other.

Mary Byrd reached out one hand and took Betsy's, with her other hand she took mine. Softly she started to sing.

"Row, row, row your boat . . ."

If she could do it, I could. I gritted my teeth against panic, and at the appropriate moment I joined in. A few bars later, Betsy's shrill little voice picked up the old round.

"Merrily, merrily, merrily, merrily, life is but a dream." No, like a nightmare, I thought, but we kept singing, over and over, our voices getting louder, until we were shouting the repetitive words at the tops of our lungs.

As I paused for breath I heard what seemed an echo—but the voices were deeper. Male voices. "Row, row, row your boat," they sang determinedly, and from beyond the door came the noise of heavy objects being moved, the crash of broken glass, the scrape of things being pulled across other things. I jumped to my feet and rushed at the door, pounding on it.

"Hello out there! Let us out! We're stuck in here! Let us out!"

"Just what we're aimin' to do, ma'am," came a deep, cheery voice. "It's a right poor mess out here. You all right?"

"Oh yes! Yes! Who are you?"

"Just three friendly old Southern boys—just you sit tight now."

And then another voice, filled with distress. "Miss Rosemary—is Betsy in there? You got my baby with you?"

"Yes, Amanda," I shouted, "she's here—she's all right!"

Betsy was beside me, beating on the door with her small fist. "Mamma! Mamma! I told Miss Romy 'bout the candles. I 'membered Dada showing me! I did, Mamma, I did!"

"Bless you, Betsy," Amanda said in a voice that wasn't quite steady.

And then the strong masculine voice again. "Stand back from the door, ladies. Stand back."

I took Betsy's hand and moved back to stand beside Mary Byrd, Woof quivering at my knee. With a tremendous wrenching sound the door was pulled open, leaving a space filled with faces. Amanda's, smiling through tears, and three others—men I had seen before—where? Then I recalled. They were men who had begged for the scrapings from Amanda's kitchen bowl. Dirt-streaked, sweating, haggard, and thin, with torn uniforms and bleeding hands—they were all grinning as they faced us in that almost impassable basement.

I thought my heart would burst open with joy.

I guided Betsy to the opening, noting with relief that whatever ailment she had been suffering earlier had disappeared in (I assumed) the pleasant importance of knowing where light might be found. I kissed her soft cheek as she was lifted straight into her mother's arms.

Then, leaning over Mary Byrd, I placed my arms under hers. "See if you can make it up on your good foot. I'll hold you."

With a tiny wince of pain she pushed herself up until she was standing. The men watched carefully.

"You hurt, ma'am?" one asked. "Why, it's Miss Blair, isn't it? You hurt, Miss Blair?"

"It's nothing. I just twisted my ankle a bit. . . ."

The soldier set one foot into the tunnel, leaned forward and scooped Mary Byrd up as if she had been an armload of feathers. I blew out the candle and stepped out, Woof following closely. Out! I took a deep breath and was almost overcome by the suffocating smell of wine from dozens of broken bottles. The poor Bartletts who owned this house! I hoped they wouldn't think we had drunk all of it.

I turned toward the kitchen stairs. The broken steps were covered with debris.

"How did you get in?" I asked the men.

"The same way the shell did. Through that hole," one said, and pointed to a wide gap in the wall. "We heard the explosion, and this here lady—" he indicated Amanda, "she was afeared someone might be down here. So we came in, and we heard you-all singin' in there. It sounded real pretty!"

Betsy was boosted through the open space, with Amanda after her, and then one of the men pulled himself through and turned to lift Mary Byrd out, seating her gently on the grass. Then it was my turn, and there was an assist for Woof.

Poor Woof! There had been a time when he could have jumped the distance, but not now. I made sure the men climbed out safely and watching them, wondered where they had found the strength to rescue us. Their bodies were close to skeletal from hunger, their faces drawn. And yet they still smiled. When Mary Byrd, in her stained hospital apron, with dirt streaks on her face and cobwebs in her hair, pulled from somewhere a ravishing smile of her own, the men grinned delightedly.

"You're just the sweetest little ol' boys I've had the pleasure of meetin'," she said. "You must give me your names so I can invite you the next time we have a party."

MEET PATRICIA CLAPP, AUTHOR

Patricia Clapp describes how reading the diary of an unknown woman who lived through the seige of Vicksburg influenced her to write a novel about this time: "I read the facts as she had written them—skinned rats and mule meat hanging in the butcher's window, the closing of shops with nothing to sell, the Northern ships clogging the Mississippi River, so that nothing came into the city and nothing went out of it. No food, no medicines, no fresh troops, no household items—nothing. What must it have been like? . . . I read and read and began to 'be there.' "

She describes the research she does for each historical novel she writes: "I have access to two excellent libraries, and I come home weighted down with assorted volumes and submerge myself for weeks. Architecture, clothing, food, pastimes, politics, education, language—all of these must be as familiar to me as the events I am writing about. Every period has its own flavor and unless that is clearly conveyed the reader will lose half the story."

UNDER SIEGE

from VOICES FROM THE CIVIL WAR
by Milton Meltzer

The most wearing time in war for soldiers—and civilians—is the siege. A siege may last for weeks, months, or even years. It is the time when an army is positioned in front of a fortified place in order to force its surrender. The besiegers simply wait for the army penned up inside to give up because supplies and morale are low, or they may hasten surrender by bombardment and a series of assaults.

The siege of Vicksburg, a city high on a bluff above the Mississippi River, was a prime target of the Union campaign for the river. General Grant hoped to cut off the West from the other Rebel states, and to open up passage from the Gulf of Mexico to the North. By the spring of 1862, much of this had been achieved, except for taking Vicksburg and Port Hudson.

Grant made two attacks upon Vicksburg, but was repulsed. Then he decided to lay siege to the city, with an army of seventy thousand and over two hundred guns. After a six week bombardment, on July 4, 1863, General Pemberton surrendered the city and over thirty thousand troops, the largest haul of manpower up to that time.

A Union woman (we don't know her name), caught somehow inside Vicksburg amid the Southerners, describes the tension and danger in a diary she kept:

This watercolor by an unknown artist shows General Grant's attack on Vicksburg on May 19, 1863.

Pencil and watercolor. M. & M. Karolik Collection,
Museum of Fine Arts, Boston

MARCH 20, 1863—The slow shelling of Vicksburg goes on all the time, and we have grown indifferent. It does not at present interrupt or interfere with daily avocations [chores], but I suspect they are only getting the range of different points; and when they have them all complete, showers of shot will rain on us all at once. Noncombatants have been ordered to leave or prepare accordingly. Those who are to stay are having caves built. Cave-digging has become a regular business; prices range from twenty to fifty dollars, according to size of cave. Two diggers worked at ours a week and charged thirty dollars. It is well made in the hill that slopes just in the rear of the house, and well propped with thick posts, as they all are. It has a shelf also, for holding a light or water. When we went in this evening and sat down, the earthy, suffocating feeling, as of a living tomb, was dreadful to me. I fear I shall risk death outside rather than melt in that dark furnace. The hills are so honeycombed with caves that the streets look like avenues in a cemetery. . . .

APRIL 28—I never understood before the full force of those questions—what shall we eat? what shall we drink? and wherewithal shall we be clothed? We have no prophet of the Lord at whose prayer the meal and oil will not waste. Such minute attention must be given the wardrobe to preserve it that I have learned to darn like an artist. Making shoes is now another accomplishment. Mine were in tatters. H. came across a moth-eaten pair that he bought me, giving ten dollars, I think, and they fell into rags when I tried to wear them; but the soles were good, and that has helped me to shoes. A pair of old coat sleeves saved—nothing is thrown away now—was in my trunk. I cut an exact pattern from my old shoes, laid it on the sleeves, and cut out thus good uppers and sewed them carefully; then soaked the soles and sewed the cloth to them. I am so proud of these homemade shoes, think I'll put them in a glass case when the war is over, as an heirloom. . . .

I have but a dozen pins remaining, so many I gave away. Every time these are used they are straightened and kept from rust. All these curious labors are performed while the shells are leisurely screaming through the air; but as long as we are out of range we don't worry. For many nights we have had but little sleep, because the Federal gunboats have been running past the batteries. The uproar when this is happening is phenomenal. The first night the thundering artillery burst the bars of sleep, we thought it an attack by the river. To get into garments and rush upstairs was the work of a moment. From the upper gallery we have a fine view of the river, and soon a red glare lit up the scene and showed a small boat, towing two large barges, gliding by. The Confederates had set fire to a house near the bank. Another night, eight boats ran by, throwing a shower of shot, and two burning houses made the river clear as day. One of the batteries has a remarkable gun they call "Whistling Dick," because of the screeching, whistling sound it gives, and certainly it does sound like a tortured thing. Added to all this is the indescribable Confederate yell, which is a soul-harrowing sound to hear. . . . Yesterday the *Cincinnati* attempted to go by in daylight, but was disabled and sunk. It was a pitiful sight; we could not see the finale, though we saw her rendered helpless. . . .

MAY 28—The regular siege has continued. We are utterly cut off from the world, surrounded by a circle of fire. Would it be wise like the scorpion to sting ourselves to death? The fiery shower of shells goes on day and night. H.'s occupation, of course, is gone; his office closed. Every man has to carry a pass in his pocket. People do nothing but eat what they can get, sleep when they can, and dodge the shells. There are three intervals when the shelling stops, either for the guns to cool or for the gunners' meals, I suppose—about eight in the morning, the same in the evening, and at noon. In that time we have both to prepare and eat ours. Clothing cannot be washed

This painting by Howard Pyle shows a Confederate soldier and two women shrinking back from a Federal shell with a sputtering fuse. Behind them is the entrance to a cave.

Oil on canvas. Private collection.
Photo: © Brandywine River Museum

or anything else done. On the 19th and 22d, when the assaults were made on the lines, I watched the soldiers cooking on the green opposite. The half-spent balls coming all the way from those lines were flying so thick that they were obliged to dodge at every turn. At all the caves I could see from my high perch, people were sitting, eating their poor suppers at the cave doors, ready to plunge in again. As the first shell again flew they dived, and not a human being was visible. The sharp crackle of the musketry firing was a strong contrast to the scream of the bombs. I think all the dogs and cats must be killed or starved; we don't see any more pitiful animals prowling around. . . .

JUNE 25—A horrible day. The most horrible yet to me, because I've lost my nerve. We were all in the cellar, when a shell came tearing through the roof, burst upstairs, tore up that room, and the pieces coming through both floors down into the cellar, one of them tore open the leg of H.'s pantaloons. This was tangible proof the cellar was no place of protection from them. On the heels of this came Mr. J. to tell us that young Mrs. P. had had her thighbone crushed. When Martha went for the milk she came back horror-stricken to tell us the black girl there had her arm taken off by a shell. For the first time I quailed [lost heart]. I do not think people who are physically brave deserve much credit for it; it is a matter of nerves. In this way I am constitutionally brave, and seldom think of danger till it is over; and death has not the terrors for me it has for some others. Every night I had lain down expecting death, and every morning rose to the same prospect, without being unnerved. It was for H. I trembled. But now I first seemed to realize that something worse than death might come: I might be crippled, and not killed. Life, without all one's powers and limbs, was a thought that broke down my courage. I said to H., "You must get me out of this horrible place; I cannot stay; I know I shall be crippled." Now the regret comes that I lost control, because H. is worried, and has lost his composure, because my coolness has broken down. . . .

EMANCIPATION

from To Be a Slave
by Julius Lester
illustrated by Lyle Miller

Julius Lester's book To Be a Slave *consists of selections from collections of interviews done shortly after the Civil War. In the chapter "Emancipation," former slaves talk about their reactions to the news that they are free.*

Granma used to tell this story to everybody that would listen, and I expect I heard it a hundred times. Granma say she was hired out to the Randolphs during the war. One day while she was weeding corn another slave, Mamie Tolliver, come up to her and whispered, "Sarah, they tell me that Massa Lincoln done set all us slaves free." Granma say, "Is that so?" and she dropped her hoe and run all the way to the Thacker's place—seven miles it was—and run to ol' missus and looked at her real hard. Then she yelled, "I'm free! Yes, I'm free! Ain't got to work for you no more. You can't put me in your pocket now!" Granma say Missus Thacker started boo-hooing and threw her apron over her face and run in the house. Granma knew it was true then.

BETTY JONES
The Negro in Virginia, p. 209

Some slave owners moved to Texas with their slaves when it appeared that the South might lose the war. By moving to Texas they hoped that they might hold on to their slaves a while longer.

We wasn't there in Texas long when the soldiers marched in to tell us that we were free. Seems to me like it was on a Monday morning when they come in. Yes, it was a Monday. They went out to the field and told them they was free. Marched them out of the fields. They come a-shouting. I remembers one woman. She jumped on a barrel and she shouted. She jumped off and she shouted. She jumped back on again and shouted some more. She kept that up for a long time, just jumping on a barrel and back off again.

ANNA WOODS
Library of Congress

The news that they were free was the fulfillment of the dream they had taken to bed each night and risen with each morning. How many times they had tried to imagine what that moment would be like, and now it had come. Some found it hard to believe.

One day I was out milking the cows. Mr. Dave come down into the field and he had a paper in his hand. "Listen to me, Tom," he said. "Listen to what I read you." And he read from a paper all about how I was free. You can't tell how I felt. "You're joking me," I says. "No, I ain't," says he. "You're free." "No," says I, "it's a joke." "No," says he, "it's a law that I got to read this paper to you. Now listen while I read it again."

But still I wouldn't believe him. "Just go up to the house," says he, "and ask Mrs. Robinson. She'll tell you." So I went. "It's a joke," I says to her. "Did you ever know your master to tell you a lie?" she says. "No," says I, "I ain't." "Well," she says, "The war's over and you're free." By that time I thought maybe she was telling me what was right. "Miss Robinson," says I, "can I go over to see the Smiths?" They was a colored family that lived nearby. "Don't you understand," says she, "you're free. You don't have to ask me what you can do. Run along, child." And so I went. And do you know why I was a-going? I wanted to find out if they was free, too. I just couldn't take it all in. I couldn't believe we was all free alike.

Was I happy? You can take anything. No matter how good you treat it—it wants to be free. You can treat it good and feed it good and give it everything it seems to want—but if you open the cage—it's happy.

Tom Robinson
Library of Congress

Most slaves, though, had no difficulty at all believing the news when they heard it.

The news come on a Thursday and all the slaves been shoutin' and carryin' on till everybody was tired out. I remember the first Sunday of freedom. We was all sittin' around restin' and tryin' to think what freedom meant and everybody was quiet and peaceful. All at once ol' Sister Carrie who was near 'bout a hundred started into talking:

Tain't no mo' sellin' today.
Tain't no mo' hirin' today.
Tain't no mo' pullin' off shirts today.
It's stomp down freedom today.
Stomp it down!

And when she says, "Stomp it down," all the slaves commence to shoutin' with her:

Stomp down freedom today.
Stomp it down!
Stomp down freedom today.

Wasn't no more peace that Sunday. Everybody started in to sing and shout once more. First thing you know they done made up music to Sister Carrie's stomp song and sang and shouted that song all the rest of the day. Child, that was one glorious time!

CHARLOTTE BROWN
The Negro in Virginia, p. 212

❀ 124 ❀

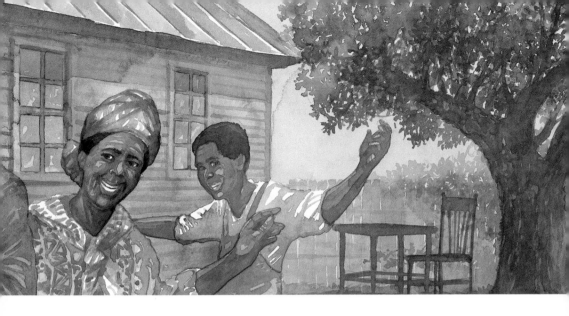

Daddy was down to the creek. He jumped right in the water up to his neck. He was so happy he just kept on scoopin' up handfulls of water and dumpin' it on his head and yellin', "I'se free! I'se free! I'se free!"

LOUISA BOWES ROSE
The Negro in Virginia, p. 208

The war was over and when the South surrendered to the North at Appomattox, it was appropriate that there were blacks present to watch the official end of the war and slavery.

General Lee tipped his hat first and then General Grant tipped hissen. General Lee got off his horse, and General Grant got off hissen. General Lee got on a new uniform with gold braid and lots of buttons, but General Grant got on an old blue coat that's so dirty it look black. They stood there talking about half an hour and then they shake hands and us what was watching know that Lee done give up. Then General Lee tipped his hat and General Grant tipped hissen, and General Lee rode over to the rebel side. General Grant rode over to our side and the war was over.

TOM HESTER
The Negro in Virginia, p. 204.

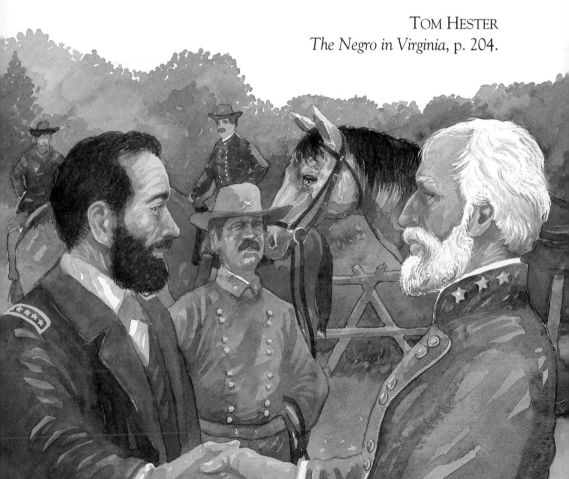

Freedom. One day they had been awakened by the sound of the overseer's horn. The next day they were not. One morning they had gone to the fields and before the sun set, they had left their hoes, their plows, their cotton sacks lying in the furrows. And they put the full meaning of it into one eloquent phrase, which they sang over and over.

Free at last,
Free at last,
Thank God A-Mighty,
I'm free at last.

THE GETTYSBURG ADDRESS

delivered at Gettysburg,
Pennsylvania, November 19, 1863
by Abraham Lincoln

The Bettmann Archive

Fourscore and seven years ago our fathers brought forth upon this continent a new nation, conceived in liberty, and dedicated to the proposition that all men are created equal.

Now we are engaged in a great civil war, testing whether that nation, or any nation so conceived and so dedicated, can long endure. We are met on a great battlefield of that war. We have come to dedicate a portion of that field as a final resting place for those who here gave their lives that that nation might live. It is altogether fitting and proper that we should do this.

But in a larger sense we cannot dedicate, we cannot consecrate, we cannot hallow this ground. The brave men, living and dead, who struggled here, have consecrated it far above our poor power to add or detract. The world will little note, nor long remember, what we say here; but it can never forget what they did here.

It is for us, the living, rather to be dedicated here to the unfinished work which they who fought here have thus far so nobly advanced. It is rather for us to be here dedicated to the great task remaining before us, that from these honored dead we take increased devotion to that cause for which they gave the last full measure of devotion; that we here highly resolve that these dead shall not have died in vain; that this nation, under God, shall have a new birth of freedom, and that government of the people, by the people, and for the people, shall not perish from the earth.

BIBLIOGRAPHY

The Civil War by the editors of Time-Life Books. The 28 volumes of this series include maps, photographs, and detailed information about many aspects of the war.

A Civil War Treasury of Tales, Legends, and Folklore edited by B. A. Botkin. This collection of stories from newspapers, magazines, diaries, letters, and other sources shows how people of the time viewed the Civil War.

Escape to Freedom: A Play About Young Frederick Douglass by Ossie Davis. You might enjoy performing this play based on the life of Frederick Douglass, an important leader in the fight against slavery.

Harriet Tubman: Conductor on the Underground Railroad by Ann Petry. This biography tells about how Tubman escaped slavery and helped other runaways.

A Month of Seven Days by Shirley Climo. A Southern girl tries to protect her home and family from Northern soldiers.

A Separate Battle: Women and the Civil War by Ina Chang. Who were the women who served as soldiers, nurses, or spies during the Civil War? This book tells their stories.

Stonewall by Jean Fritz. How did Stonewall Jackson get his name? This biography of the Confederate general will tell you.

The 290 by Scott O'Dell. A young English boy helps to construct and then serves as a crewman on the Confederate battleship *Alabama*.

THE AMERICAN
WEST

Buffalo Hunter. Artist unknown. c. 1844.

Oil on canvas. Gift of Harriet Cowles Hammet Graham, in memory of Buell Hammet,
Santa Barbara Museum of Art

BUFFALO HUNT
from the book by Russell Freedman

A GIFT FROM THE GREAT SPIRIT

Over blazing campfires on winter nights, Indian story-tellers spoke of the buffalo. They told tales of buffalo giants and buffalo ghosts, of buffalo that changed magically into men, of children who were raised by buffalo and understood their language.

In olden times, it was said, buffalo used to eat Indians. They ate so many Indians that a legendary figure called Old Man had to put a stop to it. He organized a race between the buffalo and the Indians to decide who should eat whom. The Indians won.

On the Great Plains of North America, every Indian tribe had a rich and ready store of buffalo tales and legends. According to the Comanche, buffalo came from gigantic caves somewhere on the windswept ranges of the Texas Panhandle. Each spring, the Great Spirit sent throngs of buffalo from those hidden caves onto the open plains, as a gift to the Indian people.

Up North, the Blackfoot said that a lake in Canada was the place where the buffalo began. They were born beneath the water, in the darkest depths of the lake. If you could visit that sacred spot on the right night, at exactly the right time, you would hear an eerie rumbling coming from the middle of the lake. Then you would see the buffalo rise out of the water and crowd onto the shore, their shaggy fur wet and dripping, their curved horns gleaming in the moonlight.

To the Plains Indians, the buffalo, or American bison, was the most important animal on earth. This snorting, lumbering beast provided almost everything the Indians needed to stay alive. The buffalo kept their bellies full and their bodies warm. It supplied raw materials for their weapons, tools, ornaments, and toys. The rhythm of their daily lives was ruled by the comings and goings of the great buffalo herds.

It is little wonder that the Indians worshiped the buffalo as a sacred animal. Before and after every hunt, they praised the spirit of the buffalo and thanked him for giving his meat. Men, women, and children carried buffalo-shaped rocks and fossils for good luck. They believed in the powerful magic of buffalo dreams. When they died, they hoped to go to a happy hunting ground in the sky where buffalo flourished. Looking into the night sky, the Pawnee believed that the Milky Way was formed by dust left behind by the spirit buffalo.

As recently as 150 years ago, countless millions of buffalo still roamed the prairies and plains. They ranged from the Mississippi River westward to the Rockies, and from Canada down to the Rio Grande. Native American hunters had been stalking the animals for many thousands of years. During most of that time, the Indians had neither horses nor guns. They hunted on foot, and they killed their prey with stone-tipped arrows and spears. They knew how to creep up on a grazing herd, how to surround the buffalo, and how to drive them into corrals or stampede them over cliffs.

Without horses, the Indians had to travel on foot whenever they moved their encampments. Back then, they used big shaggy dogs as pack animals to help carry their tipis and other belongings. Sometimes on a long journey the dogs would grow tired and begin to droop and lag and hang their tongues. Then someone would cry, "Buffalo ahead! Fresh meat in plenty!" And the dogs would bound forward as though they had just set out. Later, the Indians would remember that era as their Dog Days.

The first horses were brought to North America by Spanish explorers in the 1500s. Within a century or so, runaway horses had drifted northward from Spanish settlements in Mexico and were roaming the plains in wild herds. The Indians learned to capture and tame those wild horses, and the horses changed their lives.

Now they could travel long distances to find the buffalo. They could chase the herds and kill the choicest animals. And with pack horses, they could carry bigger tipis and more possessions with them as they traveled across the plains. In time, the Indians became some of the world's finest horsemen, experts at hunting and fighting on horseback.

When white trappers and traders began to visit the Great Plains in the early 1800s, about 250,000 Indians were living in the region. They belonged to some two dozen distinct tribes, each with its own language and customs. Many of these tribes had migrated from the woodlands of the East, but only a few, like the Pawnee of Kansas and Nebraska, still practiced the old arts of farming and fishing.

Most of the Plains Indians had given up the settled life of farmers and fishermen to follow the buffalo herds. They spent the winter in sheltered camps. But in spring they folded their tipis and roamed the plains. They hunted other animals beside the buffalo, of course—deer, antelope, elk, and an occasional bear. But buffalo meat was their staple food, buffalo hunting their main occupation.

A Plains tribe was made up of many small, independent bands. Once or twice a year, all the bands belonging to a tribe would assemble for a great religious ceremony, a tribal council, or a communal hunt. But mostly, the bands moved about on their own. Each band had its own encampments, or villages. And each band hunted in a different part of the tribal territory.

Hunting was a man's responsibility. Every able-bodied boy was taught that he should become a fearless hunter and warrior. Small boys ran about yip-yapping in play hunts, dreaming of the day when they would be big enough to ride after a herd of stampeding buffalo. A successful hunter could provide for many people. He became a man of influence, entitled to honors and privileges.

Women were responsible for putting the buffalo and other game to good use. It was a woman's job to skin and butcher the buffalo, to preserve the meat and tan the hides. As Indian girls grew up, they learned from their mothers and grandmothers the art of transforming a dead buffalo into a thousand practical and useful objects.

The buffalo was the biggest animal on the plains. A full-grown bull stood six feet tall at the humped shoulders and weighed a ton or more. An angry bull could stab a bear to death. He could toss a wolf so high into the air that the wolf would be killed by the fall.

The Silk Robe.
c. 1890. Charles M. Russell.

Oil on canvas. Amon Carter Museum,
Fort Worth, Texas. 1961.135

Painted elkskin robe. Late
19th century. Crow.

The National Museum of the American Indian,
Smithsonian Institution. 3249

While buffalo were somewhat dim-sighted, they could hear the faintest sounds and smell enemies from three miles away. And when they sensed danger, they moved fast. A bull or cow could wheel about on its slim hind legs and run as fast as a horse. When a whole herd stampeded, the earth trembled.

White explorers were astonished at the size of the herds they saw as they crossed the Great Plains. There were times when buffalo stretched endlessly across the countryside as far as the eye could see. Artist George Catlin described these herds when he traveled west during the 1830s to study and paint the Indians. "Buffalo graze in immense herds and almost incredible numbers," he wrote. "And they roam over vast tracts of country."

No one really knows how many buffalo roamed the prairies and plains before the white man came. The Indians thought there were enough buffalo to last forever. It seemed impossible that they could ever disappear.

THE HUNT

On the day set for starting a hunt, everyone was up at sunrise. The women went right to work, packing their household belongings and getting everything ready for the move. Youngsters rounded up the horses and dogs. The men gathered in small groups to discuss the day's plans.

After a quick morning meal, the leaders of the hunt, the marshals, assembled. They took their feathered banners in their hands, mounted their horses, and gave the signal to break camp.

With that, the Indian village disappeared almost like a puff of smoke. Tipis dropped to the ground as the women removed the buffalo-skin walls and took down the long poles that held the tipis erect.

The poles were now put to a different use. Lashed to the sides of a horse so they trailed behind on the ground, the poles supported a sturdy rawhide platform called a travois (tra-VOY). This platform held the folded tipi walls and the family's household goods. Sometimes small children or sick people sat on top of the pile to be hauled along by a strong packhorse. Dogs also worked as pack animals, pulling travois designed to fit their size and strength.

When the horses and dogs were harnessed and loaded and ready to go, the people and their animals moved out across the plains. The warriors, mounted on the best hunting horses, rode along in front. They were followed by boys and girls driving the herd of extra horses. Behind them came the women leading the packhorses, along with the small children and the old folks, some riding, some walking, and some being

Band of Sioux Moving Camp with Dogs and Horses. 1837–39. George Catlin.

Oil on canvas. National Museum of American Art, Smithsonian Institution. Photo: Art Resource

carried on the travois. Every woman had a heavy pack on her back. The men never carried packs. They kept their arms free to use their weapons in case of a surprise attack.

Scouts rode far ahead of the marching people, and far to either side, watching for signs of buffalo or lurking enemies. Other warriors acted as a rear guard. They followed the group at a distance, seeing that no one lagged behind.

Strung out across the prairie, the Indians formed a grand procession. People sang as they marched along, dogs barked, horses whinnied, bells jingled. They moved forward each day by easy stages, so their horses would be in good condition when they found the buffalo.

At the end of a day's march, the marshals picked the spot where they would pitch camp. The women quickly put up the tipis and prepared the evening meal as the men gathered to chat and smoke. On the open plains, the Indians usually camped in a circle, with the doorway of each tipi facing east to catch the morning sun.

When they reached the territory where they expected to hunt, the scouts fanned out across the countryside, looking for buffalo. Everyone else waited in the hushed camp. Marshals moved quietly from one tipi to the next. They reminded people in low tones not to sing or shout or make any loud noise that might scare off the buffalo, which could hear weak and distant sounds.

The scouts, meanwhile, searched for buffalo signs. Sometimes they relied on animal helpers. The Comanche watched for ravens. They thought that if a raven circled four times overhead and cawed, it would then fly off toward the buffalo. A Cheyenne hunter would find a cricket, hold it in his hand,

and wait to see which way its antennae pointed. The buffalo, he believed, would be found in that direction.

When a herd was sighted, the successful scout rushed back to camp. As he arrived, people crowded around, greeting him with congratulations and thanks. First he smoked a ceremonial pipe with one of the band's elders. Then he reported what he had seen.

The chase usually started the next morning. As soon as it was light enough to see, the hunters mounted their horses. Riding close together, they stayed downwind from the herd, so the buffalo would not catch their scent.

When they were as close as they could get without disturbing the buffalo, they paused and waited. The marshals looked over the area and selected the best spot to launch the attack. Silently, they led the hunters forward and spaced them evenly, so that each would have a fair start. Then one of the marshals rode out in view of both hunters and buffalo. He waved his hand above his head, and the chase began.

Bending low over their horses, the Indians galloped toward the grazing herd. At first the buffalo paid little attention. Often the hunters would almost reach the herd before the buffalo became alarmed and started to run.

Each man acted on his own now. Holding his bow in his left hand, urging his horse on with the whip strapped to his right wrist, a hunter picked his target and went after it at full speed. His horse was trained to approach the buffalo from the right, so the rider could shoot his arrow to the left, toward the animal. As he closed in, he aimed for a spot just behind the buffalo's last rib, where the arrow would pierce the animal's lungs. A single well-aimed arrow could kill the biggest buffalo.

Sometimes an arrow would strike with such force that it would be completely buried. It might pass all the way through the animal, come out the other side, and drop to the ground. If an arrow failed to go deep enough, the hunter might reach over, pull it out of the buffalo, and use it again.

Once an arrow hit its mark, the hunter instantly took off after another buffalo. His horse understood exactly what to do. Running free, guided only by words or knee pressure, a trained hunting pony would leap away from a buffalo's horns as soon as it heard the twang of the bowstring.

Some men found the bow and arrow too tame. They preferred to use spears, for it took more strength and courage to spear a buffalo. To carry only a spear on the hunt was a mark of daring and pride.

With any weapon, the chase was risky. Horses stumbled in prairie-dog holes. Wounded buffalo lashed out with their

The Buffalo Hunt No. 39. 1919. Charles M. Russell.

Oil on canvas. Amon Carter Museum, Fort Worth, Texas. 1961.146

horns. Sometimes an enraged bull crashed headlong into a horse and rider. The buffalo claimed many victims as hunters were trampled in the dust or died of broken bones.

While the chase was thrilling, it wasn't always the best way to hunt. During a typical chase on horseback, each hunter might bring down two or three buffalo. Under the right conditions, the Indians could get better results with less danger by hunting in the old way—on foot.

In that case, they would stake their horses and creep up on the buffalo, crawling on hands and knees through tall grass. As long as the Indians were hidden, the buffalo would go right on grazing, even as arrows flew silently around them. Each man might shoot several buffalo in quick succession before the others became frightened and ran off.

In winter, when the grass offered little cover, a hunter might sneak up on a herd disguised in a buffalo robe. Or he could drape himself in the skin of a white wolf. Healthy buffalo in herds did not fear wolves and didn't run when they saw one.

If a herd was small enough, the Indians sometimes surrounded the buffalo on foot. Approaching downwind, they fanned out, moved in from all sides, and formed a tight ring. Then they ran in circles around the herd, whooping and yelling and waving their arms as the terrified animals milled about in confusion. Slowly the Indians closed the circle until they were close enough to let go with their arrows and spears.

The first buffalo to be hit would fall near the outside of the circle, blocking the path of those inside the ring. As more buffalo fell, their bodies trapped the others. Sometimes not a single animal escaped alive.

Buffalo Chase with Bows and Lances. 1832–33. George Catlin.

Oil on canvas. National Museum of American Art, Smithsonian Institution. Photo: Art Resource

On horseback, the Indians could surround bigger herds, galloping around them in a circle. One afternoon in 1832, the artist George Catlin, armed with his pencil and sketchbook, watched from a distance as 500 Sioux horseman surrounded a herd near the present site of Pierre, South Dakota. By sundown, the hunters had killed 1,400 buffalo.

FROM THE BRAINS TO THE TAIL

A successful hunt called for a feast. Beside the campfire that evening, a medicine man offered prayers of thanksgiving. He thanked the spirits for their aid during the chase, and he thanked the buffalo for giving his meat to the people. Choice bits of meat were sliced off, held up for the spirits to see, then buried as an offering.

There was plenty for everyone to eat. A single fat buffalo cow supplied enough meat to feed a hundred hungry people. They gorged themselves on fresh tongue roasted over the open fire, on tasty morsels cut from the buffalo's hump. They ate hot, dripping ribs and steaks. And they feasted on yards of roasted gut, turned inside out, stuffed with chunks of meat, and seared over glowing coals. The sweet, nutritious bone marrow was saved for the old folks. It was the only meat their toothless gums could chew.

Most of the meat taken during a big hunt was preserved for the future. The women cut the meat into strips and hung it over high poles to dry. After several days, this sun-dried meat, called jerky, was so well preserved that it would last for months. It could be carried anywhere and would not spoil, even during the hottest months.

Some of the dried meat was pounded to a pulp, mixed with buffalo fat, and flavored with crushed nuts, berries, and fruit. This was called pemmican. Packed in buffalo-skin bags, pemmican would last for years without spoiling. Sliced and dipped in wild honey, it was nourishing and delicious, a favorite food among the Indians, and later the white fur traders as well.

Every part of the buffalo that could be chewed, swallowed, and digested was used for food. And every other part was put to some use.

Indian women spent a great deal of time and effort tanning buffalo hides. After a hunt, the fresh hides were spread out on the ground, hairy side down, and pegged in place. Using scrapers made of buffalo bone, the women scraped all the flesh, fat, and blood from the hides. They cured and bleached the hides in the sun, and soaked them in a tanning fluid of buffalo brains, liver, and fat mixed with water. Then they worked the hides for several days—rubbing, kneading, squeezing, stretching—to make them soft and supple. A good hunter might have several wives working on hides taken from the animals he had killed.

If the hides were to be used as winter robes, the hair was left in place. Thick-furred buffalo robes made warm and comfortable cloaks and bedding. They could be cut and stitched into caps, earmuffs, leggings, and mittens. The finest robes came from buffalo killed during the winter, when nature gave the animal a full coat to protect it from snow and cold.

With the hair scraped off, the hides were smoked over fires to make them waterproof. They could then be fashioned into dozens of useful articles. They were used for the walls of tipis, for clothing and moccasins, for pouches, purses, and saddlebags. Babies were carried in cradleboards lined with the softest buffalo calfskin. The dead were laid to rest wrapped in buffalo-hide winding sheets.

Thick rawhide from the necks of old bulls was stretched to make tough war shields and the soles of winter moccasins. Strong sinews from the neck and back of the buffalo provided bowstrings and thread. The buffalo's hair was twisted into ropes and bridles, woven into ornaments, stuffed into leather balls. Its stomach became a water jug, its tail a flyswatter.

Buffalo horns were used for cups, ladles, and spoons, and to carry hot coals to the next campground. The hooves produced glue; the fat, soap. The bones were shaped into knives, spears, and tools of many kinds. On the northern plains, the backbone with ribs attached made a toboggan for children in winter.

Comanche Village in Texas, Women Dressing Robes and Drying Meat.
1834–35. George Catlin.

Oil on canvas. National Museum of American Art, Smithsonian Institution. Photo: Art Resource

Even the buffalo's droppings were valuable. On the treeless plains, firewood was scarce. But there was an endless supply of sundried buffalo dung left behind by the grazing herds. These prized "buffalo chips" burned slowly, produced a hot fire, and were ideal for cooking. They were used for that purpose by the Indians, and later by white settlers too.

A fall buffalo hunt would continue until the band had all the hides and meat it needed for the winter. Then the Indians would settle down in their winter camps. Every band had its favorite winter camping sites near woods, in a sheltered canyon, or along a river bottom. Instead of camping in a circle, as they did on the open plains, the Indians pitched their winter tipis in a line that sometimes stretched for miles along the canyon floor or the river's banks.

A tipi provided a warm and cozy winter home. Because it was shaped like a cone, it could withstand the most violent winds and blizzards. Its walls were waterproof. An open fire in the center of the tipi furnished heat, light, and a stove for indoor cooking. The smoke spiraled up through an adjustable smoke hole at the top of the tipi. At night, firelight would shine through the translucent buffalo-skin walls, and from the outside, the tipi glowed like a lantern.

Tipis were usually owned by the women who made them. A typical tipi measured perhaps fifteen feet across at the base, allowing sufficient living space for the family and its possessions. It could be put up in fifteen minutes by the women of the household. It could be taken down in five minutes. And it could be packed on a horse travois and carried anywhere.

When the hunting was good, the Indians went into winter camp with tons of sun-dried buffalo meat. They didn't have to hunt day after day, all winter long, for fear of starving. Between hunts, they were free to do as they wished. "It was a great life," said Tom Le Forge, a white man who lived several years with the Crows. "At all times I had ample leisure for lazy loafing and dreaming and visiting."

Year after year without fail, the buffalo drifted back and forth across the plains in tune with the seasons. Usually they traveled in small bands. But during the late summer rutting season, they gathered in enormous herds that numbered hundreds of thousands of animals. A truly great herd might be fifty miles long and take days to pass by.

Indians had hunted the buffalo for thousands of years without making much of a dent in the herds. Sometimes they killed more animals than they could use. When they drove a herd over a cliff, they could not always carry away all the meat. But for the most part, the Indians were not wasteful. They hunted when they needed meat and hides.

As white people came to the plains, the buffalo herds began to dwindle. By the early 1800s, trading posts were springing up all over the West. White traders wanted buffalo robes and tongues for profitable markets in the East. In exchange, they offered guns, tools, tobacco, whiskey, and trinkets. The Indians had always hunted for their own needs. Now, by killing a few more buffalo, they could obtain the white man's goods.

Soon the Indians were killing buffalo for their hides and tongues alone. Tongues packed in salt were shipped in barges down the Missouri River, to be sent to the cities of the East, where they were sold as an expensive delicacy. Buffalo robes became fashionable as lap robes and blankets. White people had them made into fur coats. During the 1830s and 1840s, hundreds of thousands of robes were shipped east.

By then, white hunters were beginning to kill more buffalo than the Indians. Pioneers traveling westward in covered wagons shot the animals for food along the way, scaring off entire herds. Before long, few buffalo could be found along the great trails leading west. Then the United States Army hired professional hunters to supply buffalo meat to western military posts. And as railroads were built across the prairies and plains, white hunters furnished buffalo meat for the railroad construction crews.

Buffalo hunting became a popular sport. Many travelers felt that a trip west wasn't complete unless they had shot themselves a buffalo. American millionaires and European noblemen toured the West in style, with servants to hand them their guns and champagne to drink after the hunt. Railroads began to feature special excursion trains through buffalo country. As the trains chugged along, passengers could poke their guns through the open windows and fire away at the grazing herds.

By the 1860s, Indian tribes found that the buffalo were disappearing from their traditional hunting grounds. When they went elsewhere to hunt, they were followed almost immediately by white hunters, soldiers, and settlers. "Wherever the whites are established, the buffalo is gone," complained the Sioux Chief White Cloud, "and the red hunters must die of hunger."

Indians who once had been friendly to white people vowed to go on the warpath. Alarmed by the large-scale slaughter of their herds, angry warriors from many tribes banded together. They began to attack wagon trains, ranch houses, and railroad construction crews.

There were still about eight million buffalo left on the plains in 1870, when a newly invented tanning process sealed the fate of the remaining herds. For the first time, commercial tanneries in the East could turn buffalo hides into expensive leather. A single hide now brought as much as $3—more than a factory worker earned in a week in those days. A professional hide hunter could bag as many as two hundred buffalo in one day.

Organized bands of hide hunters shot their way south from Kansas to Texas. Armed with powerful long-range rifles with telescopic sights, they began to slaughter buffalo at the rate of a million a year. As the animals fell, gangs of skinners stripped them of their valuable hides and left the carcasses to rot on the prairie.

Indian war parties attacked the hide hunters wherever they found them, but the hunters could not be stopped. Within a few years, the Indians saw their main source of food, clothing, and shelter vanish.

At one time, perhaps sixty or seventy million buffalo had roamed the plains. By the early 1880s, the endless herds had been wiped out. Only a few hundred wild buffalo were still hiding out in remote mountain valleys.

With the buffalo gone, the proud and independent Plains Indians became a conquered people. Their way of life was destroyed, their hunting grounds taken over by white ranchers and settlers. Swept by starvation and disease, the great hunting tribes were confined to reservations, where they depended on government food rations. Their children were sent to boarding schools to learn the language and customs of the white man.

The days of the buffalo hunters had faded like a dream. But Indian storytellers still gather on winter nights to keep the old tales alive. They speak of a time when buffalo ruled the plains, and Indian warriors rode out to meet them.

> I go to kill the buffalo.
> The Great Spirit sent the buffalo.
> On hills, in plains and woods.
> So give me my bow; give me my bow;
> I go to kill the buffalo.
> —SIOUX SONG

Last of the Buffalo. 1888. Albert Bierstadt.

MEET GEORGE CATLIN AND CHARLES M. RUSSELL, ARTISTS

GEORGE CATLIN *of Philadelphia made a series of journeys into unmapped Indian territory between 1830 and 1836, visiting most of the major tribes from the Upper Missouri River to the Mexican Territory in the far Southwest. Carrying his canvases, paints, and notebooks, he wandered alone from tribe to tribe, fearlessly entering Indian villages, where he was greeted with courtesy and friendship. At the time, only a few fur trappers and traders had penetrated the region. The outside world knew practically nothing about the people who lived in the wilderness beyond the Mississippi. "Catlin's Indian Gallery," as the artist himself called it, consisted of hundreds of paintings and drawings portraying scenes of Indian life.*

CHARLES M. RUSSELL *was born in St. Louis in 1864. As a child, Russell loved to sketch and model animals, cowboys, and Native Americans. He visited the Montana Territory when he was sixteen and soon made that part of the country his home. He worked as a hunter for two years and as a cowboy for ten years, while continuing to paint and sculpt in his spare time. In 1892, he became a full-time artist and soon became famous for his paintings and sculptures of cowboy life.*

THE WHOLE WORLD IS COMING

Sioux Indian

The whole world is coming,
A nation is coming, a nation is coming,
the eagle has brought the message to the tribe.
Over the whole earth they are coming;
the buffalo are coming, the buffalo are coming,
the crow has brought the message to the tribe.

illustrated by Stella Ormai

THE FLOWER-FED BUFFALOES

Vachel Lindsay

The flower-fed buffaloes of the spring
In the days of long ago,
Ranged where the locomotives sing
And the prairie flowers lie low:
The tossing, blooming, perfumed grass
Is swept away by the wheat,
Wheels and wheels and wheels spin by
In the spring that still is sweet.
But the flower-fed buffaloes of the spring
Left us, long ago.
They gore no more, they bellow no more,
They trundle around the hills no more:
With the Blackfeet, lying low,
With the Pawnees, lying low,
Lying low.

OLD YELLER & THE BEAR

from OLD YELLER by Fred Gipson
illustrated by Charles Shaw

*Fourteen-year-old Travis lives with his family in
Texas during the 1860s. Travis feels responsible for his mother
and brother while his father is away on a long cattle drive.
Travis thinks the big yellow dog that adopts his family is a
useless nuisance until a bear shows him how wrong he is.*

That Little Arliss! If he wasn't a mess! From the time
he'd grown up big enough to get out of the cabin,
he'd made a practice of trying to catch and keep every
living thing that ran, flew, jumped, or crawled.

Every night before Mama let him go to bed, she'd make
Arliss empty his pockets of whatever he'd captured during the
day. Generally, it would be a tangled-up mess of grasshoppers
and worms and praying bugs and little rusty tree lizards. One
time he brought in a horned toad that got so mad he swelled
out round and flat as a Mexican tortilla and bled at the eyes.
Sometimes it was stuff like a young bird that had fallen out of
its nest before it could fly, or a green-speckled spring frog or a
striped water snake. And once he turned out of his pocket a

wadded-up baby copperhead that nearly threw Mama into spasms. We never did figure out why the snake hadn't bitten him, but Mama took no more chances on snakes. She switched Arliss hard for catching that snake. Then she made me spend better than a week, taking him out and teaching him to throw rocks and kill snakes.

That was all right with Little Arliss. If Mama wanted him to kill his snakes first, he'd kill them. But that still didn't keep him from sticking them in his pockets along with everything else he'd captured that day. The snakes might be stinking by the time Mama called on him to empty his pockets, but they'd be dead.

Then, after the yeller dog came, Little Arliss started catching even bigger game. Like cottontail rabbits and chaparral birds and a baby possum that sulled and lay like dead for the first several hours until he finally decided that Arliss wasn't going to hurt him.

Of course, it was Old Yeller that was doing the catching. He'd run the game down and turn it over to Little Arliss. Then Little Arliss could come in and tell Mama a big fib about how he caught it himself.

I watched them one day when they caught a blue catfish out of Birdsong Creek. The fish had fed out into water so shallow that his top fin was sticking out. About the time I saw it, Old Yeller and Little Arliss did, too. They made a run at it. The fish went scooting away toward deeper water, only Yeller was too fast for him. He pounced on the fish and shut his big mouth down over it and went romping to the bank, where he dropped it down on the grass and let it flop. And here came Little Arliss to fall on it like I guess he'd been doing every-

thing else. The minute he got his hands on it, the fish finned him and he went to crying.

But he wouldn't turn the fish loose. He just grabbed it up and went running and squawling toward the house, where he gave the fish to Mama. His hands were all bloody by then, where the fish had finned him. They swelled up and got mighty sore; not even a mesquite thorn hurts as bad as a sharp fish fin when it's run deep into your hand.

But as soon as Mama had wrapped his hands in a poultice of mashed-up prickly-pear root to draw out the poison, Little Arliss forgot all about his hurt. And that night when we ate the fish for supper, he told the biggest windy I ever heard about how he'd dived 'way down into a deep hole under the rocks and dragged that fish out and nearly got drowned before he could swim to the bank with it.

But when I tried to tell Mama what really happened, she wouldn't let me. "Now, this is Arliss's story," she said. "You let him tell it the way he wants to."

I told Mama then, I said: "Mama, that old yeller dog is going to make the biggest liar in Texas out of Little Arliss."

But Mama just laughed at me, like she always laughed at Little Arliss's big windies after she'd gotten off where he couldn't hear her. She said for me to let Little Arliss alone. She said that if he ever told a bigger whopper than the ones I used to tell, she had yet to hear it.

Well, I hushed then. If Mama wanted Little Arliss to grow up to be the biggest liar in Texas, I guessed it wasn't any of my business.

All of which, I figure, is what led up to Little Arliss's catching the bear. I think Mama had let him tell so many big yarns about his catching live game that he'd begun to believe them himself.

When it happened, I was down the creek a ways, splitting rails to fix up the yard fence where the bulls had torn it down. I'd been down there since dinner, working in a stand of tall slim post oaks. I'd chop down a tree, trim off the branches as far up as I wanted, then cut away the rest of the top. After that I'd start splitting the log.

I'd split the log by driving steel wedges into the wood. I'd start at the big end and hammer in a wedge with the back side of my axe. This would start a little split running lengthways of the log. Then I'd take a second wedge and drive it into this split. This would split the log further along and, at the same time, loosen the first wedge. I'd then knock the first wedge loose and move it up in front of the second one.

Driving one wedge ahead of the other like that, I could finally split a log in two halves. Then I'd go to work on the halves, splitting them apart. That way, from each log, I'd come out with four rails.

Swinging that chopping axe was sure hard work. The sweat poured off me. My back muscles ached. The axe got so heavy I could hardly swing it. My breath got harder and harder to breathe.

An hour before sundown, I was worn down to a nub. It seemed like I couldn't hit another lick. Papa could have lasted till past sundown, but I didn't see how I could. I shouldered my axe and started toward the cabin, trying to think up some excuse to tell Mama to keep her from knowing I was played clear out.

That's when I heard Little Arliss scream.

Well, Little Arliss was a screamer by nature. He'd scream when he was happy and scream when he was mad and a lot of times he'd scream just to hear himself make a noise. Generally, we paid no more mind to his screaming than we did to the gobble of a wild turkey.

But this time was different. The second I heard his screaming, I felt my heart flop clear over. This time I knew Little Arliss was in real trouble.

I tore out up the trail leading toward the cabin. A minute before, I'd been so tired out with my rail splitting that I couldn't have struck a trot. But now I raced through the tall trees in that creek bottom, covering ground like a scared wolf.

Little Arliss's second scream, when it came, was louder and shriller and more frantic-sounding than the first. Mixed with it was a whimpering crying sound that I knew didn't come from him. It was a sound I'd heard before and seemed like I ought to know what it was, but right then I couldn't place it.

Then, from way off to one side came a sound that I would have recognized anywhere. It was the coughing roar of a charging bear. I'd just heard it once in my life. That was the time Mama had shot and wounded a hog-killing bear and Papa had had to finish it off with a knife to keep it from getting her.

My heart went to pushing up into my throat, nearly choking off my wind. I strained for every lick of speed I could get out of my running legs. I didn't know what sort of fix Little Arliss had got himself into, but I knew that it had to do with a mad bear, which was enough.

The way the late sun slanted through the trees had the trail all cross-banded with streaks of bright light and dark shade. I ran through these bright and dark patches so fast that the changing light nearly blinded me. Then suddenly, I raced out into the open where I could see ahead. And what I saw sent a chill clear through to the marrow of my bones.

There was Little Arliss, down in that spring hole again. He was lying half in and half out of the water, holding onto the hind leg of a little black bear cub no bigger than a small coon. The bear cub was out on the bank, whimpering and crying and clawing the rocks with all three of his other feet, trying to pull away. But Little Arliss was holding on for all he was worth, scared now and screaming his head off. Too scared to let go.

How come the bear cub ever to prowl close enough for Little Arliss to grab him, I don't know. And why he didn't turn on him and bite loose, I couldn't figure out, either. Unless he was like Little Arliss, too scared to think.

But all of that didn't matter now. What mattered was the bear cub's mama. She'd heard the cries of her baby and was coming to save him. She was coming so fast that she had the brush popping and breaking as she crashed through and over it. I could see her black heavy figure piling off down the slant on the far side of Birdsong Creek. She was roaring mad and ready to kill.

And worst of all, I could see that I'd never get there in time!

Mama couldn't either. She'd heard Arliss, too, and here she came from the cabin, running down the slant toward the spring, screaming at Arliss, telling him to turn the bear cub loose. But Little Arliss wouldn't do it. All he'd do was hang with that hind leg and let out one shrill shriek after another as fast as he could suck in a breath.

Now the she bear was charging across the shallows in the creek. She was knocking sheets of water high in the bright sun, charging with her fur up and her long teeth bared, filling the canyon with that awful coughing roar. And no matter how fast Mama ran or how fast I ran, the she bear was going to get there first!

I think I nearly went blind then, picturing what was going to happen to Little Arliss. I know that I opened my mouth to scream and not any sound came out.

Then, just as the bear went lunging up the creek bank toward Little Arliss and her cub, a flash of yellow came streaking out of the brush.

It was that big yeller dog. He was roaring like a mad bull. He wasn't one-third as big and heavy as the she bear, but when he piled into her from one side, he rolled her clear off her feet. They went down in a wild, roaring tangle of twisting bodies and scrambling feet and slashing fangs.

As I raced past them, I saw the bear lunge up to stand on her hind feet like a man while she clawed at the body of the yeller dog hanging to her throat. I didn't wait to see more. Without ever checking my stride, I ran in and jerked Little Arliss loose from the cub. I grabbed him by the wrist and yanked him up out of that water and slung him toward Mama like he was a half-empty sack of corn. I screamed at Mama. "Grab him, Mama! Grab him and run!" Then I swung my chopping axe high and wheeled, aiming to cave in the she bear's head with the first lick.

But I never did strike. I didn't need to. Old Yeller hadn't let the bear get close enough. He couldn't handle her; she was too big and strong for that. She'd stand there on her hind feet, hunched over, and take a roaring swing at him with one of those big front claws. She'd slap him head over heels. She'd knock him so far that it didn't look like he could possibly get back there before she charged again, but he always did. He'd hit the ground rolling, yelling his head off with the pain of the blow; but somehow he'd always roll to his feet. And here he'd come again, ready to tie into her for another round.

I stood there with my axe raised, watching them for a long moment. Then from up toward the house, I heard Mama calling: "Come away from there, Travis. Hurry, son! Run!"

That spooked me. Up till then, I'd been ready to tie into that bear myself. Now, suddenly, I was scared out of my wits again. I ran toward the cabin.

But like it was, Old Yeller nearly beat me there. I didn't see it, of course; but Mama said that the minute Old Yeller saw

we were all in the clear and out of danger, he threw the fight to that she bear and lit out for the house. The bear chased him for a little piece, but at the rate Old Yeller was leaving her behind, Mama said it looked like the bear was backing up.

But if the big yeller dog was scared or hurt in any way when he came dashing into the house, he didn't show it. He sure didn't show it like we all did. Little Arliss had hushed his screaming, but he was trembling all over and clinging to Mama like he'd never let her go. And Mama was sitting in the middle of the floor, holding him up close and crying like she'd never stop. And me, I was close to crying, myself.

Old Yeller, though, all he did was come bounding in to jump on us and lick us in the face and bark so loud that there, inside the cabin, the noise nearly made us deaf.

The way he acted, you might have thought that bear fight hadn't been anything more than a rowdy romp that we'd all taken part in for the fun of it.

NAT LOVE

Harold W. Felton
illustrated by John Fulweiler

*After the Civil War, about eight thousand former
slaves headed west to become cowboys. In fact, at least one-
fourth of the cowboys on the Great Plains and in the Southwest
were African Americans. Born a slave in 1854, Nat Love
headed west when he was fifteen. In the autobiography he wrote
at the end of his life, Love explained that he won a very valuable
horse in a lottery and used the one hundred dollars he got by
selling the horse to go west. This selection tells about some
events that happened during Love's last years as a cowboy.*

On a bright clear September morning, Nat and twenty of the best men from the Texas and Arizona ranges started on a mustang hunt. They carried four days' rations of dried beef, crackers, potatoes, and coffee. A mess wagon with provisions for two months had left for the wild horse country four days before.

Swinging into the saddle the group fired their guns in noisy farewell and started on a dead run across the prairies. They missed the chuck wagon, but in ten days sighted a band of about seventy-five mustangs.

Nat Love, an African American who became one of
the most famous cowboys of all time, poses with
his lariat and saddle. Love was nicknamed
"Deadwood Dick" after winning a shooting contest
in Deadwood, South Dakota, on July 4, 1869.

South Dakota State Historical Society

"A mustang is a wild critter," Pete Gallinger said.

"We got to surround them," said Nat.

"Right. Here is how we'll do it." Pete drew a circle on the ground. "We'll form a circle like this, about ten miles across. Then, we'll take places around it. One man will be two or three miles from the other. Then, slow like, we'll start ridin' for the center of the circle, narrowin' it all the time.

"Each man will have to work sideways and cover that two or three miles, takin' good care to keep the mustangs in the circle. Remember, go slow. The herd is wild and when they see you, you'll be a mile or so away. They'll run away from you and they'll run seven or eight miles until they see one of our men on the other side of the circle." Pete described the plan carefully.

"Then," he added, "they'll run back again."

"That way," said Nat, "the wild mustangs will run maybe fifty to seventy miles or so, and will be getting pretty tired, while our horses will stay fresh."

"Just keep closin' in slow an' easy," Pete said. "The wild horses will do all the running."

"And very little eatin'." Nat added.

"Speakin' of eatin', when do we eat? We ain't got no chuck wagon," said Bill Mitchell.

"We'll hunt some meat. Buffalo is all around here. We'll jerk it and carry some with us. Two of the boys can hunt meat and bring it to us, or maybe each man will get a chance to kill his own meat," said Nat.

The buffalo were killed, and the meat cut into strips and dried in the sun. Jerked meat can support a man for a long time.

The men took their stations and formed the giant circle. Nat spotted the wild herd first. They were a mile and a half away when they saw him. As predicted, they wheeled and ran. Although he saw them at a distance several times in the days that followed, they didn't often approach him directly.

The crew worked the wild mustangs back and forth for almost thirty days. They were finally hemmed up in a canyon, so thin and tired they were easy to handle.

"I kind of hate to break 'em," Nat said. "The poor critters have been on the run for thirty days with very little to eat and almost no sleep. But we've got to rope and ride 'em now. After that we can drive 'em back to the ranch. Then they'll get some rest and enough to eat. They'll turn into good saddle horses."

On the way home, they discovered the burned shell of the chuck wagon, the remains of an Indian massacre. Signs showed that the cook and his helper had put up a good fight.

It's a rough life on the prairie, Nat thought. But it was rough in Tennessee too. I guess it's rough everywhere. A man's got to keep at it and do a job every day. A few men can catch a herd of wild mustangs easy, if they know how. It's all in learnin' an' knowin' your business. Usually if a man knows what he's doin', and if he tries hard, he can get along all right.

The next spring Nat went with a drive of a herd of horses from the home ranch in Arizona to Junction City, Kansas.

Horses on a drive move much faster than cattle and are quite as easy to stampede. They are much more difficult to control.

Everything went well for a few days. Then the storm that everyone knew would come scowled darkly from a line of low clouds in the west. It struck the camp during the second watch, a genuine, old-fashioned, Texas storm.

The herd was uneasy during the low thunder of the storm's steady approach. A hard, sharp flash of lightning roused them into action. Although it was close, the roar of the restless feet hammering against the prairie sod came before the thunder reached the camp.

The fury of wind and rain lasted all night as the men worked in an effort to keep the herd together. It was the next day before the job was over and the frightened creatures were under control.

After breakfast the tired men continued the drive. They had a river to cross near Junction City. The heavy rain of the night before had filled its banks to the top. But the men were eager to reach their goal, and Nat decided the best thing was to push on and deliver the horses to their new owners.

The cowboys, shouting and waving their hats, and pressing from the sides and rear, urged the herd into the swollen stream. Screaming and whinnying, the frightened horses slid down the wet bank into the surging water, the leaders pushed by those in the rear.

With shouts and spurs Nat sent his horse into the dark, brown flood. The other cowboys followed. The shouting died down. Men and horses were intent on the task of survival in the deep water.

Nat heard a sound. It was not wholly a cry, more of a gasp. He turned and saw Loyd Hoedin threshing wildly in the water. The sight lasted for only a moment. Loyd and his horse

completely disappeared below the surface. The current swirled and frothy brown bubbles covered the place where horse and man had been.

The water was broken as the two heads came through. There was another sound, half cry for help, half a gasping cough as the man fought for air. They sank again.

Nat's rope was coiled on the pommel. He seized it, and automatically separated the coils. It was something he had done a thousand times on a horse and on land, but never in the water where he and his mount both fought to keep their heads free of the river's reach.

Calling on all his strength, he lifted his arm and the loop left his hand. The coils dropped from the other and straightened out as the wet, water-soaked rope stretched away toward the drowning man.

Nat's aim was good and the force of the throw was enough. The small loop splashed down within Loyd Hoedin's reach. He grasped it and held on with one hand. With his other hand he held the reins and gave his horse support and guidance. Nat pulled them to the far shore.

The other trail hands had watched the scene with awe and with fear for the safety of the two men and their horses. They crowded around when Nat and Loyd moved up on to solid earth.

There weren't enough words for Loyd to express his feelings, but he found a few that served. "Thanks, Nat. I would have been a goner if it hadn't been for you," he said.

Nat took his outstretched hand. "Come on. We got to ride or the herd will get away from us," he replied.

The years passed and the great wild West Nat Love found so exciting began to fade. Covered wagons came. Men broke the soil with plows and planted seed.

Sod houses rose from the prairie. Fences cut across the open ranges and the homes that were built of turf were replaced with dwellings of wood and brick. Towns grew, factories were built. Steel rails stretched over the plains and wound through the mountains.

There were no more long trail drives. Trains carried the longhorns to market.

"The West is gone," said Nat. "It ain't no fun bein' a cowboy anymore. I got to find something else to do."

"We still have ponies and there's still longhorns," said Bill Mitchell.

"But it ain't the same. Anyway, fancy cattle are comin' in too. Shorthorns, Angus, and Herefords may make beef, but longhorns got to have better cowboys. Nope. I got to find something else to do," said Nat.

"Yeah. But what?"

There was a faraway look in Nat's dark eyes. "During my life so far I had no chance to get an education, except the education of the plains and the cattle business. But this is a time of change and as long as the world is changin', I got to change too."

"The cards are stacked against you. If you ain't a cowboy, you'll have to be a farm hand or something like that," said Bill with the sound of defeat in his voice.

"Oh, no," Nat answered brightly. "Not at all. Anybody can still learn."

"Learn!" Bill exploded. "Why, you're over thirty-five years old. What more are you goin' to learn?"

"I'll figure out something," said Nat.

"Sure, you got to live. You got to have a job. But you're a black man and you don't know nothin' but being a cowboy."

"I can't argue with that, Bill. But look. What's the biggest change you see out here on the prairies?"

Bill Mitchell thought for a moment. "Why, trains," he said. "Trains, engines, iron tracks, iron horses. That's what's made the prairie different."

"Sure," said Nat easily. "So it is trains that have taken my job. If trains have done it, why, I'll get me a job on the railroad."

"You crazy?"

"Yep. Crazy like Billy Blood, Joe Turner, and E. W. Gillett. They are working for the railroads, and there are good jobs there for a black man like me."

"Sure. On a section gang, a track layin' crew, or a tunnel driver."

"Well, I guess you never heard of George Pullman and his Pullman Palace cars," Nat replied.

"You're right. Never heard of him."

"On those long trains there are Pullman cars where people can eat and sleep. Pullman Palace cars, they call 'em and each car is in the charge of a man. And it's a first-class job. It ought to be, because those cars are for first-class passengers." Nat grinned at his joke.

"But you're a cowpuncher. How are you goin' to deal with first-class passengers?"

"I've dealt with some first-class cowpunchers—and some low-class ones, too. It can't be much different on the railroads. People are just people. Besides, I can learn."

"By golly," Bill said, "I think you really could."

" 'Course I can. And I aim to be the best Pullman porter in the country," Nat said.

So, like many other men of the Old West, Nat Love turned to the railroads to fill a life made empty by them. Like many others, he found a full and happy life and new adventures with the iron horses and steel rails that took the place of the mustangs and the western trails.

Nat enjoyed his work with the railroad. It was easy to get along with people, and it was still exciting to ride across the prairies and mountains, even if it was on a train instead of a horse.

In later years he decided to write about all his adventures in a book, and in 1907 it was published. It was called *The Life and Adventures of Nat Love: Better Known in the Cattle Country as "Deadwood Dick"—By Himself*, and in it Nat described his days on the range, his exciting trail rides, the Indian fights, the friends he made, the changes brought by the coming of the railroads. They had been good days. He had lived a good life. He was satisfied. Every job he had he did well. He enjoyed life. No man can do better than that.

DEATH OF THE
IRON HORSE
Paul Goble

L ong ago, long before the white people ever came to this land, the Cheyenne Prophet, called Sweet Medicine, had a terrible dream: In his dream he saw strange hairy people coming from the East. There were more of them than buffaloes—as many, even, as the grasshoppers. They killed his people, and those few who were left alive were made to live in little square houses. And Sweet Medicine saw them kill all

the buffaloes, so there was nothing left to eat, and the people starved. He saw the hairy people tear open our Mother, the earth, exposing her bones, and they bound her with iron bands. Even the birds and animals were afraid, and no longer spoke with people. It was a terrible dream, and they say that Sweet Medicine died of awful sadness not long afterward.

And then, one day, white people did come from the East. First a few came, and then more and more: they wanted all the land for themselves. Soldiers attacked and burned the tipi villages. They killed women and children, and drove off the horses. The people fought back bravely to protect themselves and to keep the land they loved. But they lived in fear. People said that those things which Sweet Medicine had foretold were surely coming true.

One day scouts galloped into camp, and told of something they called the Iron Horse:

"It is huge! It breathes out smoke and has the voice of Thunder. It is coming this way. The white men are making an iron road for it go on. *Nothing* can stop the Iron Horse!" They tried to describe it. People had terrifying images in their minds.

Was it an enormous snake, or even an underwater monster which had crawled out of the river? Was this what Sweet Medicine had spoken about? Then there was even greater fear. In the minds of the children fear grew that the Iron Horse would suddenly come over the hill, right into camp.

Spotted Wolf, Porcupine, Red Wolf, Yellow Bull, Big Foot, Sleeping Rabbit, Wolf Tooth, and many others whose names are not now remembered, wanted to protect the people from the Iron Horse. They were not much older than boys, and knew they would have to be brave, even ready to die, like the warriors who had died defending the helpless ones.

"The soldiers have defeated us and taken everything that we had, and made us poor. We have no more time to play games around camp. Let us go and try to turn back this Iron Horse." They left camp without telling anyone.

They rode all night and most of the next day, and came to a ridge overlooking the wide valley of the river. Thick black smoke was rising in the far distance.

"It is a grass fire," said one.

"No, the smoke has a strange shape. *Look!* The smoke is coming this way, *against the wind!*"

"Impossible," said another, "fire cannot go against the wind. . . ."

But the smoke kept on coming, and underneath it something was growing larger.

"It is the Iron Horse; nothing else can make smoke go against the wind. See, it puffs and puffs like a white man's pipe."

When the Iron Horse had disappeared in the distance, the young men went on again.

"Let us see the trail it leaves," they said to each other. But nobody had ever seen anything like its tracks.

"These must surely be the iron bands binding our Mother, earth, which Sweet Medicine dreamed about. We must cut them apart and set her free."

With only tomahawks and knives it seemed an impossible task. But they dug down and chopped the ties in the middle, and hacked out spikes until the rails no longer joined together. The moon had long passed overhead when they finished.

Dawn was just showing when they saw a small light over the level plain.

"Morning Star is rising," someone said.

"No," said another, "it is the eye of the Iron Horse shining."

548

Those with the fastest horses galloped up the track to find out.

When they saw it was indeed the Iron Horse, they turned around, but their horses were not fast enough. The Iron Horse came up behind, huffing and panting, and belching out clouds of black smoke. It thundered alongside, sending forth screams and hissing and shooting sparks high into the air:

puff-a-puff-a-puff-a-puff-a-puff-a-puff-a-puff-a-puff-a-puff-a-puff-a-puff-a-puff-a-

The young men shot their arrows; one tried to throw a rope over the engine, but the horses were terrified and ran from the monster. Suddenly the locomotive jumped right into the air, and all the boxcars slammed and zig-zagged together with a dreadful crash.

Everything was twisted up in clouds of dust and smoke and steam.

The dust blew away. The hissing steam faded. There was silence. One white man was on the ground; another was in the cab. They were both dead.

"The Iron Horse does not breathe any longer," someone said. The sun rose as they stood looking in bewilderment at what they had done. Suddenly a door in the caboose opened; a man jumped down and started running back up the track. He died full of arrows.

"Come on; let us see what white people carry in these wagons."

They broke open the first car; inside was a jumble of broken boxes and barrels. The first box was filled with axes. Then everyone was hacking open cases, excited to see what was inside. They had never seen so many different things;

they did not know what most of them were. But there were pans and kettles; china plates and glass vases; cups, files, and knives, like those which cost many buffalo robes in trade with the white men. Everyone found something useful. There were mountains of boxes: shoes, shirts, pants, jackets, tall black hats, and hats with ribbons and feathers. They scattered them everywhere. Best of all, there were soldiers' uniforms and blankets, and glasses which the soldier chiefs used for looking into the distance. They even found flags, and someone uncovered a beautiful shiny bugle.

In the caboose there were things to eat, and bottles of sweet juice. There was also a heavy tin box which would not open. They knocked off the lock; it was filled with bags of silver coins and bundles of little bits of green paper. The coins they took because the women knew to make holes in them

and hang them on their dresses. But they threw the bits of green paper into the air and watched them blowing like leaves.

There were bolts of cloth in another boxcar; cloth of every color and pattern.

"Ha! Look at all this! Here is more than the stingy traders have! This is all ours! Look how much!"

"Well, this one is mine," someone said, and he ran off, holding onto an end while the cloth unrolled behind him.

"I am taking this one," said another, and he jumped on his horse and galloped away with the cloth unfurling and floating after him like a long ribbon. And then everybody did it. When one tied an end to his pony's tail, others tried to step on the cloth, hoping to jerk him out of the saddle. They had great fun. The horses joined in the excitement, galloping this way and that over the prairie with the lengths of cloth sailing behind them. When they became old men they loved to laugh about that day . . .

It was only a smudge on the horizon, but first one, then another one stopped galloping to look.

"Another Iron Horse is coming. This time there will be soldiers with horses in the wagons."

They quickly gathered up all the precious things they could carry. And then someone said: "We will burn this and leave nothing for the soldiers."

Taking red-hot coals out of the locomotive, they set the boxcars alight. They reached the high ridge and looked back. The valley was filled with smoke.

"Now our people need not fear the Iron Horse. We will make them glad when we give them all these things. Let's go."

MEET PAUL GOBLE, AUTHOR AND ILLUSTRATOR

Paul Goble was born in England and worked as an industrial designer there. On vacations, however, he traveled in the western part of the United States. He says about his interest in American Indians, "I have been interested in everything Indian since I can remember. . . . [Their world] was so different from the crowded island where I lived. And yet perhaps growing up so far from this country sharpened my need to know more. Over many years I acquired a considerable library of the better books concerning Native Americans and I really studied those books."

Since 1970 Goble has lived and worked in the Black Hills of South Dakota. For Death of the Iron Horse, Goble used Cheyenne accounts and other accounts of an incident that took place on August 7, 1867. A Union Pacific freight train that was traveling through Nebraska was derailed by a group of young Cheyenne men. Goble says, "The derailment was only a minor incident, but one that the Cheyenne people have remembered with pride and amusement. . . . From this distance in time we can see that the Cheyenne were simply fighting for their lives, liberty, and their own pursuit of happiness."

THE COMING OF THE LONG KNIVES

from SING DOWN THE MOON
by Scott O'Dell
illustrated by Howard Post

The year is 1864. Bright Morning, a fourteen-year-old Navaho girl, lives with her family in what is now Arizona. Bright Morning, her family, and her friend Tall Boy, who was crippled saving Bright Morning from Spanish slave traders, have no idea that an encounter with the United States soldiers they call the Long Knives will change their lives forever.

The pinto beans pushed up through the earth and the peaches began to swell. Wool from the shearing was stored away for the winter weaving. My father and brother went into the mountains and brought back deer meat which we cut into strips and dried. It was a good summer and a good autumn.

Then early one winter morning three Long Knives came. They were from the white man's fort and they brought a message from their chief. When all of our people were gathered in the meadow one of the soldiers read the message, using Navaho words. He read fast and did not speak clearly, but this is what I remember.

The Long Knife read more from the paper which I do not remember. Then he fastened the paper to a tree where all in the village could see it and the three soldiers rode away.

There was silence after the soldiers left. Everyone was too stunned to speak or move. We had been threatened before by the Long Knives, but we lived at peace in our canyon, so why should they wish to harm us?

Everyone stared at the yellow paper fastened to the cottonwood tree, as if it were alive and had some evil power. Then, after a long time, Tall Boy walked to the tree. Grasping the paper, he tore it into many pieces and threw them into the river. We watched the pieces float away, thinking as they disappeared that so had the threat of the white men. But we were wrong. At night, in the dark of the moon, the Long Knives came.

The morning of that day we knew they were coming. Little Beaver, who was tending his mother's sheep, saw them from the high mesa. He left his flock and ran across the mesa and down the trail, never stopping.

He fell in front of his mother's hogan and lay there like a stone until someone threw a gourd of water in his face. By that time all the people in the village stood waiting for him to speak. He jumped to his feet and pointed into the south.

"The white men come," he cried. "The sun glints on their knives. They are near."

"How many?" Tall Boy said.

"Many," cried Little Beaver, "too many."

My father said, "We will take our goods and go into the high country. We will return when they are gone."

"We will go," said the other men.

But Tall Boy held up his hand and shouted, facing the elder Indians, "If we flee they will follow. If we flee, our goods will remain to be captured. It is better to stay and fight the Long Knives."

"It is not wise to fight," my father said.

"No, it is not," my uncle said, and all the older men repeated what he said.

It was decided then that we should go. But Tall Boy still would not yield. He called to five of the young men to join him in the fight. They went and stood by him.

"We will need you," my father said to the six young men. "We will have to go into high country. Your strength will help us there."

Tall Boy was unbending. My father looked at him, at his arm held helplessly at his side.

"How is it, Tall Boy, that you will fight?" he said. "You cannot string a bow or send a lance. Tell me, I am listening."

I watched Tall Boy's face darken.

"If you stay and cannot fight, what will happen?" my father asked him. "You will be killed. Others will be killed."

Tall Boy said nothing. It hurt me to watch his face as he listened to words that he knew were true. I left them talking and went down to the river. When I came back Tall Boy had gathered his band of warriors and gone.

We began to pack at once. Each family took what it could carry. There were five horses in the village and they were driven up the mesa trail and left there. The sheep and goats were driven a league away into a secret canyon where they could graze. My flock, my thirty sheep, went too, with the rest. I would have gone with them if I had not thought that in a few days the Long Knives would leave and we could come back to our village. I would never have abandoned them.

When the sun was high we filed out of the village and followed the river north, walking through the shallow water. At

dusk we reached the trail that led upward to the south mesa. Before we went up the trail the jars were filled with water. We took enough to last us for a week and five sheep to slaughter. The cornmeal we carried would last that long. By that time the soldiers would be gone.

The soldiers could not follow our path from the village because the flowing water covered our footsteps as fast as they were made. But when we moved out of the river our steps showed clear in the sand. After we were all on the trail some of the men broke branches from a tree and went back and swept away the marks we had left. There was no sign for the soldiers to see. They could not tell whether we had gone up the river or down.

The trail was narrow and steep. It was mostly slabs of stone which we scrambled over, lifting ourselves from one to the other. We crawled as much as we walked. In places the sheep had to be carried and two of them slipped and fell into a ravine. The trail upward was less than half a mile long, but night was falling before we reached the end.

We made camp on the rim of the mesa, among rocks and stunted piñon trees. We did not think that the soldiers would come until morning, but we lighted no fires and ate a cold supper of corncakes. The moon rose and in a short time shone down into the canyon. It showed the river winding toward the south, past our peach orchards and corrals and hogans. Where the tall cliffs ended, where the river wound out of the canyon into the flatlands, the moon shone on white tents and tethered horses.

"The soldiers have come," my uncle said. "They will not look for us until morning. Lie down and sleep."

We made our beds among the rocks but few of us slept. At dawn we did not light fires, for fear the soldiers would see the rising smoke, and ate a cold breakfast. My father ordered everyone to gather stones and pile them where the trail entered the mesa. He posted a guard of young men at the trail head to use the stones if the soldiers came to attack us. He then sent three of the fastest runners to keep watch on the army below.

I was one of the three sent. We crawled south along the rim of the mesa and hid among the rocks, within sight of each other. From where I crouched behind a piñon tree, I had a clear view of the soldiers' camp.

As the sun rose and shone down into the narrow canyon I could see the Long Knives watering their horses. They were so far below me that the horses seemed no larger than dogs. Soon afterward six of the soldiers rode northward. They were riding along the banks of the river in search of our tracks. Once they got off their horses and two of them climbed up to Rainbow Cave where cliff dwellers had lived long ago. But they found the houses deserted.

The soldiers went up the river, past the trail that led to the place where we were hidden. They did not return until the sun was low. As they rode slowly along, they scanned the cliff that soared above them, their eyes sweeping the rocks and trees, but they did not halt. They rode down the river to their tents and unsaddled the horses. We watched until they lighted their supper fires, then we went back to our camp.

Tall Boy was sitting on a rock near the top of the trail, at work on a lance. He held the shaft between his knees, using his teeth and a hand to wrap it with a split reed.

I was surprised to see him sitting there, for he and the other young warriors had ridden out of the canyon on the morning the Long Knives came. No one had heard from them since that day. Even his mother and father and sisters, who were hiding with us on the mesa, did not know where he was. At first I thought that he had changed his mind and come back to help protect them. But this was not the reason for his return.

Mumbling something that I could not understand, he went on with his work. I stood above him and as I looked down I noticed a deep scratch across his forehead and that a loop of his braided hair had pulled loose.

"Did you hurt yourself climbing the trail?" I said.

He knotted the reed around the shaft and bit the ends off with his teeth. His right arm hung useless at his side.

"The climb is not difficult," he said.

It was a very difficult climb, but I did not say so, since he wanted me to think otherwise. "Where are the warriors?" I asked him. "Are they coming to help us?"

"They have left the canyon," he said.

"But you did not go," I said, noticing now that he had lost one of his moccasins.

For an instant he glanced up at me. In his eyes I saw a look of shame, or was it anger? I saw that the young warriors had left him behind with the women and old men and children. He was no longer of any use to them.

He held up the lance and sighted along the shaft. "It has an iron point," he said. "I found it in the west country."

"It will be a mighty weapon against the Long Knives," I said.

"It is a weapon that does not require two hands."

"One hand or the other," I said, "it does not matter."

That night we ate another cold supper, yet everyone was in good spirits. The white soldiers had searched the canyon and found no trace of us. We felt secure. We felt that in the morning they would ride away, leaving us in peace.

In the morning guards were set again at the head of the trail. Running Bird and I crawled to our places near the piñon tree and crouched there as the sun rose and shone down on the camp of the Long Knives. Other lookouts hid themselves along the rim of the mesa, among the rocks and brush.

Nothing had changed in the night. There were the same number of tents among the trees and the same number of horses tethered on the riverbank. Our hogans were deserted. No smoke rose from the ovens or the fire pits. There was no sound of sheep bells.

The camp of the Long Knives was quiet until the sun was halfway up the morning sky. Men strolled about as if they had nothing to do. Two were even fishing in the river with long willow poles. Then—while Running Bird and I watched a

squirrel in the piñon tree, trying to coax him down with a nut—I saw from the corner of an eye a puff of smoke rise slowly from our village. It seemed no larger than my hand. A second puff rose in the windless air and a third.

"Our homes are burning!"

The word came from the lookout who was far out on the mesa rim, closest to the village. It was passed from one lookout to the other, at last to me, and I ran with it back to our camp and told the news to my father.

"We will build new homes," he said. "When the Long Knives leave we will go into the forest and cut timber. We will build hogans that are better than those the soldiers burned."

"Yes," people said when they heard the news, "we will build a new village."

Tall Boy said nothing. He sat working on his lance, using his teeth and one hand, and did not look up.

I went back to the piñon and my father went with me. All our homes had burned to the ground. Only gray ashes and a mound of earth marked the place where each had stood. The Long Knives were sitting under a tree eating, and their horses cropped the meadow grass.

My father said, "They will ride away now that they have destroyed our village."

But they did not ride away. While we watched, ten soldiers with hatchets went into our peach orchard, which still held its summer leaves. Their blades glinted in the sunlight. Their voices drifted up to us where we were huddled among the rocks.

Swinging the hatchets as they sang, the soldiers began to cut the limbs from the peach trees. The blows echoed through the canyon. They did not stop until every branch lay on the ground and only bare stumps, which looked like a line of scarecrows, were left.

Then, at the last, the Long Knives stripped all the bark from the stumps, so that we would not have this to eat when we were starving.

"Now they will go," my father said, "and leave us in peace."

But the soldiers laid their axes aside. They spurred their horses into a gallop and rode through the cornfield, trampling the green corn. Then they rode through the field of ripening beans and the melon patch, until the fields were no longer green but the color of the red earth.

"We will plant more melons and corn and beans," my father said.

"There are no seeds left," I said. "And if we had seeds and planted them they would not bear before next summer."

We watched while the soldiers rode back to their camp. We waited for them to fold their tents and leave. All that day and the next we watched from the rim of the mesa. On the third day the soldiers cut alder poles and made a large lean-to, which they roofed over with the branches. They also dug a fire pit and started to build an oven of mud and stones.

It was then we knew that the Long Knives did not plan to leave the canyon.

"They have learned that we are camped here," my father said. "They do not want to climb the cliff and attack us. It is easier to wait there by the river until we starve."

Clouds blew up next morning and it began to rain. We cut brush and limbs from the piñon pines and made shelters. That night, after the rain stopped, we went to the far side of the mesa where our fires could not be seen by the soldiers and cooked supper. Though there was little danger that the soldiers would attack us, my father set guards to watch the trail.

We were very careful with our jars of water, but on the sixth day the jars were empty. That night my father sent three of us down the trail to fill the jars at the river. We left soon after dark. There was no moon to see by so we were a long time getting to the river. When we started back up the trail we covered our tracks as carefully as we could. But the next day the soldiers found that we had been there. After that there were always two soldiers at the bottom of the trail, at night and during the day.

The water we carried back lasted longer than the first. When the jars were nearly empty it rained hard for two days and we caught water in our blankets and stored it. We also discovered a deep stone crevice filled with rainwater, enough for the rest of the summer. But the food we had brought with us, though we ate only half as much as we did when we were home in the village, ran low. We ate all of the corn and slaughtered the sheep we had brought. Then we ground up the sheep bones and made a broth, which was hard to swallow. We lived on this for two days and when it was gone we had nothing to eat.

Old Bear, who had been sick since we came to the mesa, died on the third day. And that night the baby of Shining Tree died. The next night was the first night of the full moon. It was then that my father said that we must leave.

Dawn was breaking high over the mesa when we reached the bottom of the trail. There was no sign of the soldiers.

My father led us northward through the trees, away from our old village and the soldiers' camp. It would have been wiser if we had traveled in the riverbed, but there were many who were so weak they could not walk against the current.

As soon as it grew light we found patches of wild berries among the trees and ate them while we walked. The berries were ripe and sweet and gave us strength. We walked until the sun was overhead. Then, because four of the women could go no farther, we stopped and rested in a cave.

We gathered more berries and some roots and stayed there until the moon came up. Then we started off again, following the river northward, traveling by the moon's white glow. When it swung westward and left the canyon in darkness we lay down among the trees. We had gone no more than two leagues in a day and part of a night, but we were hopeful that the soldiers would not follow us.

In the morning we built a small fire and roasted a basket of roots. Afterward the men held council to decide whether to go on or to stay where we were camped.

"They have burned our homes," my father said. "They have cut down the trees of our orchard. They have trampled our gardens into the earth. What else can the soldiers do to us that they have not already done?"

"The Long Knives can drive us out of the canyon," my uncle said, "and leave us to walk the wilderness."

At last it was decided that we stay.

We set about the cutting of brush and poles to make shelters. About mid-morning, while we were still working on the lean-tos, the sound of hoofs striking stone came from the direction of the river.

Taking up his lance, Tall Boy stepped behind a tree. The rest of us stood in silence. Even the children were silent. We were like animals who hear the hunter approach but from terror cannot flee.

The Long Knives came out of the trees in single file. They were joking among themselves and at first did not see us. The leader was a young man with a red cloth knotted around his neck. He was looking back, talking to someone, as he came near the place where Tall Boy stood hidden.

Tall Boy stepped from behind the tree, squarely in his path. Still the leader did not see him.

Raising the lance, Tall Boy quickly took aim and drew back, ready to send it toward the leader of the Long Knives.

He had practiced with the lance before we came down the mesa, time after time during all of one day, trying to get used to throwing it with his left hand. With his right hand he had been the best of all the warriors. It was with a lance that he had killed the brown bear beyond Rainbow Mountain, a feat of great skill.

But now, as the iron-tipped weapon sped from his grasp, it did not fly straight. It wobbled and then curved upward, struck the branch of a tree, and fell broken at the feet of the soldier's horse.

The horse suddenly stopped, tossing its head. Only then did the soldier turn to see the broken lance lying in front of him. He looked around, searching for the enemy who had thrown it. He looked at my father, at my uncle, at me. His eyes swept the small open space where we stood, the women, the children, the old people, all of us still too frightened to move or speak.

Tall Boy, as soon as he had thrown the lance, dodged behind the tree where he had hidden before, backed away into the brush and quietly disappeared. I saw his face as he went past me. He no longer looked like a warrior. He looked like a boy, crushed and beaten, who flees for his life.

The rest of the Long Knives rode up and surrounded us. They searched us one by one, making certain that no one carried a weapon, then they headed us down the canyon.

We passed the ruined fields of beans and corn and melons, the peach trees stripped of their bark and branches, our burned-out homes. We turned our eyes away from them and set our faces. Our tears were unshed.

Soon we were to learn that others bore the same fate, that the whole nation of the Navahos was on the march. With the Long Knives at their backs, the clans were moving—the Bitter-Water, Under-His-Cover, Red-House, Trail-to-the-Garden, Standing-House, Red-Forehead, Poles-Strung-Out—all the Navahos were marching into captivity.

FINE ART
THE AMERICAN
WEST

Buffalo hide shield. c. 1875.
Probably Mandan.

Deerskin, feathers, and beads. National Museum of
the American Indian, Smithsonian Institution. 3771

The Becker sisters on a ranch near
Alamosa, Colorado. 1894.

Photograph. Colorado Historical Society

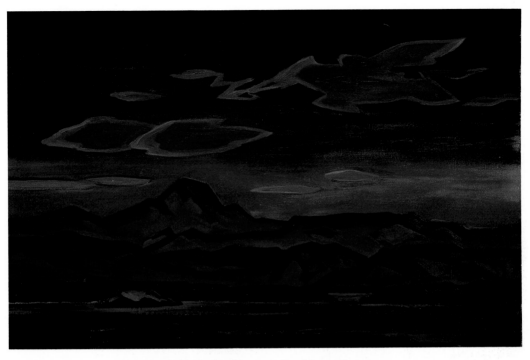

Rider in the Midnight Sky. 1928. Emil James Bisttram.

Oil on canvas. George A. Hearn Fund, by exchange, 1984, The Metropolitan Museum of Art.
1984.372. Photo: © 1985 The Metropolitan Museum of Art

The Bronco Buster. 1895.
Frederic Remington.

Bronze. Amon Carter Museum,
Fort Worth, Texas. 1961.3

THE WEST BEGINS

from BY THE SHORES OF SILVER LAKE
by Laura Ingalls Wilder
illustrated by Julie Ecklund

*Laura's father had gone ahead of the family
to take a job with the railroad in the Dakota territory. Now
reunited, Laura, her mother and father, and her three sisters
travel the last part of the journey from Minnesota to the railroad
camp that will be their new home.*

Early next morning they were all in the wagon again. It had not been unloaded so everything was ready to go. Nothing was left of the camp but Aunt Docia's shanty. Over the worn-out grass and the dead spots where shanties had been, surveyors were measuring and driving stakes for a new town that would be built.

"We'll be along as soon as Hi gets his business settled," Aunt Docia said.

"I'll see you at Silver Lake!" Cousin Lena called to Laura, while Pa chirruped to the horses and the wheels began to turn.

The sun shone brightly on the uncovered wagon, but the wind was cool and riding was pleasant. Here and there, men were working in their fields, and now and then a team and wagon passed.

Soon the road curved downward through rolling land and Pa said, "The Big Sioux River's ahead."

Laura began to see out loud for Mary. "The road's going down a low bank to the river, but there aren't any trees. There's just the big sky and grassy land, and the little, low creek. It's a big river sometimes, but now it's dried up till it's no bigger than Plum Creek. It trickles along from pool to pool, by dry gravel stretches and cracked dry mud flats. Now the horses are stopping to drink."

"Drink hearty," Pa said to the horses. "There's no more water for thirty miles."

Beyond the low river the grassy land was low curve behind curve and the road looked like a short hook.

"The road pushes against the grassy land and breaks off short. And that's the end of it," said Laura.

"It can't be," Mary objected. "The road goes all the way to Silver Lake."

"I know it does," Laura answered.

"Well, then I don't think you ought to say things like that," Mary told her gently. "We should always be careful to say exactly what we mean."

"I was saying what I meant," Laura protested. But she could not explain. There were so many ways of seeing things and so many ways of saying them.

Beyond the Big Sioux there were no more fields, no houses, no people in sight. There really was no road, only a dim wagon trail, and no railroad grade. Here and there Laura glimpsed a little wooden stake, almost hidden in the grasses. Pa said they were surveyors' stakes for the railroad grade that was not started yet.

Laura said to Mary, "This prairie is like an enormous meadow, stretching far away in every direction, to the very edge of the world."

The endless waves of flowery grasses under the cloudless sky gave her a queer feeling. She could not say how she felt. All of them in the wagon, and the wagon and team, and even Pa, seemed small.

All morning Pa drove steadily along the dim wagon track, and nothing changed. The farther they went into the west, the smaller they seemed, and the less they seemed to be going anywhere. The wind blew the grass always with the same endless rippling, the horses' feet and the wheels going over the grass made always the same sound. The jiggling of the board seat was always the same jiggling. Laura thought they might go on forever, yet always be in this same changeless place, that would not even know they were there.

Only the sun moved. Without ever seeming to, the sun moved steadily upward in the sky. When it was overhead, they stopped to feed the horses and to eat a picnic lunch on the clean grass.

It was good to rest on the ground after riding all the morning. Laura thought of the many times they had eaten under the sky, while they were traveling all the way from Wisconsin to Indian Territory in Oklahoma and back again to Minnesota. Now they were in Dakota Territory going farther west. But this was different from all the other times, not only because there was no cover on the wagon and no beds in it, but some other reason. Laura couldn't say how, but this prairie was different.

"Pa," she asked, "when you find the homestead, will it be like the one we had in Indian Territory?"

Pa thought before he answered. "No," he said finally. "This is different country. I can't tell you how, exactly, but this prairie is different. It feels different."

"That's likely enough," Ma said sensibly. "We're west of Minnesota, and north of Indian Territory, so naturally the flowers and grasses are not the same."

But that was not what Pa and Laura meant. There was really almost no difference in the flowers and grasses. But there was something else here that was not anywhere else. It was an enormous stillness that made you feel still. And when you were still, you could feel great stillness coming closer.

All the little sounds of the blowing grasses and of the horses munching and whooshing in their feedbox at the back of the wagon, and even the sounds of eating and talking could not touch the enormous silence of this prairie.

Pa talked about his new job. He would be the company storekeeper, and the timekeeper at Silver Lake railroad camp. He would run the store and he would keep straight in his books the charge account of every man on the job, and know exactly how much money was due each man for his work, after his board bill and his account at the store had been subtracted. And when the paymaster brought the money each payday, Pa would pay every man. That was all he had to do, and for that he would be paid fifty dollars every month.

"And best of all, Caroline, we're among the very first out here!" said Pa. "We've got the pick of the land for our homestead. By George, our luck's turned at last! First chance at new land, and fifty dollars a month for a whole summer to boot!"

"It is wonderful, Charles," said Ma.

But all their talking did not mean anything to the enormous silence of that prairie.

All that afternoon they went on, mile after mile, never seeing a house or any sign of people, never seeing anything but grass and sky. The trail they followed was marked only by bent and broken grasses.

Laura saw old Indian trails and buffalo paths worn deep in the ground and now grassed over. She saw strange large depressions, straight-sided and flat-bottomed, that had been buffalo wallows, where now the grass was growing. Laura had never seen a buffalo, and Pa said it was not likely that she would ever see one. Only a little while before the vast herds of thousands of buffaloes had grazed over this country. They had been the Indians' cattle, and white men had slaughtered them all.

On every side now the prairie stretched away empty to far, clear skyline. The wind never stopped blowing, waving the tall prairie grasses that had turned brown in the sun. And all the afternoon, while Pa kept driving onward, he was merrily whistling or singing. The song he sang oftenest was:

"Oh, come to this country,
And don't you feel alarm,
For Uncle Sam is rich enough
To give us all a farm!"

Even baby Grace joined in the chorus, though she did not bother to follow the tune.

"Oh, come away! Come away!
Come away, I say!
Oh, come away! Come away!
Come right away!
Oh, come to this country
And have no fear of harm
Our Uncle Sam is rich enough
To give us all a farm!"

The sun was lowering in the west when a rider appeared on the prairie behind the wagon. He came following behind not very fast, but coming a little nearer mile after mile while the sun was slowly sinking.

"How much farther is it to Silver Lake, Charles?" Ma asked.

"About ten miles," said Pa.

"There isn't anybody living nearer, is there?"

"No," said Pa.

Ma did not say anything more. Neither did anyone else. They kept glancing back at that rider behind them, and each time they looked, he was a little nearer. He was surely following them and not meaning to overtake them until the sun sank. The sun was so low that every hollow between the low prairie swells was filled with shadow.

Each time that Pa glanced back, his hand made a little motion, slapping the horses with the lines to hurry them. But no team could pull a loaded wagon as fast as a man could ride.

The man was so near now that Laura could see two pistols in leather holsters on his hips. His hat was pulled low over his eyes, and a red bandana was tied loosely around his neck.

Pa had brought his gun west, but it was not in the wagon now. Laura wondered where it was, but she did not ask Pa.

She looked back again and saw another rider coming on a white horse. He wore a red shirt. He and the white horse were far behind and small, but they came fast, galloping. They overtook the first rider, and the two came on together.

Ma said in a low voice, "There's two of them now, Charles."

Mary asked frightened, "What is it? Laura, what's the matter?"

Pa looked back quickly, and then he was comfortable. "Everything's all right now," he said. "That's Big Jerry."

"Who's Big Jerry?" Ma asked.

"He's a half-breed, French and Indian," Pa answered carelessly. "A gambler, and some say a horse thief, but a darned good fellow. Big Jerry won't let anybody waylay us."

Ma looked at him astonished. Her mouth opened and then it shut; she did not say anything.

The riders came up beside the wagon. Pa lifted his hand and said, "Hullo, Jerry!"

"Hullo, Ingalls!" Big Jerry answered. The other man gave them all a snarling look and went galloping on ahead, but Big Jerry rode along by the wagon.

He looked like an Indian. He was tall and big but not one bit fat, and his thin face was brown. His shirt was flaming red. His straight black hair swung against his flat, high-boned cheek as he rode, for he wore no hat. And his snow-white horse wore no saddle or bridle. The horse was free, he could go where he wanted to go, and he wanted to go with Big Jerry wherever Big Jerry wanted to ride. The horse and the man moved together as if they were one animal.

They were beside the wagon only a moment. Then away they went in the smoothest, prettiest run, down into a little hollow and up and away, straight into the blazing round sun on the far edge of the west. The flaming red shirt and the white horse vanished in the blazing golden light.

Laura let out her breath. "Oh, Mary! The snow-white horse and the tall, brown man, with such a black head and a bright red shirt! The brown prairie all around—and they rode right into the sun as it was going down. They'll go on in the sun around the world."

Mary thought a moment. Then she said, "Laura, you know he couldn't ride into the sun. He's just riding along on the ground like anybody."

But Laura did not feel that she had told a lie. What she had said was true too. Somehow that moment when the beautiful, free pony and the wild man rode into the sun would last forever.

Ma still feared that the other man might be lying in wait to rob them, but Pa told her, "Don't worry! Big Jerry's gone ahead to find him and stay with him till we get into camp. Jerry'll see that nobody molests us."

Ma looked back to see that her girls were all right, and she held Grace snugly on her lap. She did not say anything because nothing she could say would make any difference. But Laura knew that Ma had never wanted to leave Plum Creek and did not like to be here now; she did not like traveling in that lonely country with night coming on and such men riding the prairie.

The wild calls of birds came down from the fading sky. More and more dark lines streaked the pale-blue air overhead—straight lines of wild ducks, and long flying wedges of wild geese. The leaders called to their flocks behind them, and each bird answered in turn. The whole sky twanged, "Honk? Honk! Honk! Quanck? Quanck. Quanck."

"They're flying low," said Pa. "Settling down for the night on the lakes."

There were lakes ahead. A thin silvery line at the very edge of the sky was Silver Lake, and little glimmers south of it were the Twin Lakes, Henry and Thompson. A wee dark blob between them was the Lone Tree. Pa said it was a big cottonwood, the only tree to be seen between the Big Sioux River and the Jim; it grew on a little rise of ground no wider than a road, between the Twin Lakes, and it grew big because its roots could reach water.

"We'll get some seeds from it to plant on our homestead," Pa said. "You can't see Spirit Lake from here, it's nine miles northwest of Silver Lake. You see, Caroline, what fine hunting country this is. Plenty of water and good feeding ground for wild fowl."

"Yes, Charles, I see," said Ma.

The sun sank. A ball of pulsing, liquid light, it sank in clouds of crimson and silver. Cold purple shadows rose in the east, crept slowly across the prairie, then rose in heights on heights of darkness from which the stars swung low and bright.

The wind, which all day long had blown strongly, dropped low with the sun and went whispering among the tall grasses. The earth seemed to lie breathing softly under the summer night.

Pa drove on and on beneath the low stars. The horses' feet went softly thump-thumping on the grassy ground. Far, far ahead a few tiny lights pricked through the dark. They were the lights of Silver Lake camp.

"Don't need to see the trail for these next eight miles," Pa told Ma. "All a man's got to do is keep driving toward the lights. There's nothing between us and camp but smooth prairie and air."

Laura was tired and chilly. The lights were far away. They might be stars after all. The whole night was glittering of stars. Close overhead and down on all sides great stars glittered in patterns on the dark. The tall grass rustled against the turning wagon wheels; it kept on rustling, rustling against the wheels that kept on turning.

Suddenly Laura's eyes jerked open. There was an open doorway and light streaming out. And in the dazzle of lamplight Uncle Henry was coming, laughing. So this must be Uncle Henry's house in the Big Woods when Laura was little, for that was where Uncle Henry was.

"Henry!" Ma exclaimed.

"It's a surprise, Caroline!" Pa sang out. "I thought I wouldn't tell you Henry's out here."

"I declare, it takes my breath, I am so surprised," said Ma.

And then a big man was laughing up at them, and he was Cousin Charley. He was the big boy who had bothered Uncle Henry and Pa in the oat field, and been stung by thousands of yellow jackets. "Hello, Half-pint! Hello, Mary! And here's baby Carrie, a big girl now. Not the baby any longer, uh?" Cousin Charley helped them down from the wagon, while Uncle Henry took Grace and Pa helped Ma over the wheel, and here came Cousin Louisa, bustling and talking and herding them all into the shanty.

Cousin Louisa and Charley were both grown up now. They were keeping the boarding shanty, cooking for the men who were working on the grade. But the men had eaten supper long ago, and now they were all sleeping in the bunkhouses. Cousin Louisa talked about all this, while she dished up the supper she had been keeping hot on the stove.

After supper Uncle Henry lighted a lantern and led the way to a shanty that the men had built for Pa.

"It's all new lumber, Caroline, fresh and clean as a whistle," Uncle Henry said, holding up the lantern so they could see the new board walls and the bunks built up against them. There was a bunk on one side for Ma and Pa, and on the other side two narrow bunks, one above the other, for Mary and Laura and Carrie and Grace. The beds were already spread in the bunks; Cousin Louisa had seen to that.

In no time at all, Laura and Mary were cuddled on the rustling fresh hay-mattress with the sheet and quilts drawn up to their noses, and Pa blew out the lantern.

MEET LAURA INGALLS WILDER, AUTHOR
Laura Ingalls Wilder was over sixty when she began to write the story of her childhood. During the years she wrote about, her family lived in Wisconsin, Kansas, Minnesota, Iowa, and the Dakota territory.

In 1879, just before the time described in "The West Begins," her sister Mary became ill with what was called "brain fever." When Mary recovered, she was blind. Wilder's father asked her to describe for Mary the things that Mary could not see for herself. Wilder later said that this was when she began to see the world as a writer would see it. She explains why she wanted to write about her life:
"I understood that in my own life I represented a period of American history. . . . I had seen the whole frontier, the woods, the Indian country of the great plains, the frontier towns, the building of railroads in wild, unsettled country, homesteading, and farmers coming in to take possession. I realized that I had seen and lived it all—all the successive phases of the frontier."

McBROOM THE RAINMAKER

Sid Fleischman
illustrated by Cat Bowman Smith

I dislike to tell you this, but some folks have no regard for the truth. A stranger claims he was riding a mule past our wonderful one-acre farm and was attacked by woodpeckers.

Well, there's no truth to that. No, indeed! Those weren't woodpeckers. They were common prairie mosquitoes.

Small ones.

Why, skeeters grow so large out here that everybody uses chicken wire for mosquito netting. But I'm not going to say an unkind word about those zing-zanging, hot-tempered, needle-nosed creatures. They rescued our farm from ruin. That was during the Big Drought we had last year.

Dry? Merciful powers! Our young'uns found some tadpoles and had to teach them to swim. It hadn't rained in so long those tadpoles had never seen water.

That's the sworn truth—certain as my name's Josh McBroom. Why, I'd as soon grab a skunk by the tail as tell a falsehood.

Now, I'd best creep up on the Big Drought the way it crept up on us. I remember we did our spring plowing, as usual, and the skeeters hatched out, as usual. The bloodsucking rapscallions could be mighty pesky, but we'd learned to distract them.

"Willjillhesterchesterpeterpollytimtommarylarryandlittleclarinda!" I called out. "I hear the whine of gallinippers. We'd better put in a patch of beets."

Once the beets were up, the thirsty skeeters stuck in their long beaks like straws. Didn't they feast though! They drained out the red juice, the beets turned white, and we harvested them as turnips.

The first sign of a dry spell was when our clocks began running slow. I don't mean the store-bought kind—no one can predict the weather with a tin timepiece. We grew our own clocks on the farm.

Vegetable clocks.

Now, I'll admit that may be hard to believe, but not if you understand the remarkable nature of our topsoil. Rich? Glory be! Anything would grow in it—lickety-bang. Three or four crops a day until the confounded Big Dry came along.

Of course, we didn't grow clocks with gears and springs and a name on the dial. Came close once, though. I dropped my dollar pocket watch one day, and before I could find it, the thing had put down roots and grown into a three-dollar alarm clock. But it never kept accurate time after that.

It was our young'uns who discovered they could tell time by vegetable. They planted a cucumber seed, and once the vine leaped out of the ground, it traveled along steady as a clock.

"An inch a second," Will said. "Kind of like a second hand."

"Blossoms come out on the minute," Jill said. "Kind of like a minute hand."

They tried other vegetable timepieces, but pole beans had a way of running a mite fast and squash a mite slow.

As I say, those homegrown clocks began running down. I remember my dear wife, Melissa, was boiling three-and-a-half-minute eggs for breakfast. Little Clarinda planted a cucumber seed, and before it grew three blossoms and thirty inches, those eggs were hard-boiled.

"Mercy!" I declared. "Topsoil must be drying out."

Well, the days turned drier and drier. No doubt about it—our wonderful topsoil was losing some of its get-up-and-go. Why, it took almost a whole day to raise a crop of corn. The young'uns had planted a plum tree, but all it would grow was prunes. Dogs would fight over a dry bone—for the moisture in it.

"Willjillhesterchesterpeterpollytimtommarylarryandlittleclarinda!" I called. "Keep your eyes peeled for rain."

They took turns in the tree house scanning the skies, and one night Chester said, "Pa, what if it doesn't rain by Fourth of July? How'll we shoot off firecrackers?"

"Be patient, my lambs," I said. We used to grow our own firecrackers, too. Don't let me forget to tell you about it. "Why, it's a long spell to Fourth of July."

My, wasn't the next morning a scorcher! The sun came out so hot that our hens laid fried eggs. But no, that wasn't the Big Dry. The young'uns planted watermelons to cool off and beets to keep the mosquitoes away.

"Look!" Polly exclaimed, pointing to the watermelons. "Pa, they're rising off the ground!"

Rising? They began to float in the air like balloons! We could hardly believe our eyes. And gracious me! When we cut those melons open, it turned out they were full of hot air.

Well, I was getting a mite worried myself. Our beets were growing smaller and smaller, and the skeeters were growing larger and larger. Many a time, before dawn, a rapping at the windows would wake us out of a sound sleep. It was those confounded, needle-nosed gallinippers pecking away, demanding breakfast.

Then it came—the Big Dry.

Mercy! Our cow began giving powered milk. We pumped away on our water pump, but all it brought up was dry steam. The oldest boys went fishing and caught six dried catfish.

"Not a rain cloud in sight, Pa," Mary called from the tree house.

"Watch out for gallinippers!" Larry shouted, as a mosquito made a dive at him. The earth was so parched, we couldn't raise a crop of beets and the varmints were getting downright ornery. Then, as I stood there, I felt my shoes getting tighter and tighter.

"Thunderation!" I exclaimed. "Our topsoil's so dry it's gone in reverse. It's *shrinking* things."

Didn't I lay awake most of the night! Our wonderful one-acre farm might shrink to a square foot. And all night long the skeeters rattled the windows and hammered at the door. Big? The *smallest* ones must have weighed three pounds. In the moonlight I saw them chase a yellow-billed cuckoo.

Didn't that make me sit up in a hurry! An idea struck me. Glory be! I'd break that drought.

First thing in the morning I took Will and Chester to town with me and rented three wagons and a birdcage. We drove straight home, and I called everyone together.

"Shovels, my lambs! Heap these wagons full of topsoil!"

But Larry and little Clarinda were still worried about Fourth of July. "We won't be able to grow fireworks, Pa!"

"You have my word," I declared firmly.

Before long, we were on our way. I drove the first wagon, with the young'uns following along behind in the other two. It might be a longish trip, and we had loaded up with picnic hampers of food. We also brought along rolls of chicken wire and our raincoats.

"Where are we going, Pa?" Jill called from the wagon behind.

"Hunting."

"Hunting?" Tom said.

"Exactly, my lambs. We're going to track down a rain cloud and wet down this topsoil."

"But how, Pa?" asked Tim.

I lifted the birdcage from under the wagon seat. "Presto," I said, and whipped off the cover. "Look at that lost-looking, scared-looking, long-tailed creature. Found it hiding from the skeeters under a milk pail this morning. It's a genuine rain crow, my lambs."

"A rain crow?" Mary said. "It doesn't look like a crow at all."

"Correct and exactly," I said, smiling. "It looks like a yel-low-billed cuckoo, and that's what it is. But don't folks call 'em rain crows? Why, that bird can smell a downpour coming sixty miles away. Rattles its throat and begins to squawk. All we got to do is follow that squawk."

But you never heard such a quiet bird! We traveled miles and miles across the prairie, this way and the other, and not a rattle out of that rain crow.

The Big Dry had done its mischief everywhere. We didn't see a dog without his tongue dragging, and it took two of them to bark at us once. A farmer told us he hadn't been able to grow anything all year but baked potatoes!

Of course, we slept under chicken wire—covered the horses, too. My, what a racket the gallinippers made!

Day after day we hauled our three loads of topsoil across the prairie, but that rain crow didn't so much as clear its throat.

The young'uns were getting impatient. "Speak up, rain crow," Chester muttered desperately.

"Rattle," Hester pleaded.

"Squawk," said Peter.

"Please," said Mary. "Just a little peep would help."

Not a cloud appeared in the sky. I'll confess I was getting a mite discouraged. And the Fourth of July not another two weeks off!

We curled up under chicken wire that night, as usual, and the big skeeters kept banging into it, so you could hardly sleep. Rattled like a hailstorm. And suddenly, at daybreak, I rose up laughing.

"Hear that?"

The young'uns crowded around the rain crow. We hadn't been able to hear its voice rattle for the mosquitoes. Now it turned in its cage, gazed off to the northwest, opened its yellow beak, and let out a real, ear-busting rain cry.

"*K-kawk! K-kawk! K-kawk!*"

"Put on your raincoats, my lambs!" I said, and we rushed to the wagons.

"*K-kawk! K-kawk! K-kawk!*"

Didn't we raise dust! That bird faced northwest like a dog on point. There was a rain cloud out there and before long Jill gave a shout.

"I see it!"

And the others chimed in one after the other. "Me, too!"

"*K-kawk! K-kawk! K-kawk!*"

We headed directly for that lone cloud, the young'uns yelling, the horses snorting, and the bird squawking.

Glory be! The first raindrops spattered as large as quarters. And my, didn't the young'uns frolic in that cloudburst! They lifted their faces and opened their mouths and drank right out of the sky. They splashed about and felt mud between their toes for the first time in ages. We all forgot to put on our raincoats and got wet as fish.

Our dried-up topsoil soaked up raindrops like a sponge. It was a joy to behold! But if we stayed longer, we'd get stuck in the mud.

"Back in the wagons!" I shouted. "Home, my lambs, and not a moment to lose."

Well, home was right where we left it.

I got a pinch of onion seeds and went from wagon to wagon, sowing a few seeds in each load of moist earth. I didn't want to crowd those onions.

Now, that rich topsoil of ours had been idle a long time—it was rarin' to go. Before I could run back to the house, the greens were up. By the time I could get down my shotgun, the tops had grown four or five feet tall—onions are terrible slow growers. Before I could load my shotgun, the bulbs were finally bursting up through the soil.

We stood at the windows watching. Those onion roots were having a great feast. The wagons heaved and creaked as the onions swelled and lifted themselves—they were already the size of pumpkins. But that wasn't near big enough. Soon they were larger'n washtubs and began to shoulder the smaller ones off the wagons.

Suddenly we heard a distant roaring in the air. Those zing-zanging, hot-tempered, blood-sucking prairie mosquitoes were returning from town with their stingers freshly sharpened. The Big Dry hadn't done their dispositions any good—their tempers were at a boil.

"You going to shoot them down, Pa?" Will asked.

"Too many for that," I answered.

"How big do those onions have to grow?" Chester asked.

"How big are they now?"

"A little smaller'n a cow shed."

"That's big enough," I nodded, lifting the window just enough to poke the shotgun through.

Well, the gallinippers spied the onions—I had planted red onions, you know—and came swarming over our farm. I let go at the bulbs with a double charge of buckshot and slammed the window.

"Handkerchiefs, everyone!" I called out. The odor of fresh-cut onion shot through the air, under the door, and through the cracks. Cry? In no time our handkerchiefs were wet as dishrags.

"Well! You never saw such surprised gallinippers. They zing-zanged every which way, most of them backwards. And weep? Their eyes began to flow like sprinkling cans. Onion tears! The roof began to leak. Mud puddles formed everywhere. Before long, the downpour was equal to any cloudburst I ever saw. Near flooded our farm!

The skeeters kept their distance after that. But they'd been mighty helpful.

With our farm freshly watered we grew tons of great onions—three or four crops a day. Gave them away to farmers all over the country.

The newspaper ran a picture of the whole family—the rain crow, too.

McBROOM THE RAINMAKER BREAKS BIG DROUGHT

The young'uns had a splendid Fourth of July. Grew all the fireworks they wanted. They'd dash about with bean shooters—shooting radish seeds. You know how fast radishes come up. In our rich topsoil they grew quicker'n the eye. The seeds hardly touched the ground before they took root and swelled up and exploded. They'd go off like strings of firecrackers.

And, mercy, what a racket! Didn't I say I'd rather catch a skunk by the tail than tell a fib? Well, at nightfall a scared cat ran up a tree, and I went up a ladder to get it down. Reached in the branches and caught it by the tail.

I'd be lying if I didn't admit the truth. It was a skunk.

THE SEARCH

from . . . And Now Miguel
by Joseph Krumgold
illustrated by Mary C. Gilman

*Miguel Chavez's great wish is to be allowed
to accompany his father, uncles, and older brothers on their
annual move to the Sangre de Cristo Mountains with the
family's sheep herds. Miguel feels that at twelve he is old enough
to spend the summer with the men of the family in the
mountains rather than stay at home with his mother and
younger brother and sister. When some of the family's sheep are
lost as the result of a spring storm, Miguel thinks that his chance
has come to prove his worth as a shepherd. He intends to find
the sheep. However, fearing that Miguel will only get in the
way, his father will not allow him to join the search.*

My friend Juby was playing basketball when I came to
the yard of the schoolhouse. That is, Juby and some
of the others were playing just shooting for baskets,
and as soon as he saw me, he waved his hand and quit, and
came over.

"How're you doing?" he asked me.

I said, "Pretty good," because what's the use telling everybody your troubles?

"D'you folks lose any sheep?" he asked me.

"What?" I made one grab at his arm and held tight.

"Sheep," he said. "What's the matter?"

"Now look, Juby," I said. "What's the use talking you and me? How do you know we got missing sheep? What about them?"

"I saw them."

"What?"

"At least I think they're yours. From the shape of the numbers they look like yours." We don't put our brand on the sheep until after we shear them. But our numbers had a different shape to them than any of the others in the neighborhood.

"Where?"

"Then you did lose some sheep?"

"Juby!" I was a little excited. "What's the use, Juby? Just to talk? Where did you see them?"

"Well—you know Carlotta?"

"Who?"

"Our milk cow."

"Cows? What about the sheep?"

"I'm telling you. She got loose last night, Carlotta, and when I went to herd her back I saw those sheep."

"Where? Where? Where?"

"What's the matter with you, Mike? Something wrong?"

"Juby," I said. "You and me, you're my oldest friend, aren't you?"

"Sure."

"Then tell me, where are the sheep?"

"Give me a chance. I saw them across the river. Maybe fifteen, ewes and lambs. They looked like they were heading straight for Arroyo Hondo." It was just in the opposite direction from where my older brother Blasito and the sheep wagon was, from where he looked this morning. "Were they yours?"

"You don't know what this could mean, Juby. That is for me."

But just then the bell started to ring, and Mrs. Mertian, who is the teacher of our school over there in Los Cordovas, she came to the door and told everybody to come in.

"Let's go." Juby went with the others into the class.

And that's the way things stood.

On one side, Mrs. Mertian with the bell ringing. And on the other side the big mountains, looking very dark and a little mad, if you can think of mountains like they were mad. But that was the way they looked, and at that moment there came thunder from behind them.

And in the middle, I stood. If it ever happened that I came home with the missing sheep? Could anything ever be better?

Mrs. Mertian said, "Miguel."

From the Sangre de Cristo there came thunder, very low.

I did not stand too long. Because there was no question about it! Nothing, that is to say, nothing at all could ever be better.

I headed straight for the *Boys* on the other side of the yard.

"Miguel!" It was Mrs. Mertian yelling. I didn't even look back. I jumped into this whole bunch of bushes and started down the hill.

Big champion jumps, every one breaking a world's record, that's the way I came down that hill. With each jump, everything went flying. My books banging at the end of the rope in my hand, swinging all around. My arms, like I had a dozen of them, each one going off by itself. My feet, like I was on a bike, working away to keep my balance. But I couldn't balance. Except by jumping. I couldn't stop. Each jump bigger than the last. I cleared a bush, then a big cracked rock. Then, I wasn't going to make it but I did, a high cactus. Each jump I thought was the last. Each jump was going to end with a cracked head, a split rib, or maybe two broken legs. But it didn't. I don't know why. There was nothing I could do. I came down that hill, like a boulder bumping in bigger and bigger bumps, bumping its way down a cliff. Straight for the river. Until I wasn't scared of falling anymore. I had to fall! Or land in the river. But how? I grabbed a bush. That didn't stop me. And then my books caught, between a couple of rocks. I slipped, grabbed at another bush. Slid a couple of feet, and then took off again. And then I landed. On my face. I landed in a whole piled up bunch of mesquite. No one, I'm sure ever since that hill was first there, ever came down it so fast.

I wasn't hurt. Except for a scratch stinging near my eye, I was all right. It didn't even bleed. All I needed was to catch my breath. I lay there in the bushes until I did. Breathing and listening for Mrs. Mertian, in case she came to the top of the hill and was yelling down at me. But I didn't hear any yelling. When I looked she wasn't there. The school bell stopped, too. All there was to hear was the thunder, now and then, far off, and the wind blowing quiet.

I got up thinking, I'd done it. After what Juby told me there was only one thing to do, and now I'd done it. Here I was, just me, Miguel, getting the sheep that were lost, all alone. And there would be no one bringing them home but me. All I had

to do was to get up there, on the mesa across the river, round up the bunch and march them back to where everyone could see. It would be something worth watching, me herding the ewes and lambs that were lost back into the corral at home. My father would tell me how sorry he was about what happened at breakfast, the way he wouldn't let me go help. And I would tell my father, it was nothing, he didn't have to feel sorry.

I felt good. Looking at the mountains, and the mountains looking down at me as if to see what I was going to do next.

I hopped across the river. The easy place to cross was downstream a way, where there were more rocks to jump on. I didn't bother to go to the easy place. I could have made it even if the rocks were twice as far from each other, feeling good like I was, and all in practice from the way I'd come jumping down the hill. I only slipped into the water twice, without much water getting into my shoes at all.

To get up the cliff on the other side was not easy. It was steep in this place and wet and slippery with the rain, the stones high and smooth with nothing to grab on to except sometimes a juniper bush. And besides having the books in one hand. It would be better without the books. But I couldn't leave them around or hide them, seeing they might get wet. I made it all right, pulling and crawling my way up. Steep places and books, that wasn't too hard. Not to find a bunch of lost sheep, it wasn't.

When I got up to the top and looked, I didn't see them. I guess I did expect a little bit they'd be up there waiting for me. But they weren't. I didn't mind too much. The kind of thing I was doing had to be hard. Such a big thing couldn't be too easy. It'd be like cheating. I set out, walking to the north.

Up on the mesa, it looked empty. Like one of those pictures that my little brother Pedro draws. One straight line across the middle of the page and big zigzags off to one side which is the mountains. Then dark on top for the clouds, which he makes by smudging up all the pencil lines. And dark on the bottom for the mesa, which he makes with a special black crayon. That's all there is in the picture. And that's why it's a good picture. Because that's all there is. Except for some little bushes, juniper and chaparral and sagebrush. With nothing sticking up, only a high soapweed or a crooked looking cactus. Nothing else.

Especially, no sheep.

I walked from one rise to the next. Every three or four steps turning all around as I walked. And when I got near to the top of each rise I had to run. Because I thought in the next ten, fifteen steps up top there, sure, I'd see them. The first few times I saw nothing, which I didn't mind too much. And the next few times, I saw nothing, too. Pretty soon I was getting ready to see them, because after an hour or so of walking and turning around and running I figured it was hard enough. Even for something big.

Besides I had a pebble in my left shoe. I felt it down there coming up the cliff. I didn't mind then, because it only made everything even harder. And that was all right with me. But now it was getting to hurt good. And I couldn't sit down and take it out. That would be like giving up.

Besides, I didn't have any time to waste. The mesa spread out, as far as you could see, with many breaks—everywhere little canyons and washes. And it was sure that on top of the next canyon, maybe, I was going to see them, those sheep. If I didn't waste time getting up there. Which I didn't. But all I saw was the same kind of nothing that I saw from the last high place, just this wide straight line stretching right across the middle.

Walking down was harder than walking up. For one thing, walking down on my left heel made the pebble bigger. It was getting to feel like a rock. And for another, walking down, you've already seen what there is to see all around, and there's nothing to look forward to until you start to walk up again. It got so I was running more than I was walking. Running downhill because I wanted to get that part over with, and running up because I couldn't wait to get to the top. And all the time, turning around. I got pretty good at being able to turn around and keep running at the same time.

Except what good was it, getting pretty good at anything? When the only thing counted was to get one look, one quick look at those sheep.

All the turning around did was to get me so mixed up I didn't know whether I was going north, south, east or west. Not that it made any difference, I guess. The sheep weren't particular which direction you went to find them. They weren't in any direction. There were just no sheep. There was all the dark sky, and all this straight flat plain you'd ever want to see. But, no sheep.

And after a couple of hours of seeing no sheep, I would've been glad to see any sheep, even if they weren't ours. I kept trying to see sheep so hard, it was like my eyes got dry and thirsty just to see sheep. To see nothing for two, three hours, especially sheep, it gets hard on your eyes.

It was getting hard on my left foot, too, with that big rock pressing in.

And it wasn't so easy on my hands, either, on account of the books. The books weren't heavy, but when you keep that rope wrapped around your hand it can pinch. And even if you take it off one hand and put it on the other, it don't take long before it's pinching that hand, too.

Another thing was it got to be hard breathing. Because there was no time to stop and get a good breath. There was always somewhere to go take a look, and you couldn't stop because maybe that very second the sheep were moving away out of sight, and that very second if you were up on a top you'd see them.

After so many hours of it being so hard, I figured it was hard enough by then. It was getting long past the time I ought to find our sheep. Only it didn't make any difference how I figured. They weren't there to be found. Not anywhere.

And after a while, walking, walking, every place started to look like you'd been there before. You'd see a piece of tumble weed. And you were sure it was one you saw an hour before. It didn't help to think that maybe you were just walking up and around the same hill all the time.

Then looking, looking, I thought I heard a bell. I listened hard in the wind. One of the ewes that was lost might have a bell. In the flock there are ten or a dozen sheep with bells. Each one is like the leader of a bunch. I stood still, listening. Then I heard it again, and it was for sure a bell. But it was the school bell, far away, back in Los Cordovas. It must've already become noon, and that was the bell for noontime. Soon the ringing far away stopped. And there was nothing to listen to again, except the quiet wind.

It was never the same, after I heard that bell. It made me feel hungry. Because the bell meant going home to eat. And feeling hungry, I got to feel not so good in the other parts of me. Like lonely. At the beginning being alone was the best part of it, going off by myself to bring home the sheep. But now it was getting to look like I wasn't bringing home any sheep. And that made a lot of difference about being alone, while everybody else was back there going home to eat. The only way I could go home was to find them. It wasn't only so I could bring the sheep back. I had to find them so I could go back, too.

From then on, I got very busy. I didn't stop to walk any more. I ran. Everywhere I went I kept up running, and I did most of my breathing going downhill when I didn't have to try so hard to keep running. There was hardly any breath left over to keep looking with. And that was the hardest part of all, the looking. Because there was never anything to see.

And after a long while, I heard the bell again. School was out for the day.

It was hard to figure out what to do next.

I could leave home. That's about all there was left. I couldn't go back without the sheep. Not after what my father said at breakfast, and especially not after the way he looked. And it was clear enough that in all this whole empty place I was never going to find them, those sheep. I could just as well stop, that's all. I could take some time and do a lot of breathing. I could bury my books under a bush. I could sit down and take off my shoe and get rid of that rock with all the sharp edges on it. Then I could go somewhere until I saw a lot of sheep and sit down and look at them, till I got enough again of looking at sheep. And then I could decide where I was leaving home to go to.

Maybe even to the Sangre de Cristo Mountains. On my own, by myself.

But when I looked at the mountains, I knew that was no good. It was impossible. There was only one way to go up into the Mountains of the Sangre de Cristo. And that was to make everyone see you were ready, and then you would go.

Indeed, in order that I should go this way, that's why I was looking for the sheep right now. And if I gave up looking for the sheep, then the idea of going up into the Mountains, I had to give that up, too. I guess if you are going to leave home you just left home, that's all, everything.

Except, it wasn't up to me anymore. It wasn't a question that I should give up looking for the sheep.

It was just no use.

I could keep running from the top of one rise up to the next, looking, looking with my eyes getting drier and drier, without any breath, and the bones in my hands like they were cracking, and the heel of my left foot like it was getting torn away, listening to nothing but the wind—I could keep on doing that forever. It wasn't a question of me giving up, it was a question that just everything had given up, me and everything.

So I sat down. I took a deep breath. And I started to untie the laces from my left shoe. And then—what do you think?

I smelled them.

It is not hard to know that what you're smelling is sheep. If only there are some sheep around to smell. They smell a little sweet and a little old, like coffee that's left over in a cup on the table with maybe used-up cigarettes in it. That's sort of what they smell like.

So when there was this smell, I looked around. I found out from which direction was the wind. And in that direction I went to the top of the next rise, a dozen steps. And no farther away than you could throw a rock, there they were coming up the hill toward me, about fifteen ewes and their lambs, ambling along, having a good time eating, just taking a walk like there was no trouble anywhere in all the world.

"Wahoo!" I took off. Around my head in a big circle I swung my books. Like it was a rope, and I was going to throw a loop on all fifteen at once. "Wahoo!" I took off down that hill as if I were a whole tribe of Indians and the sheep was somebody's chuck wagon that was going to get raided. "Wahoo!"

The sheep looked up, a little like they were a bunch of ladies in church and they were interested to see who was coming through the door.

I showed them who was coming through the door. Before they knew what was happening they were moving. *Whoosh*— I let my books swing out, and I hit one right in the rump. *Whish*—I kicked another one with my foot that had the rock, so that it hurt me more, I think, than the sheep. I picked up a stone and—*wango*—I let a third one have it in the rear. I got them running right in the opposite direction than they were going.

I kept them going at a gallop. Running first to the one side, then to the other, swinging the books around my head all the time. Yelling and hollering so they wouldn't even dare slow down. They looked scared, but I didn't care. I had waited too long for this. And now I wanted them to know that I was here. I ran them down the hill fast enough to be a stampede. And whichever one ran last, he was the unlucky one. There were a lot of rocks around, and I throw rocks good.

At the bottom of the hill I quieted down. Why was I acting like I was so mad? I had no reason to be mad at the sheep. It wasn't as if they started out to get me in trouble. Indeed, because of them, here I was doing a great thing. I was finding them and bringing them home. If they didn't take it into their heads to go out and get lost, I never would have this big chance.

I quieted down. I stopped and I breathed. The air was good. After the rain it was clean and it smelled sweet, like a vanilla soda in Schaeffer's Drugstore in Taos before you start to drink it with the straw. I took in the air with deep breaths. I sat down and took off my shoe. I found the rock down near the heel. But my goodness, it wasn't any kind of rock at all. Just a little bit of a chip off a stone. In my foot it felt like a boulder. But in my hand it didn't look like anything at all.

I was quieted down. We started off. It was going to be a long drive home. I didn't mind. There were so many good things to think about. What my father would say to me and my grandfather.

It is no great trouble to drive a small bunch of sheep. You just walk behind them, and if one begins to separate you start in the same direction that it starts and that makes it turn back and bunch up again. It was very little work. So there was much time to think what my uncles would say, and my big brothers. And how Pedro would watch me.

There was much time to look around. At the mountains, not so dark now and not so mad. There was much to see, walking along thinking, breathing, and looking around. How the clouds now were taking on new shapes, the dark ones separating and new big white ones coming up. And on the mesa everything looked fine. I saw flowers. Before when I was looking there were no flowers. Now, there they were. The little pink ones of the peyote plants. And there were flowers on the hedgehog cactus, too, kind of pinkish purple some, and others a real red.

I remembered my brother Gabriel's song about the little red flower. And walking along, thinking, breathing, looking around, I began to sing the song. Only the first words over and over again because I didn't remember the rest, which made no difference, because who was listening anyway? It was just I wanted something to sing.

MEET JOSEPH KRUMGOLD, AUTHOR

In 1953, filmmaker Joseph Krumgold made a documentary film about the lives of sheepherders in the Southwest. While making the film, Krumgold and his wife lived for some time with the Chavez family in Taos, New Mexico. The Chavez family had been sheepherders for hundreds of years, first in Spain and then in the American Southwest. After the film was finished, Krumgold was asked to make the story into a book. That book was . . . And Now Miguel.

BIBLIOGRAPHY

Children of the Wild West by Russell Freedman. How did children work, play, and go to school in pioneer days? Old photographs will help you understand the past.

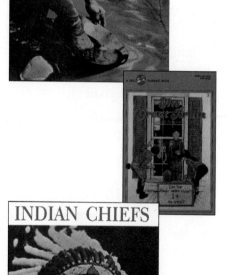

The Great American Gold Rush by Rhoda Blumberg. Why did so many people come to the West after 1849? This book explains.

The Great Brain by John D. Fitzgerald. You'll like these stories about a family of boys in early Utah.

Indian Chiefs by Russell Freedman. Photographs illustrate these short biographies of important Native Americans.

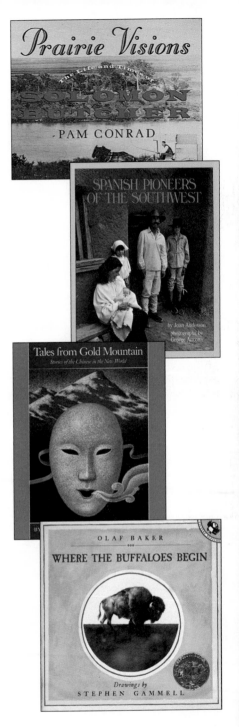

Prairie Visions: The Life and Times of Solomon Butcher by Pam Conrad. Find out about a famous photographer of pioneer times.

Spanish Pioneers of the Southwest by Joan Anderson. Photographs tell about life in New Mexico in the 1700s.

Tales from Gold Mountain: Stories of the Chinese in the New World by Paul Yee. You'll enjoy these tales about some of the many Chinese who worked on the railroads across the West.

Where the Buffaloes Begin by Olaf Baker. A Native American boy finds the lake where buffaloes originate and leads them against the enemies of his people.

JOURNEYS AND QUESTS

249

YOUNDE GOES TO TOWN

retold by Harold Courlander
and George Herzog
illustrated by Anthony Carnabuci

Once in the country of Akim, in the hills far back from the coast, there was a man named Younde. He was a simple man who had never been far from home, and he spent his time at farming and hunting like the other people of the village. He had often heard talk about the big town of Accra by the ocean, and all the wonderful things to be found there, but he had never seen it. He had never been farther from his village than the river.

But one day Younde had to go to Accra. He put on his best clothes, and took his knife and put it in his belt. He wrapped some food in a cloth and put it on his head and started out. He walked for many days, and the road was hot and dusty. After a while he was out of his own country, and people didn't speak Akim, which was his language, any more. He came closer and closer to Accra. There were many people and donkeys on the

way, all going to town or coming back from town, more people than he had ever seen on the road before.

Then he saw a great herd of cows grazing by the edge of the
road. He had never seen so many cows in his life. He stopped
and looked at them in wonder. He saw a little boy herding the
cows and he went up to him and said, "Who is the owner of all
these cattle?"

But the boy didn't understand Younde, because Younde
spoke Akim, while in Accra they spoke the Ga language, and
he replied, "Minu," which meant "I don't understand."

"Minu! What a rich man he must be to own so many cows!"
Younde said.

He continued his way into the town. He was very impressed
with everything he saw.

He came to a large building and stopped to look at it. It was made of stone, and it was very high. He shook his head. There was nothing like this back in the hills. When a woman came by on her way to market Younde spoke to her.

"What a tremendous house!" he said. "What rich person can own such a building?"

But the woman didn't know what Younde was saying, because he talked Akim and she knew only Ga, so she replied to him: "Minu."

"Minu! That man again!"

Younde was overcome. No one back in Akim had ever been so wealthy as Minu. As he went farther and farther into the town he kept seeing more wonders. He came to the market. It covered a space larger than all the houses in Younde's village. He walked through the center of it, and saw the women selling things that were rare in his village, like iron pots and iron spoons.

"Where do all these things come from?" Younde asked a little girl.

She smiled at him.

"Minu," she replied.

Younde was silent. Everything was Minu. Minu was everywhere.

The crowd was very great. People pushed and shoved, for it was the big market day and everyone within walking distance had come to sell or buy. Younde had never seen so many people in one place. The stories he had heard about Accra hadn't done it justice. He stopped an old man with a drum under his arm and said: "So many people, all at one time! What makes so many people all come to Accra?"

"Minu," the old man said.

Younde was overwhelmed. What influence that Minu had! People came to Accra in great crowds just because of him. How ignorant folks back in the village were of this great personage.

He went out of the market down to the ocean's edge. Lying in the water were many little fishing boats with sails, the first Younde had ever seen.

"Wah! To whom do all those boats belong?" he asked a fisherman standing on the beach.

"Minu," the fisherman replied.

Younde walked away, and came to where a large iron cargo ship was being loaded with palm oil and fruit. Smoke came out of its stacks in huge black clouds, and hundreds of men swarmed over its decks.

"Hah!" Younde said in great excitement to a man carrying a stalk of bananas on his head. "This must be the largest boat in the world!"

"Minu," the man said.

"Yes, I know, that much I guessed," Younde said. "But where is all the fruit going?"

"Minu," the man said, and went up onto the deck of the ship.

Younde was overcome. Minu was indeed a great man. He owned everything. He ate everything. You couldn't ask a question but what people would answer "Minu." Minu here, there, everywhere.

"I wouldn't have believed it if I hadn't seen it," Younde said. "They ought to call Accra 'Minu's Town.' How wonderful it would be to have Minu's great wealth!"

Younde then transacted his business in Accra, and again he wrapped food in his cloth and set it on his head and started out for home.

When he came to the edge of the town he saw a great procession and heard the beating of drums. He came close and saw it was a funeral. Men were carrying a coffin and women

were crying out in mourning. It was the most impressive funeral Younde had ever seen. He pushed his way into the crowd and looked. And to one of the mourners he said:

"Who is this person who has died?"

And the mourner replied sadly: "Minu."

"What! The great Minu is dead?" Younde said. "The man who owned the cattle and the tall house, the sailing boats and the iron steamship? The man whose reputation has crowded the market place beyond belief? Oh, poor Minu! He had to leave all his wealth behind. He has died just like an ordinary person!"

Younde continued his way out of the city, but he couldn't get the tragedy of Minu from his mind.

"Poor Minu!" he said over and over again. "Poor Minu!"

THE STORY OF JUMPING MOUSE

retold and illustrated by John Steptoe

O nce there was a young mouse who lived in the brush near a great river. During the day he and the other mice hunted for food. At night they gathered to hear the old ones tell stories. The young mouse liked to hear about the desert beyond the river, and he got shivers from the stories about the dangerous shadows that lived in the sky. But his favorite was the tale of the far-off land.

The far-off land sounded so wonderful the young mouse began to dream about it. He knew he would never be content until he had been there. The old ones warned that the journey would be long and perilous, but the young mouse would not be swayed. He set off one morning before the sun had risen.

It was evening before he reached the edge of the brush. Before him was the river; on the other side was the desert. The young mouse peered into the deep water. "How will I ever get across?" he said in dismay.

"Don't you know how to swim?" called a gravelly voice.

The young mouse looked around and saw a small green frog.

"Hello," he said. "What is swim?"

"This is swimming," said the frog, and she jumped into the river.

"Oh," said the young mouse, "I don't think I can do that."

"Why do you need to cross the river?" asked the frog, hopping back up the bank.

"I want to go to the far-off land," said the young mouse. "It sounds too beautiful to live a lifetime and not see it."

"In that case, you need my help. I'm Magic Frog. Who are you?"

"I'm a mouse," said the young mouse.

Magic Frog laughed. "That's not a name. I'll give you a name that will help you on your journey. I name you Jumping Mouse."

As soon as Magic Frog said this, the young mouse felt a strange tingling in his hind legs. He hopped a small hop and, to his surprise, jumped twice as high as he'd ever jumped before. "Thank you," he said, admiring his powerful new legs.

"You're welcome," said Magic Frog. "Now step onto this leaf and we'll cross the river together."

When they were safely on the other side, Magic Frog said, "You will encounter hardships on your way, but don't despair. You will reach the far-off land if you keep hope alive within you."

Jumping Mouse set off at once, hopping quickly from bush to bush. The shadows circled above, but he avoided being seen. He ate berries when he could find them and slept only when he was exhausted. Days passed. Though he was able to travel quickly, he began to wonder if he'd ever reach the other side of the desert. He then came upon a stream that coursed through the dry land. Under a large berry bush he met a fat old mouse.

"What strange hind legs you have," said the fat mouse.

"They were a gift from Magic Frog when she named me," said Jumping Mouse proudly.

"Humpf," snorted the fat mouse. "What good are they?"

"They've helped me come this far across the desert, and with luck they'll carry me to the far-off land," said Jumping Mouse. "But now I'm very tired. May I rest here a while?"

"Indeed you may," said the fat mouse. "In fact, you can stay forever."

"Thank you, but I'll stay only until I'm rested. I've seen the far-off land in my dreams and I must be on my way as soon as I'm able."

"Dreams," said the fat mouse scornfully. "I used to have such dreams, but all I ever found was desert. Why go jumping about the desert when everything anyone needs is right here?"

Jumping Mouse tried to explain that it wasn't a question of need, but something he felt he had to do. But the fat mouse only snorted again. Finally Jumping Mouse dug a hole and curled up for the night.

The next day the fat mouse warned him to stay on this side of the stream. "A snake lives on the other side," he said. "But don't worry. He's afraid of water, so he'll never cross the stream."

Life was easy beneath the berry bush, and Jumping Mouse was soon rested and strong. He and the fat mouse ate and slept and then slept and ate. Then one morning, when he went to the stream for a drink, he caught sight of his reflection. He was almost as fat as the fat old mouse!

"It's time for me to go on," thought Jumping Mouse. "I didn't come all this way to settle down under a berry bush."

Just then he noticed that a branch had gotten caught in the narrow of the stream. It spanned the water like a bridge—now the snake could cross! Jumping Mouse hurried back to warn the fat mouse. But the mousehole was empty, and there was a strange smell in the air. Snake. Jumping Mouse was too late. "Poor old friend," he thought as he hurried away. "He lost hope of finding his dream and now his life is over."

Jumping Mouse traveled throughout the night, and the next morning he saw that he had reached a grassy plain.

Exhausted, he hopped toward a large boulder where he could rest in safety. But as he got closer, he realized the boulder was an enormous, shaggy bison lying in the grass. Every once in a while it groaned.

Jumping Mouse shivered at the terrible sound. "Hello, great one," he said bravely. "I'm Jumping Mouse and I'm traveling to the far-off land. Why do you lie here as if you were dying?"

"Because I *am* dying," said the bison. "I drank from a poisoned stream, and it blinded me. I can't see to find tender grass to eat or sweet water to drink. I'll surely die."

Jumping Mouse was sad to see so wondrous a beast so helpless. "When I began my journey," he said, "Magic Frog gave me a name and strong legs to carry me to the far-off land. My magic is not as powerful as hers, but I'll do what I can to help you. I name you Eyes-of-a-Mouse."

As soon as he had spoken Jumping Mouse heard the bison snort with joy. He heard but he could no longer see, for he had given the bison his own sight.

"Thank you," said Eyes-of-a-Mouse. "You are small, but you have done a great thing. If you will hop along beneath me, the shadows of the sky won't see you, and I will guide you to the mountains."

Jumping Mouse did as he was told. He hopped to the rhythm of the bison's hooves, and in this way he reached the foot of the mountains.

"I am an animal of the plains, so I must stop here," said Eyes-of-a-Mouse. "How will you cross the mountains when you can't see?"

"There will be a way," said Jumping Mouse. "Hope is alive within me." He said good-bye to his friend; then he dug a hole and went to sleep.

The next morning Jumping Mouse woke to cool breezes that blew down from the mountain peaks. Cautiously he set out in the direction of the coolness. He had not gone far when he felt fur beneath his paws. He jumped back in alarm and sniffed the air. Wolf! He froze in terror, but when nothing happened he gathered up his courage and said, "Excuse me. I'm Jumping Mouse, and I'm traveling to the far-off land. Can you tell me the way?"

"I would if I could," said the wolf, "but a wolf finds his way with his nose, and mine will no longer smell for me."

"What happened?" asked Jumping Mouse.

"I was once a proud and lazy creature," replied the wolf. "I misused the gift of smell, and so I lost it. I have learned not to be proud, but without my nose to tell me where I am and where I am going, I cannot survive. I am lying here waiting for the end."

Jumping Mouse was saddened by the wolf's story. He told him about Magic Frog and Eyes-of-a-Mouse. "I have a little magic left," he said. "I'll be happy to help you. I name you Nose-of-a-Mouse."

The wolf howled for joy. Jumping Mouse could hear him sniffing the air, taking in the mountain fragrances. But Jumping Mouse could no longer smell the pine-scented breezes. He no longer had the use of his nose or his eyes. "You are but a small creature," said Nose-of-a-Mouse, "but you have given me a great gift. You must let me thank you. Come, hop along beneath where the shadows of the sky won't see you. I will guide you through the mountains to the far-off land."

So Jumping Mouse hopped to the rhythm of the wolf's padding paws, and in this way he reached the far-off land.

"I am an animal of the mountains, so I must stop here," said Nose-of-a-Mouse. "How will you manage if you can no longer see or smell?"

"There will be a way," said Jumping Mouse. He then said good-bye to his friend and dug a hole and went to sleep.

The next morning Jumping Mouse woke up and crawled from his hole. "I am here," he said. "I feel the earth beneath my paws. I hear the wind rustling leaves on the trees. The sun warms my bones. All is not lost, but I'll never be as I was. How will I ever manage?" Then Jumping Mouse began to cry.

"Jumping Mouse," he heard a gravelly voice say.

"Magic Frog, is that you?" Jumping Mouse asked, swallowing his tears.

"Yes," said Magic Frog. "Don't cry, Jumping Mouse. Your unselfish spirit has brought you great hardship, but it is that same spirit of hope and compassion that has brought you to the far-off land. You have nothing to fear, Jumping Mouse. Jump high, Jumping Mouse," commanded Magic Frog.

Jumping Mouse did as he was told and jumped as high as he could. Then he felt the air lifting him higher still into the sky.

He stretched out his paws in the sun and felt strangely powerful. To his joy he began to see the wondrous beauty of the world above and below and to smell the scent of earth and sky and living things.

"Jumping Mouse," he heard Magic Frog call. "I give you a new name. You are now called Eagle, and you will live in the far-off land forever."

SACAGAWEA'S JOURNEY

from SACAGAWEA by Betty Westrom Skold
illustrated by Steven Parton

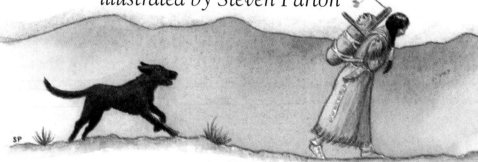

In 1803, President Thomas Jefferson purchased
the Louisiana Territory, an area that extended from the
Mississippi River to the Rocky Mountains and that doubled the
size of the United States. In 1804, he sent an expedition headed
by Meriwether Lewis and William Clark to explore this region
and to find a route through it to the Pacific Ocean. About forty-
five men set off from St. Louis and traveled up the Missouri
River to the territory of the Mandan Indians. There they met a
French fur trader, Toussaint Charbonneau, and his wife,
Sacagawea. Sacagawea was not a Mandan. She was a
Shoshone, a member of a group living in the Rocky Mountains.
Sacagawea had been captured as a young girl and brought east.
At the time she met Lewis and Clark she was sixteen or
seventeen years old and had recently given birth to a son that the
men nicknamed Pompy. She and her husband were hired to go
with the expedition as interpreters and guides.

Sacagawea stuffed a little more soft, dry grass into Pompy's cradleboard, put the child into it, and tied the rawhide thongs. Her eyes swept the room that had sheltered her through the winter, now stripped of the buffalo robes and the hunting and cooking gear. The last fire was dying on the hearth as she stepped outside.

The ground under her moccasins was spongy and damp from the melting snow. Tender new buds dotted the cottonwoods. For several days Lewis and Clark had seen swans and wild geese flying northeastward in the evening. The Hidatsas had been leaping across the ice cakes to catch the buffalo floating downstream. Soon the river would be ice-free and ready. The captains had taken charge of the final packing, carefully separating the maps, papers, and wildlife specimens that would be sent back to President Jefferson from the provisions that would go farther up the Missouri with their Corps of Discovery.

Now it was April 7, 1805. Today they would say good-bye to the Mandans and Hidatsas, who watched from the banks of the river. It would also be a day of parting for six American soldiers and two French traders, who would return to St. Louis with the keelboat and two canoes. The main part of the Corps of Discovery—Captains Lewis and Clark, Sacagawea, Pompy, Charbonneau and another interpreter, three sergeants, twenty-three privates, and a black slave named York—would follow the Missouri westward in the two long pirogues and six dugout canoes.

Shadows were lengthening into late afternoon when the big keelboat and two canoes began to move back down the Missouri toward St. Louis. Almost at the same time, the six

dugout canoes and two pirogues of the westbound party pushed away from the shoreline and started up the river.

The men were in good spirits—talking, laughing, waving at the Indians along the banks. Sacagawea began the journey more quietly. No sign of excitement showed on her face, and her voice was calm. Only months later would the others realize the depth of her feeling as she started the journey.

Sacagawea took her turn with the others, sometimes paddling in one of the boats, often walking along the shore. The world of the plains seemed to flow by. Flocks of geese fed in the young grass, while sparrow hawks wheeled across the sky.

Patches of juniper spread along the sides of the hills. Maple trees were budding and plum bushes were in bloom, but winter was not quite over. Once in a while snow would sift down briefly on a land that had already felt the touch of spring.

At Fort Mandan Sacagawea had become acquainted with the military life of the Americans. She had grown used to the uniforms, the salutes, the sentinels, the commands, and had learned the names of the thirty men whom her family had joined. As the real work of the expedition began, she came to know each person as an individual. Each one had been chosen for the skills that would help the Corps of Discovery as a whole.

Captain Lewis was a brave and thoughtful leader who enjoyed walking alone out on the prairie, studying the animals or gathering bits of plant life. It was he who learned to chart their route by the stars. Captain Lewis also served as doctor for the expedition, giving out medicines from his small leather bag. Sacagawea learned that Captain Clark's talents as mapmaker and peacemaker were equaled by his leadership skills.

Private Cruzatte, whose violin music had delighted her at Fort Mandan parties, was experienced in river travel. Sergeant Gass was a carpenter, and Private Shields was an expert gunsmith. Drewyer served as an interpreter, but he was also an able hunter. The black man, York, worked as Captain Clark's personal servant, and he provided entertainment for the whole Corps with his story-telling. Sergeant Ordway became a capable commander whenever the captains were not around. John Colter, from the Kentucky woods, had been chosen for hunting skills, and in a single day he bagged an elk, three deer, a wolf, and five turkeys. Charbonneau proved to be a surprisingly good trail cook.

Even Scannon, Captain Clark's big, black, Newfoundland dog, had his chores. An alert watchdog, he frightened away animals who wandered into camp during the night. He also helped with Pompy, lying like a faithful guardian beside the baby's cradleboard.

Sacagawea cheerfully kept pace along the trail, moving with a light, firm step. Food-gathering skills from her Shoshone childhood proved useful again and again. Just two days from Fort Mandan, when they had halted for dinner, she sharpened a digger stick and began to poke around in small piles of driftwood. She uncovered a good supply of wild artichokes, buried there by mice.

Day after day Sacagawea walked along the shore or rode in a canoe with the others, but in a sense she made the journey alone. Not even the child on her shoulders shared her experience. No one else could share her dream of homecoming.

Evenings around the campfire were a pleasant time. After supper the men would often throw quoits, a game in which they tossed rope rings at stakes. Sometimes they danced to the music of violin and mouth harp. The captains and several of the others faithfully wrote down each day's events in their journals by the dim light of the fire. Sacagawea sat cross-legged on the ground, mending buckskins and watching over Pompy.

For several days they passed through prairie country like one large grassy pasture. Gentle herds of buffalo, elk, and antelope gazed at them curiously, sometimes following the men who walked on shore. Deer peered shyly from the brush.

By late April they had reached the woodlands at the mouth of the Yellowstone River. Happy to have arrived at this first important landmark, they celebrated with music, dancing, and a small ration of spirits.

May 14 brought troubles to the expedition. Six of the hunters wounded a brown grizzly. Crazed by pain, the bear charged and chased them along the bank. The men plunged into the river, and others in the party were able to kill the bear with eight shots.

After sunset that evening the white pirogue was almost destroyed. The sail had been raised to take advantage of a brisk wind. Steering was Charbonneau, a timid and clumsy river pilot. A sudden squall struck the boat at an angle, ripping the brace of the sail from the man who held it, and the boat tipped over on its side. Charbonneau had never learned

to swim. He cried out to God in terror and dropped the rudder. Cruzatte, in the bow, threatened to shoot him if he did not take hold of the rudder and do his duty. A trembling Charbonneau obeyed.

Meanwhile Sacagawea, balancing the baby on her back, calmly reached far out over the side and grabbed the valuable cargo that had fallen overboard. After the pirogue had been dragged to shore and bailed out with kettles, the rescued articles were spread out on the ground to dry. By her quick thinking Sacagawea had saved many things of value to the expedition. She had rescued instruments for navigation, scientific books needed by the captains for their work, and trading goods needed to make peaceful contact with Indians they would meet along the way.

Almost every day the travelers reached some new tributary of the Missouri. They remembered maps drawn on skins or in the earth by Hidatsa warriors back at Fort Mandan. As each river was identified by its Hidatsa name, they could feel confident that they were on the right track. When they came to a river with water the tan color of milky tea, they named it the Milk River. This was the river known to the Hidatsas as "The River Which Scolds At All Others." Small, unnamed streams were given new names by Lewis and Clark. When a lively, clear-running river was named for Sacagawea, she accepted the honor with shy pleasure. Another stream was called Blowing Fly Creek for the hordes of flies that swarmed over their meat. Judith's River was named for a friend of Captain Clark's from Virginia.

In the high country near the mouth of Judith's River, they found the remains of a large Indian camp that had been deserted a short time before. All over the hills were the scattered ashes of cooking fires where tipis had stood. A child's ball and a moccasin found on the site were brought to Sacagawea. She looked at them carefully, then shook her head. They were not Shoshones.

In early June the party came to a branching of the river that gave them a problem. Which of the branches was the "true Missouri"? Was it the one that seemed to come from the north, or was it the branch that flowed from the southwest? Most of the Corps were sure that the northern branch was the Missouri. It looked like the river they had followed all the way from the Mississippi, broad and thick with mud. The captains, on the other hand, wanted to follow the southern branch, a clear, swift-running stream with a rock and gravel bed. They reasoned that the Missouri had its source in the mountains and that a mountain stream would be swift and clear.

A wrong decision could be a costly mistake. Already they could see snow-topped mountains in the distance. Even if they should find the "Northwest Passage," crossing the mountains in winter would be a risky business. If they should turn up the wrong river, it could waste precious weeks of summer travel time. The captains decided that a camp should be set up for a few days at the fork of the rivers. Small exploring parties would go up each of the branches and decide which fork led to the Great Falls described by the Hidatsas, and from there to Shoshone country.

Clearly it was a good time to pause. Those not in the exploring parties could spend their time dressing skins for clothing. Uniforms had fallen to shreds, and buckskin clothing had to be made to replace them. Moccasins had been so cut by the rocky trails that they had been thrown away, and the men could barely walk on their bruised feet. Many of them were exhausted from towing the boats free from sandbars or sloshing through cold water up to their armpits. Poor diet and muddy water caused diarrhea and nausea, while chilling rains brought raging fever.

Lewis was so sure that the muddy northern branch could not be the Missouri that he named it Maria's River, after his cousin, Maria Wood. Nevertheless, he agreed to take a party up this river while Captain Clark explored the southern branch. The Lewis party found out that the northern branch flowed through a picture book country of beautiful birds, wild roses, and herds of game animals, but both he and Clark were still convinced that the southern branch was the Missouri. To find out for sure, they decided that Lewis would take four men and follow the southern branch on foot in search of the Great Falls.

Lewis and a small land party pushed up into the rolling hills and across a level plain. Suddenly he heard the distant sound of falling water and saw spray rising above the horizon. He followed the sound of roaring water until he stood on a pile of rocks and looked in wonder at the water cascading over huge bluffs, nine hundred feet wide and eighty feet high. In some places the water fell in great sheets, while at other points it was broken by rocks into glittering spray. He had reached the Great Falls of the Missouri River. Back at camp, he reported that there was no way to pass this point by water. They would have to organize a portage around the falls, but they had followed the "true Missouri."

Captain Lewis learned that Sacagawea had become ill during his absence. The young woman who had met all the hardships of the journey now lay sick in the covered part of the white pirogue, shaded from the July heat. She was gripped by many pains, weak, and exhausted. Her pulse was irregular, and her fingers twitched. Captain Clark had tried medicines and had bled her, but she was no better.

The white explorers were worried. They had grown fond of this brave Shoshone woman, and she had been useful to them in finding roots, sewing buckskin, and pointing out the landmarks along the way. Now, just when they needed her most, on the very edge of Shoshone country, she lay close to death.

Finally, in desperation, Captain Lewis had mineral water brought from a nearby sulfur spring and poured it down her throat. Within minutes Sacagawea began to perspire, and her pulse grew stronger. The crisis had passed.

The captains decided that the Maria's River camp would be a good place to leave the large red pirogue and some of the provisions to lighten the load for the portage around the falls and for travel through the mountains. The men dug deep, bottle-shaped holes called caches in the ground and filled them with salt, tools, powder, and lead. Signs of the digging were removed. They dragged the pirogue up on an island, tied it to trees, and covered it with brush.

To move the six dugouts around the falls, they built makeshift wagons. The mast of the white pirogue was cut up for axles and rounds were sliced from a huge cottonwood tree to form wheels.

The eighteen-mile portage around the Great Falls was an eleven-day struggle. The explorers limped in thin moccasins over needle-sharp ground covered with buffalo tracks and prickly pear cactus, shoving the two heavy, clumsy carts. Axles cracked and wagon tongues broke, so new ones had to be made from willow trees. In a stiff breeze the men hoisted a sail on one of the canoes and the wind helped carry it along on the wagon wheels.

One day a sudden storm pelted the party with huge, bouncing hailstones. Water filled runoff channels, almost sweeping Captain Clark, Sacagawea, and Pompy away in a flash flood. They found shelter under a rock shelf and watched a wall of water moving down the creek. Pushing the mother and baby ahead of him, Captain Clark scrambled up the hill to safety just before they would have been swept away.

After they had completed the exhausting portage, they built two canoes and moved up the river, which was narrow and crowded with islands. At a place where the Missouri loops like a rattlesnake, huge rocks hung out over the banks and pressed the river into a narrow channel. Captain Lewis marveled at the scene and called it the "Gates of the Rocky Mountains."

Time had been lost in the portage, and the explorers were impatient to find the Shoshones. Each day they found new signs that the Shoshones were near, including many small, deserted camps among the hills. Sacagawea pointed out remains of willow shelters and trees that had been stripped of bark, explaining that the Shoshones used the soft underpart of the wood for food. One morning they saw smoke rising in the distance. They guessed that the Shoshones might have seen their party and set the prairie afire to warn other families that Blackfeet or Hidatsa warriors might be near.

In a green valley Sacagawea identified White Earth Creek, where her people used to gather earth for their paint. The Three Forks of the Missouri were near. For Sacagawea and for the Corps of Discovery, it was a time of hope. Soon they would set foot in the land of her people, the Land of the Shining Mountains.

Every day brought fresh signs that the Shoshones were near, creating new hope that contact could be made. Sacagawea rode in the river party with Lewis, while Captain Clark and a few others moved ahead by land, scouting for signs of the Shoshones. The Rocky Mountains crowded in close to the river like tall, rugged giants, and Captain Lewis was worried. They might be headed toward savage rapids or waterfalls. Could the river possibly run through these mountains without suddenly tossing their canoes into some wild, unexpected danger? Sacagawea assured him that the river would not suddenly change. There would be a strong and rapid flow, but no waterfalls that could wreck the canoes.

Misery followed them up the river. Shoulders ached from poling canoes between rocks. Cactus needles pierced their feet, and barbed seeds poked through their leggings. Each evening Sacagawea huddled close to the fire, protecting Pompy from the mosquitoes and gnats that swarmed around his head. They slept under mosquito biers, gauzy netting stretched over wooden frames.

On the morning of July 27, the river route opened suddenly on a beautiful stretch of plains and meadows surrounded by distant high mountains. Sacagawea grew silent and her body became tense. Her eyes moved quickly from water to shore, and then off to the forest that covered the mountain slopes. Quietly she identified this as the place of the Hidatsa raid five summers before. She pointed to the rocky shoals in the middle of the river where she had been pulled up on the horse of the Hidatsa warrior. No word from her could possibly explain the mixture of feelings that almost overwhelmed her. No word from these white men could take away the painful memory of violence. No word from them could possibly add to the joy of her return.

THE VOYAGE OF CHRISTOPHER COLUMBUS

from CHRISTOPHER COLUMBUS:
VOYAGER TO THE UNKNOWN
by Nancy Smiler Levinson

*Born in the Italian seaport of Genoa in 1451,
Christopher Columbus probably spent his childhood wondering
about the ships he saw in Genoa's harbor and the places they
visited. As Columbus was growing up, explorers were searching
for a sea route to Asia and the East Indies, the sources for
silk, precious stones, and spices. After spending some years as a
sailor and acquiring some education in geography, Columbus
became convinced that he could reach the East Indies by sailing
west. He managed to interest Queen Isabella of Spain in his
idea. In 1492 he was provided with enough money to outfit
three ships: the* Niña, *the* Pinta, *and the largest of the three,
the* Santa Maria.

O n August 3, 1492, The sailors took communion at
church, and the fleet embarked at dawn. On that
day, Columbus began a journal. (The original journal, which ended March 15, 1493, disappeared, but copies
were made, although some parts were paraphrased, omitted,
or rewritten.) That day he wrote that they departed from the

The earliest known portrait of Columbus, an engraving made in 1575.

Culver Pictures, Inc.

Palos Harbor of Saltés and "traveled with a strong breeze . . . making for the Canaries." The most momentous voyage in history had begun.

At first it was difficult to keep the tiny fleet together. The *Niña* and the *Pinta* kept moving ahead of the flagship, the *Santa Maria*, which was slower and more cumbersome, so the caravels had to restrain their speed. Even though Columbus was in command of the flagship, the *Santa Maria* was not his favorite. To him the lighter and swifter *Niña* was the most seaworthy. [Martin Pinzón and his brother Vincente were in command of the *Niña* and the *Pinta*.]

The *Santa Maria* (center) with the *Niña* and the *Pinta*.
North Wind Picture Archives

The vessels set their course south by west as they headed toward the Canary Islands. For the most part, Spain had conquered and claimed these islands, which were 800 miles away. Columbus considered them a good place to stop to secure fresh provisions of meat, cheese, water, and wood.

In a short time it became necessary to stop for repairs as well. On August 6, the *Pinta* signaled news of trouble by sending up smoke in an iron vessel used for burning charcoal. Her rudder had worked its way loose from its mounting. Three days later she reached one of the islands, the Grand Canary, and stopped there to have the rudder reattached. Contrary winds prevented the other vessels from reaching that island, so they went on to Gomera, one of the other Canary Islands, where they arrived several days later. There, in addition to gathering provisions, they replaced the triangular lateen sails on the *Niña* with *redonda*, square sails, which could withstand strong winds on the high seas better. After that they made for the Grand Canary.

The rudder repairs on the *Pinta* were not satisfactory, so Columbus decided that a new rudder had to be built. This delay caused the three vessels to remain longer than planned, and it was not until September 9 that they finally hoisted sails and departed. The course was set due west, as they headed directly for the island kingdom of Japan (called Cipangu), which according to Columbus's calculations was on the same latitude as the Canaries. Beyond Japan, then, Columbus expected to reach the Asian mainland at China.

It was dusk when they set sail out of the Canaries over calm waters. But the seamen on board were hardly calm. This time as they moved away from land, it seemed to them that the

world was disappearing. They were beginning to feel alone and frightened. Finally by nightfall, all sight of land had disappeared. A dark, mysterious, uncharted ocean now stretched before the men. They did not know how long the voyage would take, or where they would arrive, or if they would even return home.

Columbus, however, was full of optimism. To him everything looked certain and hopeful. Even the winds that were carrying them westward were glorious. These were the trade winds, always blowing in the same direction from east to west. They were constant and fair and kept the ship on the same latitude as the Canary Islands without blowing them off course.

While Columbus was optimistic, he understood the men's fears. So he decided that in addition to his daily journal, he would keep a second account of the distance the vessels traveled. The first account would be the accurate one, which he would keep privately. The other he "determined to count less than the true number so that the crew might not be dismayed if the voyage should prove long." A sea league is a unit of measurement that is about 2.82 nautical miles, although Columbus used a slightly different number that figured closer to 3.18 nautical miles to a sea league. On September 10 he noted privately that they had made 20 leagues that day. In the false journal he "reckoned only 16."

Actually no mariner at that time could accurately determine the speed of a ship. For orienting themselves, mariners had the compass, called a magnetic needle, which was a mystical instrument because it always pointed toward the North Star (Polaris). But little was known then about the pull exerted on the compass by the earth's magnetic field. Beyond the compass they were left to their own sightings and judgment at sea. It was far from scientific and not at all easy. The most common method for estimating distance was "dead reckoning"—plotting the course and position by direction, time, and speed. This meant guessing speed from a fixed point by watching an object such as a star or a piece of seaweed. In addition to the compass and dead reckoning, Columbus also navigated by soundings, which he did by lowering a tallow-covered lead weight to the sea floor to estimate depth.

For the first week out from the Canary Islands, the fleet continued to sail due west in fair weather. Columbus wrote that the "mornings were a source of great delight for all and lacked nothing to make them more enchanting, except perhaps a song of nightingales."

The sailors, bearded (except for Columbus), barefoot, and dressed in short, gray, blouselike garments and red woolen stocking caps, quickly fell into routine. They were divided into two watches of four hours each. The periods for standing watch and for sleeping were marked by the half-hour sandglass called an *ampoletta*. It was the duty of the gromets, the ships' boys, to watch all the sand filter to the bottom and then turn the glass immediately. The glass was fragile and could break easily, so many were brought along.

There was no fear of immediate hunger because there were enough stores on board to last a year. The vessels carried wine, water, salt meat and barreled salt sardines and anchovies, cheese, chick peas, lentils, beans, rice, oil, vinegar, garlic, honey, almonds, and raisins. Stowed in the driest parts were sea biscuits called hard tack, a type of bread that was baked ashore with wheat flour. The men had one hot meal a day, and they ate from wooden bowls with their fingers.

Columbus and his men were devoted Christians, sailing under the flags of the Catholic sovereigns, Queen Isabella and King Ferdinand of Spain. Every morning they faithfully recited prayers, and every evening they gathered together and sang "Salve Regina," an ancient hymn of praise to Mary, the Queen of Heaven. On a journey like this, they took comfort in knowing that God was watching over them.

So routine had ship life become after one week that some of the seamen began to show signs of boredom. But that was not to be for long. On September 16, when they were more than a thousand miles from the Canaries, events changed, and there were whispers of mutiny against the commander of the fleet.

Suddenly the men found the sea covered with a thick, floating weed. With every mile it grew thicker until finally the entire surface of the ocean appeared a yellowish green, the color of the weed. The men were greatly alarmed. Perhaps they had gone too far in tempting fate. Now they feared being stuck at sea.

As if that weren't enough, they lost the trade winds, which was puzzling and also fearful, for they wondered if there would be any winds capable of carrying them back to Spain. Some of the men began to grumble and whisper. What if they were to heave Columbus overboard? Then they could turn back, if it was not already too late. And if they made it safely, they could tell the king and queen that Columbus accidentally fell into the ocean while observing the stars.

In unfamiliar waters, even sea serpents seemed a real danger.

North Wind Picture Archives

Columbus was well aware of these grumblings. But he managed to reassure the men of westerly winds for the return voyage. He also showed them his false distance chart to make them believe they weren't as far from home as they thought. Furthermore, he convinced them they would not be trapped by the weed. Indeed, the weed did not prevent the fleet from moving forward.

A keen observer of nature, Columbus closely studied the weed. He noted in his journal that the plants were constantly growing fresh green sprouts at one end, while at the other end air-filled, berrylike globules kept the weed afloat.

Of course, it was not known then that the fleet had entered the Sargasso Sea in the midst of the North Atlantic Ocean, and that the gulfweed came from algae plants originating in prehistoric times.

The trade winds did not pick up again for a while, so the fleet sailed slowly after that. The men remained suspicious, but toward the end of September they were given new hope. Tropical birds were sighted. This meant they could not be far from land. Then, on September 25, Martin Pinzón shouted with joy over to the *Santa Maria* that he sighted land. Everyone fell to his knees to give thanks to the Lord. But, to their disappointment, after sailing for another day, they came upon no land. It was a false landfall.

By early October the men were becoming more disgruntled than ever. They had been at sea without sight of land nearly four weeks now, and they were beginning to feel doomed. Again Columbus tried to be reassuring, reminding them of the promised rewards from the fabulous Indies. But it was becoming more and more difficult to calm the sailors. Finally, on October 6 the commanders conferred on what should be done. A yawl, a small servicing boat, was lowered from the *Santa Maria* into the ocean to pick up the Pinzón brothers and bring them aboard. They both reported that most of their men

Martin Pinzón mistakes an evening cloud for land.

wanted to turn back. Martin Pinzón, himself, was undecided, but Columbus refused.

The following morning there was another false landfall, which was prompted by what turned out to be only a squall of clouds seen in the distance. But afterward, Columbus gave in to Martin Pinzón's plea to alter the course to southwest by west in order to follow a flock of birds that had flown overhead at the time of the last false landfall. They continued to follow that course for two more days, October 8 and 9. The next day, October 10, was the most crucial day of the voyage. The men lost all patience. On the *Santa Maria* there were continual rumblings of open revolt.

Of course they had long passed the position where Columbus predicted that Japan lay, but he could not give up now. This was the mission of his life, and he felt he was chosen by God to carry it forth. He had given up everything, waiting seven years for King Ferdinand and Queen Isabella to finance the voyage and send him with their blessings. And before that he had spent considerable time in Portugal preparing his ideas for this grand plan. At nearly every turn during those years, it seemed, he met with people who believed that his ideas and plan were folly. But he was sure he was right, and he needed to prove it.

Once more he tried persuading the men to allow him to complete his mission. He told them it was useless to complain since they had come so far, and that with the help of the Lord, he would find the Indies. So certain was he that he made them a promise. If they did not meet with success within two or three days, he said, he gave his word that they would turn back. Torn between fear and hope, the seamen agreed.

At the fleet's departure from Spain, the king and queen had promised a reward to the first man who sighted land—ten thousand *maravedis* every year for life. A *maravedi* was worth about seven-tenths of a cent in gold, so the reward meant $700 in gold, a considerable amount for a seaman whose wages on the voyage were only a thousand *maravedis* a month. All hands on deck were busy, but every man was alert, eager to be the one to fire the signal for land. The sailors on the *Pinta* were in the best position for doing so, since the *Pinta* led the fleet that day, October 10.

By the next morning no more complaints were heard. The air was filled with anticipation. A thorn with roseberries on it was found in the water. As the day passed, the *Niña* picked up a green branch with a flower on it, the *Pinta* found a cane or a stick that looked as if it had been carved, and a reed floated past the *Santa Maria*. Spirits were high.

At sunset a breeze turned into gale force, carrying the vessels along at considerable speed. The clouds were swept away, leaving a clear horizon. Soon afterward a bright quarter moon shone above. About 10 P.M., after the seamen had sung the "Salve Regina," the *Santa Maria* lay about thirty-five miles offshore. Standing on the forecastle deck at the bow of the ship, Columbus believed he saw a light, "like a little wax candle whose flame went up and down." Immediately he called Pedro Gutiérrez, a servant of King Ferdinand, who agreed that he too had seen such a light. But Rodrigo Sánchez, a comptroller sent by the king, said he saw nothing.

Then, at last, at 2 A.M. on October 12 a great cry went up. "Land ho! Land ho!" A bombard was fired into the air. This

time it really was land! The men wept for joy. They prayed and sang. As Christopher Columbus had told them, it was destiny.

Columbus lands on San Salvador.
North Wind Picture Archives

MEET NANCY SMILER LEVINSON, AUTHOR

When Nancy Smiler Levinson began the research for her biography of Columbus, she was, as she said later, "overwhelmed." She explains: "So many spokes came out from the center of the story that I worried how I would work in all this background information to make the story more meaningful. I wanted to get across to children that history is not just old stuff and dead stuff."

Levinson says about whether or not Columbus actually "discovered" America: "Yes, there were people here before—Indians were here before, Vikings were here. But nothing changed. After Columbus, however, the world changed forever."

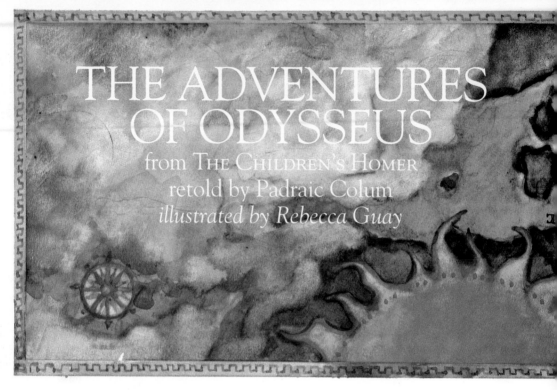

THE ADVENTURES OF ODYSSEUS

from THE CHILDREN'S HOMER
retold by Padraic Colum
illustrated by Rebecca Guay

*This selection is from a retelling of the Odyssey,
a Greek epic poem written about 700 B.C. The Odyssey tells of
the ten-year journey of the Greek warrior Odysseus from the city
of Troy, on the northwest coast of Asia Minor, to his home on the
Greek island of Ithaca. Odysseus was part of a force of Greeks
who had sailed to Troy to retrieve Helen, the most beautiful
woman in the world and the wife of a Greek king. Helen had
been carried off by a prince of Troy, and the story of the ten-year
war that was fought to bring her back is told in the Iliad,
another Greek heroic poem.*

*After the fall of Troy, Odysseus set sail for
home with twelve ships, each of which carried about fifty men.
After many troubles, Odysseus reached the island of the
Phaeacians. Here he was warmly welcomed, clothed, and fed,
and here he told the story of his adventures.*

ODYSSEUS AND THE CYCLOPS

The wind bore my ships from the coast of Troy, and with our white sails hoisted we came to the cape that is called Malea. Now if we had been able to double this cape we should soon have come to our own country, all unhurt. But the north wind came and swept us from our course and drove us wandering past Cythera.

Then for nine days we were borne onward by terrible winds, and away from all known lands. On the tenth day we came to a strange country. Many of my men landed there. The people of that land were harmless and friendly, but the land itself was most dangerous. For there grew there the honey-sweet fruit of the lotus that makes all men forgetful of their past and neglectful of their future. And those of my men who ate the lotus that the dwellers of that land offered them became forgetful of their country and of the way before them. They wanted to abide forever in the land of the lotus. They wept when they thought of all the toils before them and of all they had endured. I led them back to the ships, and I had to place them beneath the benches and leave them in bonds. And I commanded those who had not eaten of the lotus to go at once aboard the ships. Then, when I had got all my men upon the ships, we made haste to sail away.

Later we came to the land of the Cyclôpes, a giant people. There is a waste island outside the harbor of their land, and on it there is a well of bright water that has poplars growing round it. We came to that empty island, and we beached our ships and took down our sails.

As soon as the dawn came we went through the empty island, starting the wild goats that were there in flocks, and shooting them with our arrows. We killed so many wild goats there that we had nine for each ship. Afterwards we looked across to the land of the Cyclôpes, and we heard the sound of voices and saw the smoke of fires and heard the bleating of flocks of sheep and goats.

I called my companions together and I said, "It would be well for some of us to go to that other island. With my own ship and with the company that is on it I shall go there. The rest of you abide here. I will find out what manner of men live there, and whether they will treat us kindly and give us gifts that are due to strangers—gifts of provisions for our voyage."

We embarked and we came to the land. There was a cave near the sea, and round the cave there were mighty flocks of sheep and goats. I took twelve men with me and I left the rest to guard the ship. We went into the cave and found no man there. There were baskets filled with cheeses, and vessels of whey and pails and bowls of milk. My men wanted me to take some of the cheeses and drive off some of the lambs and kids and come away. But this I would not do, for I would rather that he who owned the stores would give us of his own free will the offerings that were due to strangers.

While we were in the cave, he whose dwelling it was, returned to it. He carried on his shoulder a great pile of wood for his fire. Never in our lives did we see a creature so frightful as this Cyclops was. He was a giant in size, and, what made him terrible to behold, he had but one eye, and that single eye was in his forehead. He cast down on the ground the pile of wood that he carried, making such a din that we fled in terror into the corners and recesses of the cave. Next he drove his flocks into the cave and began to milk his ewes and goats. And when he had the flocks within, he took up a stone that not all our strengths could move and set it as a door to the mouth of the cave.

The Cyclops kindled his fire, and when it blazed up he saw us in the corners and recesses. He spoke to us. We knew not what he said, but our hearts were shaken with terror at the sound of his deep voice.

I spoke to him saying that we were Agamemnon's men on our way home from the taking of Priam's City, and I begged him to deal with us kindly, for the sake of Zeus who is ever in the company of strangers and suppliants. But he answered me saying, "We Cyclôpes pay no heed to Zeus, nor to any of thy gods. In our strength and our power we deem that we are mightier than they. I will not spare thee, neither will I give thee aught for the sake of Zeus, but only as my own spirit bids me. And first I would have thee tell me how you came to our land."

I knew it would be better not to let the Cyclops know that my ship and my companions were at the harbor of the island. Therefore I spoke to him guilefully, telling him that my ship had been broken on the rocks, and that I and the men with me were the only ones who had escaped utter doom.

I begged again that he would deal with us as just men deal with strangers and suppliants, but he, without saying a word, laid hands upon two of my men, and swinging them by the legs, dashed their brains out on the earth. He cut them to pieces and ate them before our very eyes. We wept and we prayed to Zeus as we witnessed a deed so terrible.

Next the Cyclops stretched himself amongst his sheep and went to sleep beside the fire. Then I debated whether I should take my sharp sword in my hand, and feeling where his heart was, stab him there. But second thoughts held me back from doing this. I might be able to kill him as he slept, but not even with my companions could I roll away the great stone that closed the mouth of the cave.

Dawn came, and the Cyclops awakened, kindled his fire and milked his flocks. Then he seized two others of my men and made ready for his midday meal. And now he rolled away the great stone and drove his flocks out of the cave.

I had pondered on a way of escape, and I had thought of something that might be done to baffle the Cyclops. I had with me a great skin of sweet wine, and I thought that if I

could make him drunken with wine I and my companions might be able for him. But there were other preparations to be made first. On the floor of the cave there was a great beam of olive wood which the Cyclops had cut to make a club when the wood should be seasoned. It was yet green. I and my companions went and cut off a fathom's length of wood, and sharpened it to a point and took it to the fire and hardened it in the glow. Then I hid the beam in a recess of the cave.

The Cyclops came back in the evening, and opening up the cave drove in his flocks. Then he closed the cave again with the stone and went and milked his ewes and his goats. Again he seized two of my companions. I went to the terrible creature with a bowl of wine in my hands. He took it and drank it and cried out, "Give me another bowl of this, and tell me thy name that I may give thee gifts for bringing me this honey-tasting drink."

Again I spoke to him guilefully and said, "Noman is my name. Noman my father and my mother call me."

"Give me more of the drink, Noman," he shouted. "And the gift that I shall give to thee is that I shall make thee the last of thy fellows to be eaten."

I gave him wine again, and when he had taken the third bowl he sank backwards with his face upturned, and sleep came upon him. Then I, with four companions, took that beam of olive wood, now made into a hard and pointed stake, and thrust it into the ashes of the fire. When the pointed end began to glow we drew it out of the flame. Then I and my companions laid hold on the great stake and, dashing at the Cyclops, thrust it into his eye. He raised a terrible cry that made the rocks ring and we dashed away into the recesses of the cave.

His cries brought other Cyclôpes to the mouth of the cave, and they, naming him as Polyphemus, called out and asked him what ailed him to cry. "Noman," he shrieked out, "Noman is slaying me by guile." They answered him saying, "If no man is slaying thee, there is nothing we can do for thee, Polyphemus. What ails thee has been sent to thee by the gods." Saying this, they went away from the mouth of the cave without attempting to move away the stone.

Polyphemus then, groaning with pain, rolled away the stone and sat before the mouth of the cave with his hands outstretched, thinking that he would catch us as we dashed out. I showed my companions how we might pass by him. I laid hands on certain rams of the flock and I lashed three of them together with supple rods. Then on the middle ram I put a man of my company. Thus every three rams carried a man. As soon as the dawn had come the rams hastened out to the pasture, and, as they passed, Polyphemus laid hands on the first and the third of each three that went by. They passed out and Polyphemus did not guess that a ram that he did not touch carried out a man.

For myself, I took a ram that was the strongest and fleeciest of the whole flock and I placed myself under him, clinging to the wool of his belly. As this ram, the best of all his flock, went by, Polyphemus, laying his hands upon him, said, "Would that you, the best of my flock, were endowed with speech, so that you might tell me where Noman, who has blinded me, has hidden himself." The ram went by him, and when he had gone a little way from the cave I loosed myself from him and went and set my companions free.

We gathered together many of Polyphemus' sheep and we drove them down to our ship. The men we had left behind would have wept when they heard what had happened to six of their companions. But I bade them take on board the sheep we had brought and pull the ship away from that land. Then when we had drawn a certain distance from the shore I could not forbear to shout my taunts into the cave of Polyphemus. "Cyclops," I cried, "you thought you had the company of a fool and a weakling to eat. But you have been worsted by me, and your evil deeds have been punished."

So I shouted, and Polyphemus came to the mouth of the cave with great anger in his heart. He took up rocks and cast them at the ship and they fell before the prow. The men bent to the oars and pulled the ship away or it would have been broken by the rocks he cast. And when we were further away I shouted to him, "Cyclops, if any man should ask who it was set his mark upon you, say that he was Odysseus, the son of Laertes."

Then I heard Polyphemus cry out, "I call upon Poseidon, the god of the sea, whose son I am, to avenge me upon you, Odysseus. I call upon Poseidon to grant that you, Odysseus, may never come to your home, or if the gods have ordained your return, that you come to it after much toil and suffering, in an evil plight and in a stranger's ship, to find sorrow in your home."

So Polyphemus prayed, and, to my evil fortune, Poseidon heard his prayer. But we went on in our ship rejoicing at our escape. We came to the waste island where my other ships were. All the company rejoiced to see us, although they had to mourn for their six companions slain by Polyphemus. We divided amongst the ships the sheep we had taken from Polyphemus' flock and we sacrificed to the gods. At the dawn of the next day we raised the sails on each ship and we sailed away.

ODYSSEUS AND THE LORD OF THE WINDS

We came to the Island where Æolus, the Lord of the Winds, he who can give mariners a good or a bad wind, has his dwelling. With his six sons and his six daughters Æolus lives on a floating island that has all around it a wall of bronze. And when we came to his island, the Lord of the Winds treated us kindly and kept us at his dwelling for a month. Now when the time came for us to leave, Æolus did not try to hold us on the island. And to me, when I was going down to the ships, he gave a bag made from the hide of an ox, and in that bag were all the winds that blow. He made the mouth of the bag fast with a silver thong, so that no wind that might drive us from our course would escape. Then he sent the West Wind to blow on our sails that we might reach our own land as quickly as a ship might go.

For nine days we sailed with the West Wind driving us, and on the tenth day we came in sight of Ithaka, our own land. We saw its coast and the beacon fires upon the coast and the people tending the fires. Then I thought that the curse of the Cyclops was vain and could bring no harm to us. Sleep that I had kept from me for long I let weigh me down, and I no longer kept watch.

Then even as I slept, the misfortune that I had watched against fell upon me. For now my men spoke together and said, "There is our native land, and we come back to it after ten years' struggles and toils, with empty hands. Different it is with our lord, Odysseus. He brings gold and silver from Priam's treasure chamber in Troy. And Æolus too has given him a treasure in an oxhide bag. But let us take something out of that bag while he sleeps."

So they spoke, and they unloosed the mouth of the bag, and behold! All the winds that were tied in it burst out. Then the winds drove our ship toward the high seas and away from our land. What became of the other ships I know not. I awoke and I found that we were being driven here and there by the winds. I did not know whether I should spring into the sea and so end all my troubles, or whether I should endure this terrible misfortune. I muffled my head in my cloak and lay on the deck of my ship.

The winds brought us back again to the floating Island. We landed and I went to the dwelling of the Lord of the Winds. I sat by the pillars of his threshold and he came out and spoke to me. "How now, Odysseus?" said he. "How is it thou hast returned so soon? Did I not give thee a fair wind to take thee to thine own country, and did I not tie up all the winds that might be contrary to thee?"

"My evil companions," I said, "have been my bane. They have undone all the good that thou didst for me, O King of the Winds. They opened the bag and let all the winds fly out. And now help me, O Lord Æolus, once again."

But Æolus said to me, "Far be it from me to help such a man as thou—a man surely accursed by the gods. Go from my Island, for nothing will I do for thee." Then I went from his dwelling and took my way down to the ship.

We sailed away from the Island of Æolus with heavy hearts. Next we came to the Æean Island, where we met with Circe, the Enchantress. For two days and two nights we were on that island without seeing the sign of a habitation. On the third day I saw smoke rising up from some hearth. I spoke of it to my men, and it seemed good to us that part of our company should go to see were there people there who might help us. We drew lots to find out who should go, and it fell to the lot of Eurylochus to go with part of the company, while I remained with the other part.

So Eurylochus went with two and twenty men. In the forest glades they came upon a house built of polished stones. All round that house wild beasts roamed—wolves and lions. But these beasts were not fierce. As Eurylochus and his men went toward the house the lions and wolves fawned upon them like house dogs.

But the men were affrighted and stood round the outer gate of the court. They heard a voice within the house singing, and it seemed to them to be the voice of a woman, singing as she went to and fro before a web she was weaving on a loom. The men shouted, and she who had been singing opened the polished doors and came out of the dwelling. She was very fair to see. As she opened the doors of the house she asked the men to come within and they went into her halls.

But Eurylochus tarried behind. He watched the woman and he saw her give food to the men. But he saw that she mixed a drug with what she gave them to eat and with the wine she gave them to drink. No sooner had they eaten the

food and drunk the wine than she struck them with a wand, and behold! The men turned into swine. Then the woman drove them out of the house and put them in the swinepens and gave them acorns and mast and the fruit of the cornel tree to eat.

Eurylochus, when he saw these happenings, ran back through the forest and told me all. Then I cast about my shoulder my good sword of bronze, and, bidding Eurylochus stay by the ships, I went through the forest and came to the house of the enchantress. I stood at the outer court and called out. Then Circe the Enchantress flung wide the shining doors, and called to me to come within. I entered her dwelling and she brought me to a chair and put a footstool under my feet. Then she brought me in a golden cup the wine into which she had cast a harmful drug.

As she handed me the cup I drew my sword and sprang at her as one eager to slay her. She shrank back from me and cried out, "Who art thou who art able to guess at my enchantments? Verily, thou art Odysseus, of whom Hermes told me. Nay, put up thy sword and let us two be friendly to each other. In all things I will treat thee kindly."

But I said to her, "Nay, Circe, you must swear to me first that thou wilt not treat me guilefully."

She swore by the gods that she would not treat me guilefully, and I put up my sword. Then the handmaidens of Circe prepared a bath, and I bathed and rubbed myself with olive oil, and Circe gave me a new mantle and doublet. The handmaidens brought out silver tables, and on them set golden baskets with bread and meat in them, and others brought cups of honey-tasting wine. I sat before a silver table but I had no pleasure in the food before me.

When Circe saw me sitting silent and troubled she said, "Why, Odysseus, dost thou sit like a speechless man? Dost

thou think there is a drug in this food? But I have sworn that I will not treat thee guilefully, and that oath I shall keep."

And I said to her, "O Circe, Enchantress, what man of good heart could take meat and drink while his companions are as swine in swinepens? If thou wouldst have me eat and drink, first let me see my companions in their own forms."

Circe, when she heard me say this, went to the swinepen and anointed each of the swine that was there with a charm. As she did, the bristles dropped away and the limbs of the man were seen. My companions became men again, and were even taller and handsomer than they had been before.

After that we lived on Circe's island in friendship with the enchantress. She did not treat us guilefully again and we feasted in her house for a year.

But in all of us there was a longing to return to our own land. And my men came to me and craved that I should ask Circe to let us go on our homeward way. She gave us leave to go.

FINE ART
JOURNEYS
AND QUESTS

Don Quixote. 1955. Pablo Picasso.

Oil on canvas. Seine-St.-Denis Municipal
Museum. © 1994 ARS, NY/SPADEM, Paris.
Photo: SCALA/Art Resource

Pilgrims. Date unknown.

Illustration for Geoffrey Chaucer's *Canterbury Tales*
(c. 1386–1400). Photo: Art Resource

Marco Polo arriving at the court of
Kublai Khan. 13th century.

Manuscript illustration. Photo: Bridgeman/Art Resource

The Return of Ulysses. 1976. Romare Bearden.

Silkscreen. Gift of Brandywine Graphic Workshop, Philadelphia
Museum of Art. © Estate of Romare Bearden

The Lady Fugitsubo watching Prince Genji departing
in the moonlight. 1853. Artist unknown.

Woodblock print. Private collection. Photo: Bridgeman/Art Resource

WHEN SHLEMIEL WENT TO WARSAW

Isaac Bashevis Singer
illustrated by
Krystyna Stasiak

Though Shlemiel was a lazybones and a sleepyhead and hated to move, he always daydreamed of taking a trip. He had heard many stories about faraway countries, huge deserts, deep oceans, and high mountains, and often discussed with Mrs. Shlemiel his great wish to go on a long journey. Mrs. Shlemiel would reply, "Long journeys are not for a Shlemiel. You better stay home and mind the children while I go to market to sell my vegetables." Yet Shlemiel could not bring himself to give up his dream of seeing the world and its wonders.

A recent visitor to Chelm had told Shlemiel marvelous things about the city of Warsaw. How beautiful the streets were, how high the buildings and luxurious the stores. Shlemiel decided once and for all that he must see this great city for himself. He knew that one had to prepare for a journey. But what was there for him to take? He had nothing but the old clothes he wore. One morning, after Mrs. Shlemiel left for the market, he told the older boys to stay home from cheder and mind the younger children. Then he took a few slices of bread, an onion, and a clove of garlic, put them in a kerchief, tied it into a bundle, and started for Warsaw on foot.

There was a street in Chelm called Warsaw Street and Shlemiel believed that it led directly to Warsaw. While still in the village, he was stopped by several neighbors who asked him where he was going. Shlemiel told them that he was on his way to Warsaw.

"What will you do in Warsaw?" they asked him.

Shlemiel replied, "What do I do in Chelm? Nothing."

He soon reached the outskirts of town. He walked slowly because the soles of his boots were worn through. Soon the houses and stores gave way to pastures and fields. He passed a peasant driving an ox-drawn plow. After several hours of

walking, Shlemiel grew tired. He was so weary that he wasn't even hungry. He lay down on the grass near the roadside for a nap, but before he fell asleep he thought, When I wake up, I may not remember which is the way to Warsaw and which leads back to Chelm. After pondering a moment, he removed his boots and set them down beside him with the toes pointing toward Warsaw and the heels toward Chelm. He soon fell asleep and dreamed that he was a baker baking onion rolls with poppy seeds. Customers came to buy them and Shlemiel said, "These onion rolls are not for sale."

"Then why do you bake them?"

"They are for my wife, for my children, and for me."

Later he dreamed that he was the King of Chelm. Once a year, instead of taxes, each citizen brought him a pot of strawberry jam. Shlemiel sat on a golden throne and nearby sat Mrs. Shlemiel, the queen, and his children, the princes and princesses. They were all eating onion rolls and spooning up big portions of strawberry jam. A carriage arrived and took the royal family to Warsaw, America, and to the river Sambation, which spurts out stones the week long and rests on the Sabbath.

Near the road, a short distance from where Shlemiel slept, was a smithy. The blacksmith happened to come out just in time to see Shlemiel carefully placing his boots at his side with the toes facing in the direction of Warsaw. The black-smith was a prankster and as soon as Shlemiel was sound asleep he tiptoed over and turned the boots around. When Shlemiel awoke, he felt rested but hungry. He got out a slice of bread, rubbed it with garlic, and took a bite of onion. Then he pulled his boots on and continued on his way.

He walked along and everything looked strangely familiar. He recognized houses that he had seen before. It seemed to him that he knew the people he met. Could it be that he had already reached another town, Shlemiel wondered. And why was it so similar to Chelm? He stopped a passerby and asked the name of the town. "Chelm," the man replied.

Shlemiel was astonished. How was this possible? He had walked away from Chelm. How could he have arrived back there? He began to rub his forehead and soon found the answer to the riddle. There were two Chelms and he had reached the second one. Still, it seemed very odd that the

streets, the houses, the people were so similar to those in the Chelm he had left behind. Shlemiel puzzled over this fact until he suddenly remembered something he had learned in cheder. "The earth is the same everywhere." And so why shouldn't the second Chelm be exactly like the first one? This discovery gave Shlemiel great satisfaction. He wondered if there was a street here like his street and a house on it like the one he lived in. And indeed, he soon arrived at an identical street and house. Evening had fallen. He opened the door and to his amazement saw a second Mrs. Shlemiel with children just like his. Everything was exactly the same as in his own household. Even the cat seemed the same. Mrs. Shlemiel at once began to scold him.

"Shlemiel, where did you go? You left the house alone. And what have you there in that bundle?"

The children all ran to him and cried, "Papa, where have you been?"

Shlemiel paused a moment and then he said, "Mrs. Shlemiel, I'm not your husband. Children, I'm not your papa."

"Have you lost your mind?" Mrs. Shlemiel screamed.

"I am Shlemiel of Chelm One and this is Chelm Two."

Mrs. Shlemiel clapped her hands so hard that the chickens sleeping under the stove awoke in fright and flew out all over the room.

"Children, your father has gone crazy," she wailed. She immediately sent one of the boys for Gimpel the healer. All the neighbors came crowding in. Shlemiel stood in the middle of the room and proclaimed, "It's true, you all look like the people in my town, but you are not the same. I came from Chelm One and you live in Chelm Two."

"Shlemiel, what's the matter with you?" someone cried. "You're in your own house, with your own wife and children, your own neighbors and friends."

"No, you don't understand. I come from Chelm One. I was on my way to Warsaw, and between Chelm One and Warsaw there is a Chelm Two. And that is where I am."

"What are you talking about. We all know you and you know all of us. Don't you recognize your chickens?"

"No, I'm not in my town," Shlemiel insisted. "But," he continued, "Chelm Two does have the same people and the same houses as Chelm One, and that is why you are mistaken. Tomorrow I will continue on to Warsaw."

"In that case, where is my husband?" Mrs. Shlemiel inquired in a rage, and she proceeded to berate Shlemiel with all the curses she could think of.

"How should I know where your husband is?" Shlemiel replied.

Some of the neighbors could not help laughing; others pitied the family. Gimpel the healer announced that he knew of no remedy for such an illness. After some time, everybody went home.

Mrs. Shlemiel had cooked noodles and beans that evening, a dish that Shlemiel liked especially. She said to him, "You may be mad, but even a madman has to eat."

"Why should you feed a stranger?" Shlemiel asked.

"As a matter of fact, an ox like you should eat straw, not noodles and beans. Sit down and be quiet. Maybe some food and rest will bring you back to your senses."

"Mrs. Shlemiel, you're a good woman. My wife wouldn't feed a stranger. It would seem that there is some small difference between the two Chelms."

The noodles and beans smelled so good that Shlemiel needed no further coaxing. He sat down, and as he ate he spoke to the children:

"My dear children, I live in a house that looks exactly like this one. I have a wife and she is as like your mother as two peas are like each other. My children resemble you as drops of water resemble one another."

The younger children laughed; the older ones began to cry. Mrs. Shlemiel said, "As if being a Shlemiel wasn't enough, he had to go crazy in addition. What am I going to do now? I won't be able to leave the children with him when I go to market. Who knows what a madman may do?" She clasped her head in her hands and cried out, "God in heaven, what have I done to deserve this?"

Nevertheless, she made up a fresh bed for Shlemiel; and even though he had napped during the day, near the smithy, the moment his head touched the pillow he fell fast asleep and was soon snoring loudly. He again dreamed that he was the King of Chelm and that his wife, the queen, had fried for him a huge panful of blintzes. Some were filled with cheese, others with blueberries or cherries, and all were sprinkled with sugar and cinnamon and were drowning in sour cream. Shlemiel ate twenty blintzes all at once and hid the remainder in his crown for later.

In the morning, when Shlemiel awoke, the house was filled with townspeople. Mrs. Shlemiel stood in their midst, her eyes red with weeping. Shlemiel was about to scold his wife for letting so many strangers into the house, but then he remembered that he himself was a stranger here. At home he would have gotten up, washed, and dressed. Now in front of

all these people he was at a loss as to what to do. As always when he was embarrassed, he began to scratch his head and pull at his beard. Finally, overcoming his bashfulness, he decided to get up. He threw off the covers and put his bare feet on the floor. "Don't let him run away," Mrs. Shlemiel screamed. "He'll disappear and I'll be a deserted wife, without a Shlemiel."

At this point Baruch the baker interrupted. "Let's take him to the elders. They'll know what to do."

"That's right! Let's take him to the elders," everybody agreed.

Although Shlemiel insisted that since he lived in Chelm One, the local elders had no power over him, several of the strong young men helped him into his pants, his boots, his coat and cap and escorted him to the house of Gronam Ox. The elders, who had already heard of the matter, had gathered early in the morning to consider what was to be done.

As the crowd came in, one of the elders, Dopey Lekisch, was saying, "Maybe there really are two Chelms."

"If there are two, then why can't there be three, four, or even a hundred Chelms?" Sender Donkey interrupted.

"And even if there are a hundred Chelms, must there be a Shlemiel in each one of them?" argued Shmendrick Numskull.

Gronam Ox, the head elder, listened to all the arguments but was not yet prepared to express an opinion. However, his wrinkled, bulging forehead indicated that he was deep in thought. It was Gronam Ox who questioned Shlemiel. Shlemiel related everything that had happened to him, and when he finished, Gronam asked, "Do you recognize me?"

"Surely. You are wise Gronam Ox."

"And in your Chelm is there also a Gronam Ox?"

"Yes, there is a Gronam Ox and he looks exactly like you."

"Isn't it possible that you turned around and came back to Chelm?" Gronam inquired.

"Why should I turn around? I'm not a windmill," Shlemiel replied.

"In that case, you are not this Mrs. Shlemiel's husband."

"No, I'm not."

"Then Mrs. Shlemiel's husband, the real Shlemiel, must have left the day you came."

"It would seem so."

"Then he'll probably come back."

"Probably."

"In that case, you must wait until he returns. Then we'll know who is who."

"Dear elders, my Shlemiel has come back," screamed Mrs. Shlemiel. "I don't need two Shlemiels. One is more than enough."

"Whoever he is, he may not live in your house until everything is made clear," Gronam insisted.

"Where shall I live?" Shlemiel asked.

"In the poorhouse."

"What will I do in the poorhouse?"

"What do you do at home?"

"Good God, who will take care of my children when I go to market?" moaned Mrs. Shlemiel. "Besides, I want a husband. Even a Shlemiel is better than no husband at all."

"Are we to blame that your husband left you and went to Warsaw?" Gronam asked. "Wait until he comes home."

Mrs. Shlemiel wept bitterly and the children cried, too. Shlemiel said, "How strange. My own wife always scolded me. My children talked back to me. And here a strange woman and strange children want me to live with them. It looks to me as if Chelm Two is actually better than Chelm One."

"Just a moment. I think I have an idea," interrupted Gronam.

"What is your idea?" Zeinvel Ninny inquired.

"Since we decided to send Shlemiel to the poorhouse, the town will have to hire someone to take care of Mrs. Shlemiel's children so she can go to market. Why not hire Shlemiel for that? It's true, he is not Mrs. Shlemiel's husband or the children's father. But he is so much like the real Shlemiel that the children will feel at home with him."

"What a wonderful idea!" cried Feivel Thickwit.

"Only King Solomon could have thought of such a wise solution," agreed Treitel Fool.

"Such a clever way out of this dilemma could only have been thought of in our Chelm," chimed in Shmendrick Numskull.

"How much do you want to be paid to take care of Mrs. Shlemiel's children?" asked Gronam.

For a moment Shlemiel stood there completely bewildered. Then he said, "Three groschen a day."

"Idiot, moron, donkey!" screamed Mrs. Shlemiel. "What are three groschen nowadays? You shouldn't do it for less than six a day." She ran over to Shlemiel and pinched him on the arm. Shlemiel winced and cried out, "She pinches just like my wife."

The elders held a consultation among themselves. The town budget was very limited. Finally Gronam announced: "Three groschen may be too little, but six groschen a day is definitely too much, especially for a stranger. We will compromise and pay you five groschen a day. Shlemiel, do you accept?"

"Yes, but how long am I to keep this job?"

"Until the real Shlemiel comes home."

Gronam's decision was soon known throughout Chelm, and the town admired his great wisdom and that of all the elders of Chelm.

At first, Shlemiel tried to keep the five groschen that the town paid him for himself. "If I'm not your husband, I don't have to support you," he told Mrs. Shlemiel.

"In that case, since I'm not your wife, I don't have to cook for you, darn your socks, or patch your clothes."

And so, of course, Shlemiel turned over his pay to her. It was the first time that Mrs. Shlemiel had ever gotten any money for the household from Shlemiel. Now when she was in a good mood, she would say to him, "What a pity you didn't decide to go to Warsaw ten years ago."

"Don't you ever miss your husband?" Shlemiel would ask.

"And what about you? Don't you miss your wife?" Mrs. Shlemiel would ask. And both would admit that they were quite happy with matters as they stood.

Years passed and no Shlemiel returned to Chelm. The elders had many explanations for this. Zeinvel Ninny believed that Shlemiel had crossed the black mountains and had been eaten alive by the cannibals who live there. Dopey Lekisch thought that Schlemiel most probably had come to the Castle of Asmodeus, where he had been forced to marry a demon princess. Shmendrick Numskull came to the conclusion that Shlemiel had reached the edge of the world and had fallen off. There were many other theories; for example, that the real Shlemiel had lost his memory and had simply forgotten that he was Shlemiel. Such things do happen.

Gronam did not like to impose his theories on other people; however, he was convinced that Shlemiel had gone to the other Chelm, where he had had exactly the same experience as the Shlemiel in this Chelm. He had been hired by the local community and was taking care of the other Mrs. Shlemiel's children for a wage of five groschen a day.

As for Schlemiel himself, he no longer knew what to think. The children were growing up and soon would be able to take care of themselves. Sometimes Shlemiel would sit and ponder: Where is the other Shlemiel? When will he come home? What is my real wife doing? Is she waiting for me, or has she got herself another Shlemiel? These were questions that he could not answer.

Every now and then Shlemiel would still get the desire to go traveling, but he could not bring himself to start out. What was the point of going on a trip if it led nowhere? Often, as he sat alone puzzling over the strange ways of the world, he would become more and more confused and begin humming to himself:

> Those who leave Chelm
> end up in Chelm.
> Those who remain in Chelm
> are certainly in Chelm.
> All roads lead to Chelm.
> All the world is one big Chelm.

MEET ISAAC BASHEVIS SINGER, AUTHOR

Isaac Singer was born in Poland in 1904 and grew up in Warsaw. He said of his childhood home: "My father was an orthodox rabbi, and our house was a house of holy books and learning. Other children had toys. I played with the books in my father's library. I began to 'write' before I even knew the alphabet. I took my father's pen, dipped it in ink, and started to scribble. At school I amazed my fellow students with fantastic stories. Once I told them that my father was a king, and they believed me."

Singer came to the United States in 1935 and learned English. He wrote all of his books first in Yiddish, however, and then translated them into English. He said of his writing for children: "Children are the best readers of genuine literature. . . . The young reader demands a real story, with a beginning, a middle, and an end, the way stories have been told for thousands of years."

ALBERIC THE WISE

Norton Juster
illustrated by Domenico Gnoli

More than many years ago when fewer things had happened in the world and there was less to know, there lived a young man named Alberic who knew nothing at all. Well, almost nothing, or depending on your generosity of spirit, hardly anything, for he could hitch an ox and plow a furrow straight or thatch a roof or hone his scythe until the edge was bright and sharp or tell by a sniff of the breeze what the day would bring or with a glance when a grape was sweet and ready. But these were only the things he had to know to live or couldn't help knowing by living and are, as you may have discovered, rarely accounted as knowledge.

Of the world and its problems, however, he knew little, and indeed was even less aware of their existence. In all his life he had been nowhere and seen nothing beyond the remote estate on which he lived and to whose lands he and his family had been bound back beyond the edge of memory. He planted and harvested, threshed and winnowed, tended the hives and the pigs, breathed the country air, and stopped now and again to listen to the birds or puzzle at the wind. There were no mysteries, hopes or dreams other than those that could be encompassed by his often aching back or impatient stomach. This was the sum of his existence and with it he was neither happy nor sad. He simply could not conceive of anything else.

Since the days were much alike he measured his life by the more discernible seasons—yet they too slipped easily by, and would have continued to do so, I'm sure, had it not been for the lone traveler who appeared unaccountably one chill morning at the close of winter. Alberic watched him make his weary way along the road until, when they stood no more than a glance apart, he paused to rest before continuing on his journey. A curious old man—his tattered tunic was patched on patches and his worn shoes left hardly a suggestion of leather between himself and the cold ground. He carried a massive bundle on his back and sighed with the pleasure of letting it slide gently from his shoulder to the ground—then just as gently let himself down upon it. He nodded and smiled, mopped his face carefully with a handkerchief easily as old as himself, then acknowledged Alberic's timid greeting and finally began to speak, and when he did it was of many, many things. Where he had come from and where he was bound, what he had seen and what there was

yet to discover—commonwealths, kingdoms, empires, counties and dukedoms—fortresses, bastions and great solitary castles that dug their fingers into the mountain passes and dared the world to pass—royal courts whose monarchs dressed in pheasant skins and silks and rich brocades of purple and lemon and crimson and bice all interlaced with figures of beasts and blossoms and strange geometric devices—and mountains that had no tops and oceans that had no bottoms.

There seemed no end to what he knew or what he cared to speak about, and speak he did, on and on through the day. His voice was soft and easy but his manner such that even his pauses commanded attention. And as he spoke his eyes sparkled and his words were like maps of unknown lands. He told of caravans that made their way across continents and back with perfumes and oils and dark red wines, sandalwood and lynx hides and ermine and carved sycamore chests, with cloves and cinnamon, precious stones and iron pots and ebony and amber and objects of pure tooled gold—of tall

cathedral spires and cities full of life and craft and industry—of ships that sailed in every sea, and of art and science and learned speculation hardly even dreamed of by most people—and of armies and battles and magic and much, much more.

Alberic stood entranced, trying desperately to imagine all these wonderful things, but his mind could wander no further than the fields that he could see and the images soon would fade or cloud.

"The world is full of wonders," he sighed forlornly, for he realized that he could not even imagine what a wonder was.

"It is everything I've said and even more," the stranger replied, and since it was by now late afternoon he scrambled to his feet and once more took up his heavy bundle. "And remember," he said with a sweep of his arm, "it is all out there, just waiting." Then down the road and across the stubble fields he went.

For weeks after the old man had gone Alberic brooded, for now he knew that there were things he didn't know, and what magic and exciting things they were! Warm wet breezes had begun to blow across the land and the frozen fields had yielded first to mud and then to early blossoms. But now this quiet hillside was not enough to hold his rushing thoughts. "It is all out there, just waiting," he said to himself again and again, repeating the old man's words. When he had repeated them often enough, they became a decision. He secretly packed his few belongings and in the early morning's mist left his home and started down into the world to seek its wonders and its wisdom.

For two days and nights and half another day again he walked—through lonely forests and down along the rushing mountain streams that seemed to know their destination far better than he knew his. Mile after mile he walked until at last the trees and vines gave way to sweeps of easy meadowland and in the distance, barely visible, the towers of a city reflected back the sun's bright rays. As he approached, the hazy form became a jumble of roofs and chimney pots spread out below, and each step closer embellished them with windows, carved gables, domes and graceful spires. All this in turn was circled by a high wall which seemed to grow higher and wider as he descended towards it until at last it filled his

vision and hid all else behind it. The stream which only days before had been so gay and playful now broadened and as if aware of its new importance assumed a slow and dignified pace as it passed through the city. Alberic paused for a moment to catch his breath, then, with a slight shiver of anticipation, passed beneath the cool dark gates and entered the city too.

What a teeming, busy place! Houses and shops, music and movement, all kinds of noises, signs and smells, and more people than he ever knew existed. He wandered along the cobbled streets delighted by each new discovery and noting with care the strange new sights and sounds so unfamiliar to his country senses. He soon learned too that he had come to a city famous above all others for the beautiful stained glass manufactured in its workshops.

"A noble and important profession," he decided soberly, "for surely beauty is the true aim of wisdom!" Without delay he went off to apprentice himself to the greatest of the master glassmakers.

"Well, well," growled the old craftsman after examining Alberic carefully, "so you want to make glass. Very well, we shall see. Your duties will be few and simple. Each morning you'll rise before the birds and with the other apprentices fetch sixty barrows of firewood from the forest. Then in each furnace bank a fire precisely hot enough to melt the lead and fuse the glass, and keep them tended constantly so that none goes out or varies even slightly in its heat. Then, of course, work the bellows, fetch the ingots from the foundry, run errands, assist the journeymen as they need, sharpen and repair all the chisels, files, knives, scrapers, shears, mallets and grozing irons so that each is in perfect order, make deliveries quickly and courteously, grind and mix the pigments, work the forge, sweep out the shop, fetch, carry, stoop, haul and bend, and in your spare time help with the household chores. You can of course eat your fill of the table scraps and sleep on the nice warm floor. Well, don't just stand there, you've only started and you're already hours behind in your work." When he finished he smiled a benevolent smile, for he was known for his generous nature.

Alberic applied himself to his new tasks with diligence, working from early morning until late at night when he would curl up in one corner of the shop to dream happily of the day's accomplishments and carefully sort and pack into his memory everything he'd learned. For some time he did only the menial jobs, but soon under the watchful eye of the master he began taking part in more important and exacting procedures. He learned to chip and shape the glass into pieces often no larger than the palm of his hand and then apply the colors mixed in gum or oil with a delicate badger brush and fire these to permanence in the glowing kilns. Then from measurements and patterns he learned to set each piece in the grooved strips of lead and solder them carefully at each joint. For almost two years he worked and watched as all these small and painstaking operations took form in great windows and medallions of saintly lives or tales of moral instruction which glowed in deep splendid blues and vivid rubies.

Finally the time came for Alberic to prove his skill and take his place among the glassmakers—to create a work entirely on his own. He was determined that it would be a rare and lovely thing and he set about it with quiet intensity.

"What will it be, Alberic?" they all asked eagerly.

"Beautiful," he replied with never a moment's doubt, and that was all he'd say.

And for weeks he worked secretly in one corner of the shop until the day came when his work was to be judged. Everyone gathered to see it. The master looked long and carefully. He stood back to view it in the light and squinted close at matters of fine detail, and then he rubbed his chin and then he tapped his finger and then he swayed and then he sighed and then he frowned.

"No," he said sadly and slowly, "certainly not. You will never be a glassmaker." And everyone agreed, for despite the best of intentions Alberic's work was poor indeed.

How miserable he was! How thoroughly miserable! Why wasn't it beautiful when he had tried so hard? How could he have learned so much and yet still fail? No one knew the answer. "There is no reason now for me to stay," he said quietly, gathering up his bundle, and without even as much as a last look back he walked out into the lonely countryside. For several days he wandered aimlessly, seeing nothing, heading nowhere, his thoughts turned inward to his unhappy failure.

But it was spring and no one who has ever worked the land can long ignore the signs this season brings. Sweet promising smells hung gently in the warm air, and all around the oxlips, daisies and celandine splashed the fields in lively yellow. A graceful bird and then another caught Alberic's eye. The busy buzz and click of small things were reassuring to his ear and even the bullfrogs' heavy thump set his heart beating once again. His spirits and then his hope revived. The world seemed large and inviting once again.

"There are other places and other things to learn," he thought. "Beauty isn't everything. The true measure of wisdom is utility. I'll do something useful." He hurried now and before long came to a city whose stonecutters and masons were renowned throughout the world for the excellence of their work. His thoughts turned to castles and cloisters, massive walls, towering vaults and steeples which only miracles of skill could hold suspended in the air.

"Everything of use and value is made of stone," he concluded and rushed to seek employment with the master stonecutter.

And for two more years he busied himself learning the secrets of this new vocation—selecting and cutting only the  finest stone from the quarry—matching, marking and extracting the giant blocks to be moved on heavy wheeled carts to each new building— and then noting carefully how each shaped stone was fitted in its place so that walls and buttresses grew and arches sprang from pier to pier with such precision that no blade however sharp could slip between the joints. Soon he learned to mix and measure mortar and operate the windlasses whose ingenious ropes and pulleys allowed one man to lift for fifty. Then to make his first careful cuts with bolster and chisel and then stop and watch again as surer hands than his cut and shaped the graceful moldings and intricate tracery which brought the stone to life. As he worked he questioned and remembered everything he saw and heard, and as each day passed, his confidence and his knowledge grew and he began to think of his future life as a great and skillful stonecutter.

When the time came for him to prove his skill to the masons and sculptors of the guild, Alberic chose a piece of specially fine, delicately veined marble and set to work. It was to be the finest carving they had ever seen. With great care he studied and restudied the block and planned his form, then

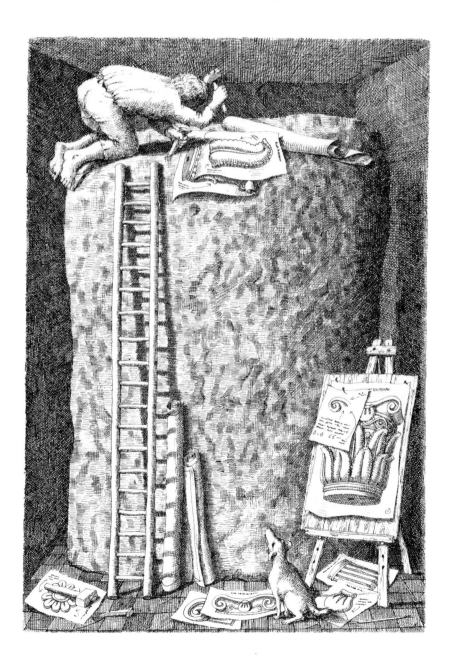

cut into the stone in search of it. He worked in a fever of excitement, his sharp chisels biting off the unwanted material in large chips and pieces. But the image he saw so clearly in his mind seemed always to be just out of sight, a little deeper in the stone. The block grew smaller and the mound of dust and chips larger, and still, like a phantom, the form seemed to recede and still he chased it. Soon there was nothing left at all. The great block of stone had disappeared and soon afterwards, the stonecutter too. For again, without a word, Alberic gathered up his belongings and passed through the city gate. He had failed once more.

"Usefulness isn't everything," he decided after roaming about disconsolately for several days. "Innovation is surely a measure of wisdom. I'll do something original."

The opportunity presented itself in the very next town, where the goldsmiths, it was said, produced objects of unsurpassed excellence and fancy. Bowls and magic boxes, mirrors, shields and scepters, crowns, rings, enchanted buckles and clasps, and candlesticks and vases of incredible grace and intricacy spilled from these workshops and found their way to every royal court and market in the land. It was here that Alberic learned to draw and shape the fine gold wire and work the thin sheets of metal into patterns and textures of light and shape and then inlay these with delicate enamels and precious stones. It was here also that he worked and hoped for the next two years of his life and it was here that for the third time he failed and for the third time took his disappointment to the lonely countryside.

And so it went, from town to town, from city to city, each noted for its own particular craft or enterprise. There were potters who turned and shaped their wet clay into graceful bowls and tall jugs fire-glazed with brilliant cobalt, manganese and copper oxides. Leather finishers who transformed smooth soft skins into shoes and boots, gloves, tunics, bombards, bottles and buckets. There were weavers and spinners who worked in wools and silks, carpenters and cabinetmakers, glassblowers, armorers and tinkers. There were scholars who spent their days searching out the secrets of ancient books, and chemists and physicians, and astronomers determining the precise distances between places that no one had ever seen. And busy ports which offered men the sea and all it touched, and smiths and scribes and makers of fine musical instruments, for anyone with such a bent. Alberic tried them all—and watched and learned and practiced and failed and then moved on again. Yet he kept searching and searching for the one thing that he could do. The secret of the wisdom and skill he so desired.

The years passed and still he traveled on—along the roads and trails and half-forgotten paths—across plains and deserts and forests whose tangled growth held terrors that were sometimes real and sometimes even worse—over hills and cruel high mountain passes and down again perhaps along some unnamed sea—until at last, alone and old and tired, he reached the ramparts of the great capital city.

"I will never find wisdom," he sighed. "I'm a failure at everything."

At the edge of the market square Alberic set his bundle down and searched longingly as all the students, artisans and craftsmen went unconcernedly about their business. He wiped the dust from his eyes and sat for a moment, thinking of his future and his past. What a strange sight he was! His beard was now quite long and gray and the cloak and hat and shoes bore evidence of some repair from every place he'd been. His great bundle bulged with the debris of a lifetime's memories and disappointments and his face was a sad scramble of much the same. As he rummaged through his thoughts, a group of children, struck by his uncommon look, stopped and gathered close around him.

"Where have you come from?"

"What do you do?"

"Tell us what you've seen," they eagerly asked, and poised to listen or flee as his response required.

Alberic was puzzled. What could he tell them? No one had ever sought his conversation before, or asked his opinion on any question. He scratched his head and rubbed his knees, then slowly and hesitantly began to speak, and suddenly the sum of all those experiences, which lay packed up in his mind as in some disordered cupboard, came back to him. He told them of a place or two he'd been and of some lands they'd never known existed and creatures that all their wildest fancies could not invent, and then a story, a legend and three dark mysterious tales remembered from a thousand years before. As he spoke, the words began to come more easily and the pleasure of them eased away his weariness. Everything he'd ever seen or heard or touched or tried was suddenly fresh and clear in his memory, and

when the children finally left for home, their faces glowing with excitement, it was to spread the news of the wonderful old man who knew so much.

Since he had no place else to go, Alberic returned to the square each day, and each day the crowds grew larger and larger around him. At first it was only the children, but soon everyone, regardless of age or size, crowded close to listen— and patiently he tried to tell them all they wished to hear. For many of their questions his own experience provided the answers, and for those he could not directly answer he always had a tale or story whose point or artifice led them to answers of their own. More and more he began to enjoy the days and soon he learned to embellish his tales with skillful detail, to pause at just the right time, to raise his voice to a roar or lower it to a whisper as the telling demanded. And the crowds grew even larger.

Workmen came to listen and stayed to learn the secret ways and methods of their own crafts. Artisans consulted him on questions of taste or skill and when they left they always knew more than when they came. Alberic told them everything he had learned or seen through all his failures and his wanderings, and before very long he became known throughout the realm as Alberic the Wise.

His fame spread so far that one day the King himself and several of his ministers came to the square to see for themselves. Cleverly disguised so as not to alert the old man to his purpose, the King posed several questions concerning matters of state and situations in far-off corners of the kingdom. Everything he asked, Alberic answered in great detail, enlarging each reply with accounts of the lore and customs of each

region, condition of the crops and royal castles, local problems and controversies, reports on the annual rainfall and the latest depredations by various discontented barons. And for added measure, two songs and a short play (in which he acted all the parts) which he had learned before being dismissed from a traveling theater company.

"You are the wisest man in my kingdom," the astonished King proclaimed, throwing off his disguise, "and you shall have a palace of your own with servants and riches as befits a man of your accomplishments."

Alberic moved into the new palace at once and was more than content with his new life. He enjoyed the wealth and possessions he had never known before, slept on feather beds, ate nothing but the most succulent and delicate foods and endlessly put on and took off the many cloaks, robes and caps the King had graciously provided. His beard was trimmed and curled and he spent his time strolling about the gardens and marble halls posing with proper dignity before each mirror and repeating to himself in various tones and accents, "Alberic the Wise, ALBERIC THE WISE, A-L-B-E-R-I-C T-H-E W-I-S-E!" in order to become accustomed to his new title.

After several weeks, however, the novelty began to wear thin, for a sable cloak is just a sable cloak and a *poulet poêla a l'estragon* is really just another roast chicken. Soon doubts began to crowd out pleasures and by degrees he grew first serious, then sober, then somber and then once again thoroughly discouraged.

"How is it possible to be a failure at everything one day and a wise man the next?" he inquired. "Am I not the same person?"

For weeks this question continued to trouble him deeply, and since he could not find a satisfactory answer he returned to the square with his doubts.

"Simply calling someone wise does not make him wise!" he announced to the eager crowd. "So you see, I am not wise." Then, feeling much better, he returned to the palace and began to make ready to leave.

"How modest," the crowd murmered. "The sign of a truly great man." And a delegation of prominent citizens was sent to prevail on him to stay.

Even after listening to their arguments Alberic continued to be troubled and the very next day he returned to the square again.

"Miscellaneous collections of fact and information are not wisdom," he declared fervently. "Therefore I am not wise!" And he returned and ordered workmen to begin boarding up the palace.

"Only the wisest of men would understand this," the people all agreed and petitions were circulated to prevent his leaving.

For several more days he paced the palace corridors unhappily and then returned for a third time.

"A wise man's words are rarely questioned," he counseled gently. "Therefore you must be very careful whom you call wise."

The crowd was so grateful for his timely warning that they cheered for fully fifteen minutes after he had returned to the palace.

Finally, in desperation, he reappeared that very afternoon and stated simply, "For all the years of my life I have sought wisdom and to this day I still do not know even the meaning of the word, or where to find it," and thinking that would convince them he ordered a carriage for six o'clock that afternoon.

The crowd gasped. "No one but a man of the most profound wisdom would ever dare to admit such a thing," they all agreed, and an epic poem was commissioned in his honor.

Once again Alberic returned to the palace. The carriage was canceled, the rooms were opened and aired. There was nothing he could say or do to convince them that he wasn't what they all thought him to be. Soon he refused to answer any more questions or, in fact, to speak at all and everyone agreed that because of the troubled times this was certainly the wisest thing to do. Each day he grew more morose and miserable, and though his fame continued to grow and spread he found no more satisfaction in his success than he had in all his failures. He slept little and ate less and his magnificent robes began to hang like shrouds. The bright optimism that had shone in his eyes through all his travels and hardships began to fade and as the months passed he took to spending all his time at the top of the great north tower, staring without any interest at nothing in particular.

"I am no wiser now than I was before," he said one afternoon, thinking back across the years. "For I still don't know what I am or what I'm looking for." But as he sat there remembering and regretting, he sensed in the air the barest suggestion of some subtle yet familiar scent that drifted in on the freshening breeze. What it was he didn't know—perhaps the pungent tangled aroma of some far eastern bazaar or the sharp and honest smell of a once-known workshop, or it might have been simply the sweet clean air of an upland field the memory of which had long been lost in detail yet retained in some more durable way; but whatever it was it grew stronger and stronger stirring something deep within him and taking hold of all his thoughts and feelings. His spirit suddenly quickened in response and each breath now came faster than the one before. And then for just a moment he sat quite still—and then at last he knew.

"I am not a glassmaker nor a stone cutter, nor a goldsmith, potter, weaver, tinker, scribe or chef," he shouted happily and he leaped up and bounded down the steep stone stairs. "Nor a vintner, carpenter, physician, armorer, astronomer, baker or boatman." Down and around he ran as fast as he could go, along the palace corridors until he reached the room in which all his old things had been stored. "Nor a blacksmith, merchant, musician or cabinetmaker," he continued as he put on the ragged cloak and shoes and hat. "Nor a wise man or a fool, success or failure, for no one but myself can tell me what I am or what I'm not." And when he'd finished he looked into the mirror and smiled and wondered why it had taken him so long to discover such a simple thing.

So Alberic picked up his bundle, took one last look through the palace and went down to the square for the last time.

"I have at last discovered one thing," he stated simply. "It is much better to look for what I may never find than to find what I do not really want." And with that he said goodbye and left the city as quietly as he'd come.

The crowd gasped and shook their heads in disbelief.

"He has given up his palace!"

"And his wealth and servants!"

"And the King's favor!"

"And he does not even know where he is going," they buzzed and mumbled. "How foolish, how very foolish! How could we ever have thought him wise?" And they all went home.

But Alberic didn't care at all, for now his thoughts were full of all the things he had yet to see and do and all the times he would stop to tell his stories and then move on again. Soon the walls were far behind and only his footsteps and the night were there to keep him company. Once again he felt the freedom and the joy of not knowing where each new step would take him, and as he walked along his stride was longer and stronger than was right somehow for a man his age.

ROADS GO EVER
EVER ON

J. R. R. Tolkien

Roads go ever ever on,
Over rock and under tree,
By caves where never sun has shone,
By streams that never find the sea;
Over snow by winter sown,
And through the merry flowers of June,
Over grass and over stone,
And under mountains in the moon.

WANDER-THIRST
Gerald Gould

Beyond the East the sunrise, beyond the West the sea,
And East and West the wander-thirst that will not let me be;
It works in me like madness, dear, to bid me say good-by!
For the seas call and the stars call, and oh, the call of the sky!

I know not where the white road runs, nor what the blue hills are,
But man can have the sun for friend, and for his guide a star;
And there's no end to voyaging when once the voice is heard,
For the river calls and the road calls, and oh, the call of a bird!

Yonder the long horizon lies, and there by night and day
The old ships draw to home again, the young ships sail away;
And come I may, but go I must, and if men ask you why,
You may put the blame on the stars and the sun and the white road
    and the sky!

347

MAPS

Dorothy Brown Thompson

High adventure
And bright dream—
Maps are mightier
Than they seem:

Ships that follow
Leaning stars—
Red and gold of
Strange bazaars—

Ice floes hid
Beyond all knowing—
Planes that ride where
Winds are blowing!

Train maps, maps of
Wind and weather,
Road maps—taken
Altogether

Maps are really
Magic wands
For home-staying
Vagabonds!

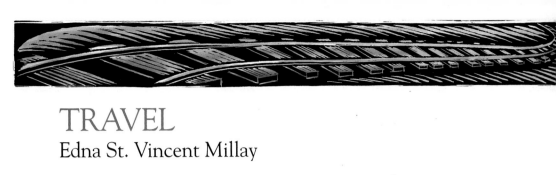

TRAVEL
Edna St. Vincent Millay

The railroad track is miles away,
And the day is loud with voices speaking,
Yet there isn't a train goes by all day
But I hear its whistle shrieking.

All night there isn't a train goes by,
Though the night is still for sleep and dreaming,
But I see its cinders red on the sky,
And hear its engine steaming.

My heart is warm with the friends I make,
And better friends I'll not be knowing,
Yet there isn't a train I wouldn't take,
No matter where it's going.

illustrated by Jennifer Hewitson

BIBLIOGRAPHY

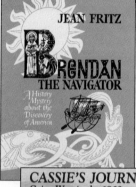

Anpao: An American Indian Odyssey by Jamake Highwater. Based on the legend of Scarface and other tales, this story tells of a young man's journey to meet his father, the Sun.

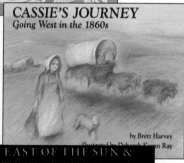

Brendan the Navigator: A History Mystery about the Discovery of America by Jean Fritz. Saint Brendan was said to have set off from Ireland in a leather boat more than 1,500 years ago and to have found Paradise. Could he have found America?

Cassie's Journey: Going West in the 1860s by Brett Harvey. This book tells the story of a young girl's journey by covered wagon from Illinois to California.

East of the Sun & West of the Moon: A Play by Nancy Willard. Will the heroine reach the castle east of the sun and west of the moon? This play based on the Scandinavian fairy tale tells the story.

The Hobbit by J. R. R. Tolkien. Travel with the hobbit Bilbo Baggins as he joins a company of dwarves to rescue a treasure from a dragon.

The Incredible Journey by Sheila Burnford. Two dogs and a cat travel almost three hundred miles across the Canadian wilderness to rejoin the people they love.

Paddle-to-the-Sea by Holling Clancy Holling. Follow a miniature carved canoe and paddler from a lake in Canada through the Great Lakes and the St. Lawrence River to the Atlantic Ocean. Maps and drawings will provide fascinating information about your journey.

The Remarkable Journey of Prince Jen by Lloyd Alexander. A young prince meets many dangers on a quest to find a mystical king.

GLOSSARY

PRONUNCIATION KEY

a as in **at**	**o** as in **ox**	**ou** as in **out**	**ch** as in **chair**
ā as in **late**	**ō** as in **rose**	**u** as in **up**	**hw** as in **which**
â as in **care**	**ô** as in **bought**	**ûr** as in **turn**;	**ng** as in **ring**
ä as in **father**	and **raw**	**germ**, **learn**,	**sh** as in **shop**
e as in **set**	**oi** as in **coin**	**firm**, **work**	**th** as in **thin**
ē as in **me**	o͝o as in **book**	ə as in **about**,	t͟h as in **there**
i as in **it**	o͞o as in **too**	**chicken**, **pencil**,	**zh** as in **treasure**
ī as in **kite**	**or** as in **form**	**cannon**, **circus**	

The mark (′) is placed after a syllable with a heavy accent,
as in **chicken** (chik′ ən).
The mark (′) after a syllable shows a lighter accent,
as in **disappear** (dis′ ə pēr′).

abide (ə bīd′) *v.* To stay; to live.

abolish (ə bol′ ish) *v.* To put an end to.

abolitionist (ab′ ə lish′ ən ist) *n.* A person who wants to end slavery.

abundant (ə bun′ dənt) *adj.* Plentiful; more than enough.

admonish (ad mon′ ish) *v.* To warn.

affliction (ə flik′ shən) *n.* A state of pain or misery.

agitation (aj′ i tā′ shən) *n.* Disturbance; excitement.

ailment (āl′ mənt) *n.* An illness; a sickness.

alder (ôl′ dər) *n.* A tree in the birch family.

allegiance (ə lē′ jəns) *n.* Loyalty.

alter (ôl′ tər) *v.* To change.

amid (ə mid′) *adv.* In the middle of; among.

anchovy (an′ chō vē) *n.* A small fish related to sardines.

anoint (ə noint′) *v.* To apply oil or ointment, especially as part of a religious ceremony.

anticipation (an tis′ ə pā′ shən) *n.* The act of expecting; hope.

appalling (ə pô′ ling) *adj.*
Frightening; filling one with
dread.

applicant (ap′ li kənt) *n.* A person
who asks for a position or job.

apprentice (ə pren′ tis) *n.* A person
learning a trade. —*v.* To bind
oneself to a craft worker in order
to learn a trade.

array (ə rā′) *n.* The order or
arrangement of something.

artifice (är′ tə fis) *n.* A clever trick
in the way a story's plot is
constructed.

artillery (är til′ ə rē) *n.* Mounted
guns.

assault (ə sôlt′) *n.* A sudden
attack.

assurance (ə sho͝or′ əns) *n.* A
statement that gives a person
confidence.

atavistic (at′ ə vis′ tik) *adj.*
Characteristic of people from a
much earlier time.

aught (ôt) *n.* Zero; nothing.

avocation (av′ ə kā′ shən) *n.*
Something a person does in
addition to or aside from his or
her regular job.

bade (bad) *v.* A past tense of **bid:**
To command.

baffle (baf′ əl) *v.* To puzzle; to
bewilder; to hinder.

bandana (ban dan′ ə) *n.* A large
handkerchief worn around the
neck.

bane (bān) *n.* Something
extremely harmful.

banish (ban′ ish) *v.* To drive away;
to force away.

barrage (bə räzh′) *n.* Any
continued attack.

bastion (bas′ chən) *n.* A part of a
fortified structure that juts out so
that defenders can fire at attackers
from several angles.

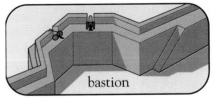
bastion

battery (bat′ ə rē) *n.* A group of
mounted guns or cannons.

bayonet (bā′ ə nit) *n.* A sword-like
weapon attached to the end of a
rifle.

benevolent (bə nev′ ə lənt) *adj.*
Kind; generous.

berate (bi rāt′) *v.* To scold harshly.

bewilder (bi wil′ dər) *v.* To confuse
completely; to puzzle.

bewilderment (bi wil′ dər mənt) *n.*
Confusion.

Pronunciation Key: at; lāte; câre; fäther; set; mē; it; kīte; ox; rōse; ô in bought; coin; bŏŏk; tōō; form; out; up; tûrn; ə sound in about, chicken, pencil, cannon, circus; **chair**; **hw** in **which**; **ring**; **shop**; **thin**; **there**; **zh** in treasure.

bice (bīs) *adj.* Blue or blue-green.

blintze (blints) *n.* Cheese or fruit wrapped in a thin layer of dough and fried.

blockade (blo kād´) *v.* To cut off an enemy's supplies.

bolt (bōlt) *n.* A roll of material or cloth.

bombard (bom´ bärd) *n.* 1. A ball or stone thrown by a cannon. 2. A leather jug or bottle.

bombardment (bom bärd´ mənt) *n.* A battering with shots and shells.

boost (bōōst) *v.* To push up.

borne (born) *v.* A past tense of **bear**: To endure suffering.

bow (bou) *n.* The front part of a ship.

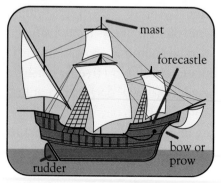

brigade (bri gād´) *n.* A large military unit, made up of two or more smaller units.

brocade (brō kād´) *n.* Woven cloth that has a raised pattern.

buttress (bu´ tris) *n.* A structure built outside a wall to give the wall support.

camphor (kam´ fər) *n.* A white substance with a strong, pleasant odor. Camphor was used as a medicine.

candor (kan´ dər) *n.* Honesty.

capital (kap´ i tl) *n.* The city that officially holds the government of a country or state. —*adj.* Excellent.

caravel (kar´ ə vel) *n.* A small sailing vessel used by the Spanish and the Portuguese from the 1300s through the 1600s. Caravels had lateen, or triangle-shaped, sails as well as square sails.

carcass (kär´ kəs) *n.* The body of a dead animal.

catapult (kat´ ə pult´) *v.* To move very quickly or with great force.

celandine (sel´ ən dīn´) *n.* A plant in the buttercup family with single yellow flowers.

ceremonial (ser′ ə mō′ nē əl) *adj.*
Having to do with a formal
celebration.

chaparral (shap′ ə ral′) *n.* An area
thick with shrubs and small trees.

cheder (hā′ dər) *n.* Religious
school for teaching Judaism.

cherish (cher′ ish) *v.* To care for.

chirrup (chēr′ əp) *v.* To chirp.

circuit (sûr′ kit) *n.* A journey
around an established territory.

cloister (kloi′ stər) *n.* A place
where religious people live away
from the world; a convent or a
monastery.

communal (kə myōōn′ l) *adj.*
Public; shared by all.

compassion (kəm pash′ ən) *n.*
Sympathy; pity.

compel (kəm pel′) *v.* To force.

compelling (kəm pel′ ing) *adj.*
Having a strong effect.

compensation (kom′ pən sā′ shən)
n. Payment.

compromise (kom′ prə mīz′) *n.* A
settlement made by both sides
giving up a little.

comptroller (kən trō′ lər) *n.* A
controller; a government official
who regulates money.

comrade (kom′ rad) *n.* A friend
who shares the same job or
responsibilities.

conceive (kən sēv′) *v.* 1. To start
something with a certain point of
view. 2. To understand.

concrete (kon′ krēt) *adj.* Real.

condemn (kən dem′) *v.* To
disapprove of something strongly;
to say that something is very bad.

confer (kən fûr′) *v.* To discuss
something together.

confine (kən fīn′) *v.* 1. To limit to.
2. To keep in a place.

confounded (kon foun′ did) *adj.*
Darned.

confrontation (kon′ frən tā′ shən)
n. A face-to-face meeting.

consecrate (kon′ si krāt′) *v.* To
make sacred.

consume (kən sōōm′) *v.* To
destroy.

cordial (kor′ jəl) *n.* A stimulating
medicine.

cornel (kor′ nl) *n.* A large shrub or
low tree that bears fruit that can
be eaten; also known as the
Cornelian cherry tree.

course (kors) *v.* To flow.

Pronunciation Key: at; lāte; câre; fäther; set; mē; it; kīte; ox; rōse; ô in bought; coin; boŏk; tōō; form; out; up; tûrn; ə sound in about, chicken, pencil, cannon, circus; chair; hw in which; ring; shop; thin; there; zh in treasure.

cradleboard (krād´ l bord´) *n.* A wooden frame that Native American women wore on their backs to carry their babies.

crucial (krōō´ shəl) *adj.* Very important.

crusader (krōō sād´ ər) *n.* A person who fights for a cause.

cumbersome (kum´ bər səm) *adj.* Clumsy; hard to handle.

deem (dēm) *v. archaic.* To believe.

defiant (di fī´ ənt) *adj.* Openly disobedient; challenging.

degradation (deg´ ri dā´ shən) *n.* Disgrace; shame.

democracy (di mok´ rə sē) *n.* A government run by the people who live under it.

depredation (dep´ ri dā´ shən) *n.* The act of attacking and robbing.

depression (di presh´ ən) *n.* A shallow hole or a dent.

destiny (des´ tə nē) *n.* Fate; what is going to happen.

devise (di vīz´) *v.* To plan; to invent.

diligence (dil´ i jens) *n.* Steady effort put forth to accomplish a task.

discernible (di sûrn´ ə bəl) *adj.* Easy to recognize as different.

disconsolately (dis kon´ sə lit lē) *adv.* In a very unhappy way; hopelessly.

disgruntled (dis grun´ tld) *adj.* Ill-tempered; in bad humor.

distinct (di stingkt´) *adj.* 1. Clear; plain. 2. Separate.

distort (di stort´) *v.* To change the meaning of something; to misrepresent.

divert (di vûrt´) *v.* To turn in another direction.

doctrine (dok´ trin) *n.* A principle or position that one believes in.

dolorous (dō´ lər əs) *adj.* Full of sorrow.

doublet (dub´ lit) *n.* A tight-fitting men's jacket, with or without sleeves.

downpour (doun´ por´) *n.* A heavy rain.

drought (drout) *n.* Dry weather that lasts a very long time.

due (dōō) *adj.* 1. Owing. 2. Suitable; expected. —*adv.* Exactly.

duly (doo′ lē) *adv.* Properly.

dwindle (dwin′ dl) *v.* To get smaller gradually.

emancipation (i man′ sə pā′ shən) *n.* The act of setting free.

embark (em bärk′) *v.* To begin a journey.

embattled (em bat′ ld) *adj.* Struggling.

embellish (em bel′ ish) *v.* To make something better or more beautiful by adding to it.

encampment (en kamp′ mənt) *n.* A camp; a temporary stopping place.

encompass (en kum′ pəs) *v.* To include.

encounter (en koun′ tər) *v.* To meet by chance.

endow (en dou′) *v.* To grant to.

engage (en gāj′) *v.* To take part; to be involved.

enumerate (i noo′ mə rāt′) *v.* To list; to count.

ermine (ûr′ min) *n.* A valuable white fur; the winter white fur coat of some weasels.

erroneous (ə rō′ nē əs) *adj.* Wrong; mistaken.

escort (i skort′) *v.* To go with and help or protect.

establish (i stab′ lish) *v.* To settle in a place.

estate (i stāt′) *n.* A large piece of land owned by one individual or family.

ewe (yoo) *n.* A female sheep.

excursion (ik skûr′ zhən) *n.* A pleasure trip; an outing.

exert (ig zûrt′) *v.* To put into action.

exhilarated (ig zil′ ə rāt′ əd) *adj.* Excited.

faction (fak′ shən) *n.* A group of people within a larger group or party.

fanatic (fə nat′ ik) *n.* A person whose devotion to a cause goes beyond reason; a person with extreme devotion.

fathom (faᵵ′ əm) *n.* A measure of water's depth; six feet.

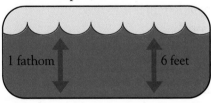

fervently (fûr′ vənt lē) *adv.* With great feeling; with emotion.

festive (fes′ tiv) *adj.* Merry.

Pronunciation Key: at; lāte; câre; fä̈ther; set; mē; it; kīte; ox; rōse; ô in bought; coin; bŏŏk; tōō; form; out; **up**; tûrn; ə sound in about, chicken, pencil, cannon, circus; **chair**; **hw** in **which**; ring; **shop**; **thin**; *th*ere; **zh** in treasure.

festoon (fe stōōn´) *v.* To hang ribbons or banners in curved shapes.

flounder (floun´ dər) *v.* To struggle.

forage cap (for´ ij kap´) *n.* A small, low military cap.

forbear (for bâr´) *v.* To hold back.

forecastle (fōk´ səl) *n.* A raised deck near the front of a ship. See illustration of **bow**.

forlornly (for lorn´ lē) *adv.* Sadly; hopelessly.

fortify (for´ tə fī´) *v.* To make stronger; to build a stronghold.

fortitude (for´ ti tōōd´) *n.* Strength; courage.

foundry (foun´ drē) *n.* A place where metal is melted and formed.

freak (frēk) *n.* A sudden odd idea; an idea based on a whim.

furrow (fûr´ ō) *n.* A trench cut by a plow.

fuse (fyōōz) *v.* To join together by melting.

gable (gā´ bəl) *n.* A part of a wall that is enclosed by sloping sides of a roof, making a triangle-shaped section on a building.

gale (gāl) *n.* A strong wind of 32–64 miles per hour.

gallinipper (gal´ ə nip´ ər) *n.* *informal.* Any of several insects that sting or bite.

gangly (gang´ glē) *adj.* Gangling; loose and awkward.

gaunt (gônt) *adj.* Very thin; bony.

globule (glob´ yōōl) *n.* A small round ball.

gore (gor) *v.* To pierce with an animal's horn or tusk.

gourd (gord) *n.* A melon-shaped fruit that can be dried and used as a bowl.

grade (grād) *n.* A slope.

groschen (grō´ shən) *n.* A form of money worth $1/100$ of a schilling. (A schilling is worth about $7^1/2$¢.)

grozing iron (grō´ zing ī´ ərn) *n.* A steel tool for cutting glass.

guilefully (gīl´ fə lē) *adv.* With slyness; with treachery.

haggard (hag´ ərd) *adj.* Exhausted-looking; gaunt.

hallow (hal´ ō) *v.* To make holy.

haversack (hav´ ər sak´) *n.* A bag
with a strap worn over one
shoulder, used to carry supplies.

hearty (här´ tē) *adj.* Big; filling.
heirloom (âr´ loॊom´) *n.* An object
handed down in a family.
hogan (hō´ gôn) *n.* A Navaho
dwelling.
holster (hōl´ stər) *n.* A leather case
for a gun, worn on the belt.
hone (hōn) *v.* To sharpen.
honeycomb (hun´ ē kōm´) *v.* To
make full of holes like a bee's
honeycomb.
humiliate (hyoॊo mil´ ē āt´) *v.* To
shame.

imminent (im´ ə nənt) *adj.* Likely
to happen at any moment.
impassioned (im pash´ ənd) *adj.*
With great feeling.
impassable (im pas´ ə bəl) *adj.*
Blocked.
impenetrable (im pen´ i trə bəl)
adj. Impossible to get through.

inalienable (in āl´ yə nə bəl) *adj.*
Not able to be sold or given away.
inappropriate (in ə prō´ prē it) *adj.*
Not fitting; not suitable.
inauguration (in ô´ gyə rā´ shən) *n.*
The ceremony in which a
president takes office.
indenture (in den´ chər) *n.* A
person bound by a contract to
work for someone else.
indescribable (in´ di skrī´ bə bəl)
adj. So extraordinary that it
cannot be described.
indifferent (in dif´ ər ənt) *adj.* Not
interested; not concerned.
inevitable (in ev´ i tə bəl) *adj.*
Certain; sure.
ingot (ing´ gət) *n.* A piece of metal
in the shape of a bar or a block.
innovation (in´ ə vā´ shən) *n.* The
act of creating something new or
original.
insurrection (in´ sə rek´ shən) *n.* A
revolt; a rebellion.
intensify (in ten´ sə fī´) *v.* To
increase; to strengthen.
intensity (in ten´ si tē) *n.* Great
strength.
interval (in´ tər vəl) *n.* A time
when action stops for a while; a
pause.

journeyman (jûr′ nē mən) *n.* A person who has completed an apprenticeship and can now work in a trade under another person.

juniper (jōō′ nə pər) *n.* An evergreen shrub with purple berries.

keelboat (kēl′ bōt′) *n.* A shallow boat built with a keel, or long beam on the bottom.

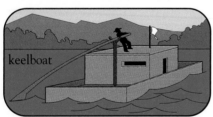

keelboat

kiln (kil) *n.* An oven for firing glass, or heating it at very high temperatures, in order to make the color permanent.

knoll (nōl) *n.* A low, rounded hill; a mound.

lance (lans) *n.* A long-shafted spear.

landfall (land′ fôl′) *n.* A sighting of land.

latitude (lat′ i tōōd′) *n.* The distance north or south of the equator.

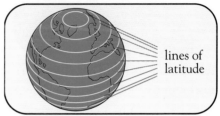

lines of latitude

legendary (lej′ ən der′ ē) *adj.* From a story that has been passed down from a people's earlier times.

leisurely (lē′ zhər lē) *adv.* In a deliberate way; without hurry.

lotus (lō′ təs) *n.* A plant mentioned in Greek myths. When travelers ate the plant's fruit, they forgot their goals and lost their desire to return to their homes.

luxurious (lug zhŏŏr′ ē əs) *adj.* Grand; rich; elegant.

lynx (lingks) *n.* A wildcat; a bobcat.

manacled (man′ ə kəld) *adj.* Handcuffed.

maneuvering (mə nōō′ vər ing) *n.* Planning and then acting according to plans.

mantle (man´ tl) *n.* A loose, sleeveless cloak.

mariner (mar´ ə nər) *n.* A sailor.

marrow (mar´ ō) *n.* 1. The soft substance in the hollow parts of bones. 2. The center; the core.

masculine (mas´ kyə lin) *adj.* Male; having to do with men.

Mass (mas) *n.* The chief service of the Roman Catholic Church.

mast (mast) *n.* 1. A pole that supports the sails of a ship or boat. See illustration of **bow**. 2. Nuts from forest trees, used as food for pigs.

matron (mā´ trən) *n.* A woman who is supervisor of a hospital.

menial (mē´ nē əl) *adj.* Humble; lowly; boring; tedious.

merciful (mûr´ si fəl) *adj.* Forgiving.

mesa (mā´ sə) *n.* A small, high plateau that stands alone, like a mountain with a flat top.

mesa

mesquite (me skēt´) *n.* A spiny shrub or tree in the legume, or pea and bean, family.

minute (mī noot´) *adj.* Detailed; careful.

mobilize (mō´ bə līz´) *v.* To put into action.

molest (mə lest´) *v.* To bother or annoy; to interfere with.

monarch (mon´ ərk) *n.* A ruler; a king or a queen.

morale (mə ral´) *n.* The level of one's confidence.

morose (mə rōs´) *adj.* Sullen; gloomy.

mutilated (myoot´ l āt´ əd) *adj.* Cut up; slashed.

mystical (mis´ ti kəl) *adj.* Mysterious.

nautical mile (nô´ ti kəl mīl´) *n.* A unit of distance at sea; 6080.20 feet.

neglectful (ni glekt´ fəl) *adj.* Careless.

nimbly (nim´ blē) *adv.* With quick, light movements.

ninepence (nīn´ pens´) *n. British.* Nine pennies.

nobly (nō´ blē) *adv.* In an honorable way.

noncombatant (non´ kəm bat´ nt) *n.* A person who is not a part of the fighting during wartime.

Pronunciation Key: at; lāte; câre; fäther; set; mē; it; kīte; ox; rōse; ô in bought; coin; bŏŏk; tōō; form; out; up; tûrn; ə sound in about, chicken, pencil, cannon, circus; chair; hw in which; ring; shop; thin; ŧħere; zh in treasure.

occupant (ok′ yə pənt) *n.* A person who takes up space on something.

ordain (or dān′) *v.* To determine beforehand.

orient (or′ ē ənt) *v.* To find out one's direction, position, or exact location.

ornery (or′ nə rē) *adj.* Mean.

orthodox (or′ thə doks′) *adj.* Having to do with the branch of the Jewish religion that most closely follows all its traditional beliefs and practices.

overseer (ō′ vər sē′ ər) *n.* A supervisor; a manager.

oxlip (oks′ lip) *n.* A flowering herb with pale-colored flowers. Oxlip developed naturally out of primrose and cowslip.

panacea (pan′ ə sē′ ə) *n.* A cure for all ills.

pantaloons (pan′ tl ōōnz′) *n.* Trousers.

parch (pärch) *v.* To become very dry.

personage (pûr′ sə nij) *n.* An important person.

peyote (pā ō′ tē) *n.* A cactus plant found in Mexico.

phenomenal (fi nom′ ə nl) *adj.* Remarkable.

piñon (pin′ yən) *n.* A kind of pine tree with edible seeds.

plight (plīt) *n.* A predicament; a bad situation; difficulty.

pommel (pum′ əl) *n.* A raised part on the front of a saddle.

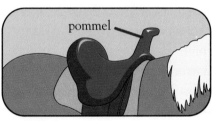
pommel

ponder (pon′ dər) *v.* To think about.

popular sovereignty (pop′ yə lər sov′ rin tē) *n.* A policy that said each state could decide whether to have slavery within its borders.

portage (por′ tij) *n.* The act of carrying boats and supplies from one waterway to another.

portage

poultice (pōl´ tis) *n.* A wad of something soft and moist that is placed over a wound to heal it.

prankster (prangk´ stər) *n.* A person who plays tricks on people for fun.

prevail on (pri vāl´ on) *v.* To persuade.

procedure (prə sē´ jər) *n.* The steps to follow in carrying out a routine or method.

proclaim (prō klām´) *v.* To announce publicly.

profound (prə found´) *adj.* Deep.

prominence (prom´ ə nəns) *n.* Fame; importance.

prominent (prom´ ə nənt) *adj.* Famous; well-known.

prophet (prof´ it) *n.* A person who tells future events before they happen.

proposition (prop´ ə zish´ ən) *n.* An idea that is presented; a principle.

prosper (pros´ pər) *v.* To succeed; to thrive.

provisions (prə vizh´ ənz) *n. pl.* Supplies, especially food or tools.

prow (prou) *n.* The curved front part of a ship; the bow. See illustration of **bow**.

pungent (pun´ jənt) *adj.* Sharp or strong smelling or tasting.

quail (kwāl) *v.* To shrink back in fear.

quota (kwō´ tə) *n.* The amount one expects to receive.

rabbi (rab´ ī) *n.* A teacher of Jewish religion and law.

rampart (ram´ pärt) *n.* A wall used as a defense for a city.

rapscallion (rap skal´ yən) *n.* A rascal; a scamp.

ration (rash´ ən) *n.* A limited share of food.

ravine (rə vēn´) *n.* A narrow, steep-sided valley worn into the earth by running water.

ravishing (rav´ i shing) *adj.* Very beautiful.

recede (ri sēd´) *v.* To go backwards; to back away.

recesses (ri ses´ əz) *n.* Areas that are more deeply inside a place or away from all the rest.

recrimination (ri krim´ ə nā´ shən) *n.* An accusation made in return for another accusation; blame given in return.

recruit (ri krōōt´) *v.* To get new members.

Pronunciation Key: at; lāte; câre; fäther; set; mē; it; kīte; ox; rōse; ô in bought; coin; bŏŏk; tōō; form; out; up; tûrn; ə sound in about, chicken, pencil, cannon, circus; chair; hw in which; ring; shop; thin; ŧhere; zh in treasure.

recruitment (ri krōōt´ mənt) *n.* Signing up new soldiers.

refuge (ref´ yōōj) *n.* A place of safety.

regiment (rej´ ə mənt) *n.* A large body of soldiers.

remote (ri mōt´) *adj.* Far away and separate from others.

render (ren´ dər) *v.* To make.

repetitive (ri pet´ i tiv) *adj.* Repeated.

repulse (ri puls´) *v.* To push back.

restrain (ri strān´) *v.* To hold back.

reveille (rev´ ə lē) *n.* The playing of a bugle to awaken soldiers.

roust (roust) *v.* To decisively defeat and chase someone out of a place; to rout.

rout (rout) *n.* A disorderly flight of beaten soldiers.

rowdy (rou´ dē) *adj.* Rough; disorderly.

rudder (rud´ ər) *n.* A broad, flat blade at the rear of a ship, used to steer. See illustration of **bow**.

rutting (rut´ ing) *n.* Mating.

sacrifice (sak´ rə fīs´) *v.* To suffer loss in helping others.

sandglass (sand´ glas´) *n.* A glass container with a narrow center, used for measuring time; an hourglass. Sand runs from the top to the bottom of the device in a certain amount of time. Then the glass is turned upside down and the process is repeated.

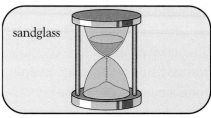

sandglass

scruple (skrōō´ pəl) *n.* A feeling of doubt.

scythe (sīŧh) *n.* A tool with a long, curved blade for cutting grass or grain by hand.

scythe

sear (sēr) *v.* To roast; to burn.

sentinel (sen´ tn l) *n.* A person who stands watch; a guard.

shanty (shan´ tē) *n.* A roughly built cabin.

shlemiel (shlə mēl´) *n. slang.* A fool who is both awkward and unlucky.

shmendrick (shmen´ drik) *n. slang.* A nincompoop; a nobody.

shroud (shroud) *n.* A covering for a dead body.

siege (sēj) *n.* An army's attempt to force surrender by surrounding the enemy's position, keeping out food and supplies.

singe (sinj) *v.* To burn the surface of something.

sinister (sin´ ə stər) *adj.* Harmful; threatening.

skedaddle (ski dad´ l) *v. informal.* To run quickly away.

skeeter (skē´ tər) *n. informal.* A mosquito.

skeletal (skel´ i tl) *adj.* Like a skeleton; so thin that the shapes of bones show.

skirmish (skûr´ mish) *n.* A fight between small forces.

slaughter (slô´ tər) *v.* To kill many animals.

smithy (smith´ ē) *n.* A blacksmith's shop; a place where horses' shoes are made.

snivel (sniv´ əl) *v.* To whine.

solace (sol´ is) *n.* Comfort.

solder (sod´ ər) *v.* To join metal pieces together by using a highly heated liquid metal at a joint, without heating the pieces themselves.

solicitous (sə lis´ i təs) *adj.* Eager to please.

solitary (sol´ i ter´ ē) *adj.* Alone; single.

soul-harrowing (sōl´ har´ ō ing) *adj.* Causing suffering to a person's innermost self.

sovereign (sov´ rin) *n.* A king, queen, or other supreme ruler.

span (span) *v.* To stretch across.

spasm (spaz´ əm) *n.* A seizure; a fit.

speculation (spek´ yə lā´ shən) *n.* Thinking about a subject; pondering.

spirits (spir´ its) *n.* A liquid containing alcohol.

staple (stā´ pəl) *n.* A basic or necessary food.

stark (stärk) *adj.* Stiff; rigid.

start (stärt) *v. archaic.* To startle; to frighten.

stifle (stī´ fəl) *v.* To hold back; to choke.

stygian (stij´ ē ən) *adj.* Dark; gloomy.

succession (sək sesh´ ən) *n.* One thing happening right after another.

successive (sək ses´ iv) *adj.* Following in order.

sufficient (sə fish´ ənt) *adj.* Enough.

sull (sul) *v.* To be balky; to stop suddenly and refuse to move.

supple (sup´ əl) *adj.* Easily bent; not stiff.

suppliant (sup´ lē ənt) *n.* A person who begs or asks for a favor.

suppress (sə pres´) *v.* To stop; to put down.

supremacy (sə prem´ ə sē) *n.* A position of the highest power.

surpass (sər pas´) *v.* To go beyond.

sway (swā) *v.* To influence.

swine (swīn) *n.* A pig or pigs.

swivet (swiv´ it) *n.* A state of worry or fear.

talisman (tal´ is mən) *n.* A lucky charm.

tallow (tal´ ō) *n.* The melted-down, hardened fat from cattle or sheep.

tan (tan) *v.* To turn animal hides into leather.

tangible (tan´ jə bəl) *adj.* Real; actual.

tarry (tar´ ē) *v.* To remain or stay; to linger.

teeming (tē´ ming) *adj.* Overflowing; swarming.

tethered (teth´ ərd) *adj.* Tied by rope to a fixed object.

thresh (thresh) *v.* 1. To throw oneself about wildly; to thrash. 2. To separate grain from the stalk by beating it.

tipi (tē´ pē) *n.* A tent of the Native Americans of the Plains; a tepee.

toboggan (tə bog´ ən) *n.* A long, narrow sled.

toil (toil) *n.* Work; labor.

tract (trakt) *n.* A large area of land.

transact (tran sakt´) *v.* To carry on business.

tributary (trib´ yə ter´ ē) *n.* A stream or river that flows into a larger one.

trifle (trī´ fəl) *n.* An unimportant thing.

trinket (tring´ kit) *n.* A small or cheap piece of jewelry.

tropical (trop´ i kəl) *adj.* From the tropics, which is a hot, humid region near the equator.

tunic (too´ nik) *n.* A short coat.

turf (tûrf) *n.* A layer of soil with grass growing in it.

unaccountably (un´ ə koun´ tə blē) *adv.* In a way that cannot be explained.

unanimously (yoo nan´ ə məs lē) *adv.* With the agreement of everyone.

uncharted (un chär´ tid) *adj.* Not shown on a map; not explored; unknown.

undermine (un´ dər mīn´) *v.* To weaken.

unfurl (un fûrl´) *v.* To open out; to unroll.

verify (ver´ ə fī´) *v.* To prove the truth.

vintage (vin´ tij) *n.* The grapes or wine produced in a vineyard in one year.

vintner (vint´ nər) *n.* A person who makes wine for a living.

vital (vīt´ l) *adj.* Very important; necessary.

vocation (vō kā´ shən) *n.* An occupation; a profession.

wallow (wol´ ō) *n.* A place where animals roll around in the mud.

waylay (wā´ lā´) *v.* To lie in wait for; to attack or stop on the road.

whey (hwā) *n.* The watery part of milk that separates from the curd when making cheese.

whither (hwith´ ər) *adv.* Where.

whopper (hwop´ ər) *n. informal.* A big lie.

windlass (wind´ ləs) *n.* A roller turned with a handle, used for lifting heavy weights.

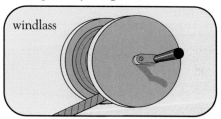

windlass

winnow (win´ ō) *v.* To remove the chaff, or husks, from grain.

wrath (rath) *n.* Anger; rage.

Yiddish (yid´ ish) *n.* A language of the Jews that developed from many other languages.

yield (yēld) *v.* To give in; to stop arguing.

continued from page 5

William Morrow and Co., Inc.: "McBroom the Rainmaker" by Sid Fleischman, copyright © 1973 by Sid Fleischman.

Penguin USA: An excerpt entitled "Emancipation" from *To Be a Slave* by Julius Lester, text copyright © 1968 by Julius Lester. "The Flower-Fed Buffaloes" from *Going to the Stars* by Vachel Lindsay, copyright 1926 by D. Appleton and Co., copyright renewed 1954 by Elizabeth C. Lindsay. "The Voyage of Christopher Columbus" from *Christopher Columbus: Voyager to the Unknown* by Nancy Smiler Levinson, copyright © 1990 by Nancy Smiler Levinson.

Sterling Lord Literistic, Inc.: "Alberic the Wise" from *Alberic the Wise and Other Journeys* by Norton Juster, illustrated by Domenico Gnoli, copyright © 1965 by Norton Juster.

Dorothy Brown Thompson: "Maps" by Dorothy Brown Thompson.

University of Nebraska Foundation, copyright owners: Excerpts from *Nat Love, Negro Cowboy* by Harold W. Felton, copyright © 1969 by Harold Felton.

Photography
35 © Charles Osgood/The Chicago Tribune
57 Janet Goble
85 UPI/Bettmann
93 © L.M.A.M.A. Orchard House
225 © 1991, Jerry Bauer
293 Marilyn Sanders

COLOPHON

This book has been designed in the classic style to emphasize our commitment to classic literature. The typeface, Goudy Old Style, was drawn in 1915 by Frederic W. Goudy, who based it on fifteenth-century Italian letterforms.

The art has been drawn to reflect the golden age of children's book illustration and its recent rebirth in the work of innovative artists of today. This book was designed by John Grandits. Composition, electronic page makeup, and photo and art management were provided by The Chestnut House Group, Inc.